Radical Freud

Radical Freud reveals a radical dimension to Sigmund Freud's sexual theory that has previously been neglected.

Thomas Olver argues that Freud's radical heritage has been transformed into an orthodox school with an internal stasis that is unassailable from within but increasingly challenged from without as irrelevant. Olver offers a return to the radical elements of Freud's work, first by reviewing the ways in which Freud's pioneering sexual theory has been vulgarised since his death, and by recentring his texts. The bisexuality thesis is then reconstructed, based on a close reading of key texts, and contrasted with the better-known Oedipus theory. Olver then explores the philosophical and clinical consequences of this parallel line of sexual theory.

Radical Freud will be of great interest to psychoanalysts as well as to academics and scholars of psychoanalytic studies, gender and queer studies, sociology, anthropology, history and philosophy.

Thomas Olver is an independent researcher and translator living in Pretoria, South Africa. He studied modern languages, comparative literature and psychology at Pretoria, Witwatersrand and Zurich. He favours a collaborative approach to epistemology. His research and teaching interests include psychoanalysis, semiotics, aesthetics, narratology, modern literature, translation and the history of ideas.

Radical Freud

Reconstructing the Bisexuality Thesis

Thomas Olver

Routledge
Taylor & Francis Group

LONDON AND NEW YORK

Designed cover image: © Cover image of Vaal Dam (South Africa) by Thomas Olver

First published 2025
by Routledge
4 Park Square, Milton Park, Abingdon, Oxon OX14 4RN

and by Routledge
605 Third Avenue, New York, NY 10158

Routledge is an imprint of the Taylor & Francis Group, an informa business

© 2025 Thomas Olver

British Library Cataloguing-in-Publication Data
A catalogue record for this book is available from the British Library

ISBN: 9781032812571 (hbk)
ISBN: 9781032812564 (pbk)
ISBN: 9781003498919 (ebk)

DOI: 10.4324/9781003498919

Typeset in Times New Roman
by codeMantra

Dedicated to the memory of my
loving and enlightened parents,
Quinton and Frances

Contents

Acknowledgements

The journey of a thousand miles begins with a single step, but it is also helped along by good fortune en route. This has certainly been the case for the book you are reading now. It was my very good fortune to stumble upon the work of Freud early in my studies, and then to have had the inestimable opportunity to study under Reingard Nethersole and Ulrike Kistner in Johannesburg. More recently, Ulrike's 2016 English translation of the 1905 edition of Freud's *Three essays* inspired me to pick up the trail of Freud's sexual theory. My journey also had the serendipity of crossing paths with Tony Pipolo, who was for many years the editor of *The Psychoanalytic Review*. Although I never had the privilege of meeting Tony in person, his generosity of spirit and sharp analytic perception stand out, and I gratefully acknowledge *The Psychoanalytic Review* for publishing the essays that document my journey of investigating radical Freud (details below: Olver, 2020; 2023a; 2023b).

The second of these essays (2023a), in which I initially introduced the bisexuality thesis, provides the main theoretical axis of this book and serves as the foundation for Chapters 2 and 3, while Chapters 4 and 5 incorporate the consequences of the thesis outlined in the third essay (2023b), although the discussion now goes substantially further. The book retreats somewhat from my original interest (2020) in the epistemological value of Freud's radical sexual theory, but even this element still plays a role in the discussion ahead.

Finally, when the third of these essays appeared in September 2023, it was my exceptional good fortune to be contacted by Susannah Frearson from Routledge. Through Susannah's intellectual acumen and serene professionalism, I was tempted and persuaded by equal measure to carry on and embark on this next stage of the journey. I cannot express sufficiently my appreciation to Susannah and the team at Routledge. I also gratefully acknowledge the strong endorsement from three Routledge reviewers.

In the end, however, the real good fortune in life is the circle of family and friends who share the journey, and I would like to thank in abundance the special people in my life who have been part of this endeavour, patiently listening to my endless explanations of Freud's radicalism while unstintingly giving encouragement and frequently delivering chocolate.

Reference list

Olver, T. (2020). The problem of value and other outstanding issues in Freud's sexual theory. *The Psychoanalytic Review*, 107(5), 405–34. (© 2020 NPAP)

Olver, T. (2023a). Radical Freud (part two): Freud's bisexuality thesis and the negation of the Oedipus complex. *The Psychoanalytic Review*, 110(2), 161–93. (© 2023 NPAP)

Olver, T. (2023b). The subject of the dialectic: Some consequences of Freud's bisexuality thesis. *The Psychoanalytic Review*, 110(3), 259–86. (© 2023 NPAP)

Introduction

Overview and methodology

This book is constructed around the central proposition that there is a radical dimension to the work of Sigmund Freud which has previously been unappreciated. This may seem both controversial and banal on the surface, and certainly few scholars would disagree that Freud's work was a radical departure from the prevailing knowledge and methodology in the field of psychology in his time. In the decades since Freud's death, however, the ideas he put forward and the clinical techniques he developed have become so mainstream that psychoanalysis today is hardly considered radical, with a fully established epistemology and a vast body of secondary literature and a clinical profession that includes its own training institutions around the world.

In the process of entering the mainstream, Freud's heritage has been transformed into an orthodox school with an internal stasis that is unassailable from within but regularly challenged from without as irrelevant. Freud himself has become a diminished figurehead who is presented as both saint and sinner. He enjoys either fading regard as the inspired founder of this school or attracts virulent criticism as the emblem of an ossified and socially conservative worldview that is increasingly out of touch with the realities of the 21st century. The clinical practice of psychoanalysis and the various splinter traditions that psychoanalysis has produced now often seem apologetic about their Freudian foundation and ready to jettison this in order to assert their own relevance today.

Since his death, Freud's texts and his ideas have been sidelined and displaced in countless revisions and vulgarisations of the original ideas, giving rise to a contemporary psychoanalytic epistemology that is Freudian largely in name only. This harsh assessment need only be weighed against the readiness of psychoanalysts to abandon the radical elements of Freud's theory, commencing as far back as 1940, the year after Freud's death, when Sandor Rado famously attacked bisexuality as a "deceptive concept" and proposed it be discarded within psychoanalysis.

This book offers a return to the radical elements of Freud's work, and starts by recentring his texts, especially those dealing with his sexual theory. Some of Freud's most radical ideas emerge in the theory of sexuality that he developed. Reasserting these ideas against the conservative orthodoxy of psychoanalysis was the initial focus of my interest, but in the process of reading Freud's texts in the

DOI: 10.4324/9781003498919-1

area of sexual theory, I was surprised to discover an entirely new level of argument that I had not recognised before in my own reading of Freud's work or encountered in the voluminous secondary literature.

Freud's early and pioneering insights into sexuality in the *Three essays* (1905) and the Oedipus theory are perhaps the best-known aspects of his enduring theory of sexuality but, in parallel and less explicitly developed, I found that Freud suggests and partially sketches an alternative thesis of universal bisexuality in humans. This book on radical aspects in Freud's work reconstructs in detail Freud's bisexuality thesis, contrasts it to the Oedipus theory and explores the consequences of this parallel line of sexual theory in Freud's work. As the book unfolds, it will become clear that there are in fact two bisexuality theories present in Freud's work: the bisexuality which is a component of the complete Oedipus complex, and the bisexuality thesis this book reconstructs; both are closely connected to the structural theory of *The ego and the id* (1923).

The discussion in this book is inspired directly by Freud's own famous rejoinder that "the *exclusive* sexual interest felt by men for women is also a problem that needs elucidating and is not a self-evident fact" (1905, p. 146, emphasis added). The book examines Freud's manifest position on bisexuality and then traces the bisexual path from infantile sexuality with its bisexual "disposition" via the bifurcations Freud identifies in the libidinal instinct as it develops from childhood through puberty into the adult forms of sexual expression. It will become clear that I boldly extend Freud's line of thinking to confirm not only the fundamental centrality of bisexuality to human sexuality but also its crucial consequence, which Freud himself implicitly recognises, namely the negation of his thesis of the Oedipus complex. This is an ambitious argument with ramifications for the theory and clinical practice of psychoanalysis which this book explores. I have not encountered this argument or even a suggestion of this line of thinking elsewhere, not within the broad orthodoxies of psychoanalytic discourse and not in the counter-discourses to psychoanalysis, such as that of Gilles Deleuze and Félix Guattari (1972, 1980), so there is no avoiding the enormity of this novel argument. That I base this argument on what boils down finally to a single sentence in *The ego and the id* (Freud, 1923) will challenge even the most sympathetic reader's patience and endurance. In this regard, I can only say that overcoming one's own deep resistances is the greatest part of the work of reconstructing and analysing Freud's bisexuality thesis, and I trust an audience trained and skilled in the analytic techniques for archaeological excavation of the mind will have the necessary self-reflexive fortitude to follow the argument to its conclusions.

Overview of chapters

The overall structure of the book falls roughly into three parts. The first part of the book (the Introduction and Chapter 1) presents the methodology and rationale for reconstructing Freud's radical theory. The second part (Chapters 2 and 3) is the reconstruction of the bisexuality thesis and the final part (Chapters 4, 5 and the Conclusion) explores the consequences of the thesis.

The Introduction describes the methodology of the book, which is guided by the *relativism* of knowledge and the two anchoring principles of evolution and emancipation. The apparent contradiction between evolution and emancipation is crystallised in a problem known as *Darwin's paradox*. This is followed by comments on the question of veracity in scientific investigation. The Introduction then highlights and explains the value of *close reading* as a technique, adopted from literature studies. The methodology of the book also relies on insights from the structural linguistics of Ferdinand de Saussure, which provide the book's main approach of focusing on system over instance. The Introduction goes on to explore Freud's methodology and shows this to be relativist and metaphorical. The Introduction ends with definitions and a discussion of three sets of core terminologies that feature in the book: identity and identification; biological sex and gender; and the terminology of sexual orientation, including gay, lesbian, bisexual, trans and queer.

Before the book proceeds in detail to Freud's radical theory, Chapter 1 reviews the ways in which Freud's radical work – especially his sexual theory – has been vulgarised and de-radicalised by his followers since his death in 1939. The chapter demonstrates how the widespread view of Freud today as representative of a conservative and heteronormative outlook is incorrect. Important thematic areas are discussed to show the ways in which Freud's theory has been sidelined, misunderstood and vulgarised. These thematic areas are: sexuality in general; homosexuality and bisexuality; the Oedipus complex; and Freud's metaphorical style. Some prominent scholarship in these areas is evaluated, including work by Roy Schafer, Judith Butler and Mark Solms. In particular, the neglect of Freud's theory of bisexuality is highlighted. This chapter sets the stage and provides the context for the radical re-evaluation that follows in subsequent chapters.

Chapter 2 is the core chapter of the book where the reconstructing of Freud's bisexuality thesis commences, using a close reading of texts by Freud. The chapter starts by examining key passages in Freud's texts where he explicitly outlines his view of the centrality of universal human bisexuality in both its object and subject components. An overview of Freud's sexual theory is then provided as the foundation to understand the Oedipus complex. The close reading in this chapter concentrates on *Three essays on the theory of sexuality* (1905), *Group psychology and the analysis of the ego* (1921) and *The ego and the id* (1923) to show how Freud's bisexuality thesis emerges in a dialectic contrast to the rivalry thesis of the Oedipus complex.

The key concept of *primary identification* emerges from Chapter 2 and becomes the focus of Chapter 3 in a comparison of the bisexuality thesis with Freud's theory of the Oedipus complex. In order to produce a genealogy of the term, two important sources in the development of my thinking around primary identification are evaluated in detail, namely Trigant Burrow and Isidor Sadger. The discussion distinguishes between primary and secondary identification in a dialectic analysis of the two forms of identification to demonstrate the value of a dialectic approach as a way of synthesising the two bisexuality theses and reconciling the apparent contradictions in Freud's work.

Developing and extending the discussion of identification in the preceding chapter, Chapter 4 examines some of the main implications and consequences suggested by Freud's bisexuality thesis. The dialectic method of analysis remains central and focuses on various conceptual bifurcations that emerge from the bisexuality thesis, including primary and secondary identification. These are shown to build on Freud's original dialectic polarities: pleasure/unpleasure, activity/passivity and subject/object. The chapter provides a deeper investigation of shame and rivalry as the mechanisms of secondary identification. This is extended to a discussion of the emergence of society and the economy with reference to the ego and superego. The dialectic movement of emergence is arrested by various acts of nomination, most notably the nomination of heterosexuality in the forms of sexual reproduction and financial profit, which have become social and economic master values in modernity. Only by keeping the dialectic open can the subject do justice to its inherent and revolutionary bisexual nature, not in the sense of transgression but rather in pursuit of the non-nomination that is the permanent *becoming* of a dialectic self.

Chapter 5 discusses further implications and consequences flowing from the reconstructed bisexuality thesis. A key evaluation in this regard is the clinical value of the bisexuality thesis, especially concerning the idea of a primal or primary repression. The first section of this chapter explores a semiotic model of the subject that is developed from the consequences of the reconstructed bisexuality thesis. There are three elements to this model: the structure of language, metaphor and narrative. This is followed by an extensive discussion of repressed and unconscious homosexuality, and the chapter then moves on to evaluate the clinical value of the bisexuality thesis. The discussion includes a comparison of Freud's clinical approach to the clinical styles of Jacques Lacan's psychopathology and Deleuze and Guattari's schizoanalysis. The chapter ends by considering the implications of the bisexuality thesis for the clinical situation as well as the social and economic environment in which the individual human emerges as an emancipated bisexual subject.

The Conclusion briefly reviews the reconstructed bisexuality thesis and returns to consider the implications of the thesis from the perspective of evolution. The bisexuality thesis confirms an understanding of bisexuality as an ancestral condition of indiscriminate sexual behaviour.

Here I would also like to mention a few practical points about the book. Firstly, I dislike footnotes and endnotes. They leave me scrambling to follow the thoughts of an author between multiple and physically different parts of the book, which really just forces the work of integration onto the reader. This process only becomes more complex in electronic versions, where it is impossible to keep a finger or bookmark in several places at the same time. For this reason, there are expressly no footnotes or endnotes in this book. All the ideas presented to the reader are integral, and the reader is assured that I have stripped the discussion down to its key components and integrated these into a single flowing text. Furthermore, I aspire to write in clear and straightforward English with the minimum of jargon and specialised terminology and, as far as possible, I avoid using the personal forms of address (I, we, you, etc.) in the text. The English language affords the remarkable ability to write in an abstract manner that does not require personalisation of statements. This allows the focus to be placed squarely on the text and on the ideas rather than on the author or reader of the ideas. I hope the conceptual utility is persuasive. There are places in the discussion, however, where it has seemed necessary to open the perspective or to highlight a particular perspective, transition or interpretation as my own, and I resort to the personal form to signal such occasions.

In these strange technological times, it now appears no longer redundant to assure the reader that, unless otherwise clearly acknowledged in the references, this book and the ideas in it are entirely the product of my own exertions, and no machine or software had any role in the production of this manuscript, except my antiquated and much-loved laptop with an ancient version of MS Word used for typing up the text.

On the matter of references, the book adopts the system of historical layering of references, based on the principle that no one writes posthumously. Historical layering makes the distinction between *source* text and *access* text. The access text is a publication actually used in the preparation of the manuscript, whereas the source text is the original version of the publication as authored by the person(s) referenced in the manuscript. In many cases, the source texts and access texts are the same, but the source date can be different from the access date, in which case *page references* used are always for the access text, but the *reference year* is that of the source text. In these cases, the relation of access text to source text is explained in the References list at the end of each chapter, including details about translations. Despite reservations I have about certain translations, I reference the standard or readily available translations as far as possible to assist with ease of re-access for readers. This is the case in particular for references to the English translation of Freud's work, which are to the *Standard edition* (and not the *Revised standard edition*).

Methodology of this book

Such is the overview of the content of the book with its aims. At this point, readers may wish to proceed directly to Chapter 1 and pursue the reconstruction of Freud's bisexuality thesis. However, the approach I take in this book is unconventional in a number of ways and may seem unusual or even strange to some readers, especially those trained in the traditional human, social and medical sciences, so I think it is prudent here to add a number of framing comments on methodology. This allows me the opportunity to delineate and make clear the underlying methodology of my project, and I hope the reader will thus be better armed for the arguments ahead.

The methodology of this book is guided by the *relativism* of knowledge. This approach to or understanding of knowledge entails certain principles and perspectives, which are outlined here in the context of this book. After this outline, I go on to demonstrate how relativism as methodology is also deeply implicated in Freud's epistemology.

The *relativism* of knowledge is well summarised by Friedrich Nietzsche's observation that there are no facts, only interpretations (1885–1887, p. 267). The extent to which knowledge is scientific is the extent to which a particular interpretation can be explained in its relationship to other interpretations. Certain interpretations claim precedence or seniority in this intersection of epistemological relations. It is not always easy to dissect and analyse these claims, and it is inevitable that starting points are adopted. The starting points for me are two basic principles that anchor this book: evolution and emancipation. After briefly laying out these two principles, I then discuss my approach to certain subsequent problems of epistemology, including pursuit of the *truth function* in science and the relationship of system and instance. In this, I am guided by a commitment to the two anchoring principles and by the inescapable relativism of knowledge.

Anchoring principles

There are two grounding principles underpinning this book: evolution and emancipation. Everything that is alive is the product of evolution and so, in order to understand any aspect of life, the underlying evolutionary paradigm must be traced and understood. The significance of Charles Darwin's pioneering paradigm cannot be overemphasised or forgotten. Nowhere is this clearer or more urgent than in the areas of the survival and reproduction of the species. All life is driven by a primary and fundamental urge to survive and to reproduce itself. In humans, the reproduction of the species is a function of sexual complementarity between male and female. There is no avoiding this basic evolutionary fact. The male and the female of the species contribute their unique gametes, which then join in the conception of new life. In a very basic and non-moral sense, this is the unavoidable logic of evolution – life is the product of evolution. So central is this logic that it can be called a natural law, in fact the only law of nature. In no way should this be understood as an endorsement of pseudo-scientific applications of this law in various ideological formations or ambitions; evolution is simply a statement of empirical fact.

In a far more recent phenomenon than evolution, humans have developed the idea of emancipation. This concept has taken millennia to be articulated and has only gradually been adopted, with the paradigm becoming especially prominent in recent centuries. The paradigm of emancipation is summarised briefly in two statements: people should be free to define who they are, and they should be free to choose who they love. While not a law in the empirical or natural sense, these can be called the two fundamental human freedoms; as a principle, they are only offset by a single basic restriction: do no harm to life (life of the self or other life). As fundamental and self-evident as these two freedoms appear, their negation has been the focus of human social development for the entire period of recorded history. The two freedoms have been thwarted and constrained by most social, economic, legal, religious and moral codes. Despite all the restraining social and economic forces, a certain degree of real and practical emancipation towards full enjoyment of these two freedoms has been accomplished in modernity (a period covering roughly the last two centuries and located in fragmented and limited geographical jurisdictions). The advancement today of this practical emancipation is still geographically and culturally limited, but many jurisdictions (by no means all) now recognise that who we are and who we love are deeply individual and personal matters that are of absolutely no concern to the rest of society, beyond adherence to the basic limitation of doing no harm to life. From a rational perspective within this emancipatory paradigm of freedom, the natural law of biological sex – the presence of the male or female chromosome – plays no defining role in who we are and who we love. Human freedom is sometimes invoked as a natural law, e.g. by John Locke, Jean-Jacques Rousseau, Thomas Paine or Karl Marx, but in reality freedom is not an empirical force analogous to evolution; freedom is always a social convention.

Clearly the principle of emancipation is a component of the social construction of human reality, whereas the principle of evolution is deduced from an empirical reality that stands outside and apart from human social constructs. A contradiction seems to arise between the two principles. If human social reality can be structured so as to favour the fullest measure of personal and intimate freedom, then this very freedom – expressed for example in same-sex desire – appears to contradict the principle of evolution, which would favour opposite-sex desire. The contradiction emerges more starkly when approached from the opposite political direction, where the logic of evolution is deployed to explain an apparent naturalness of opposite-sex desire. In turn this explanation becomes the basis and justification for persecuting and pathologising a range of non-reproductive sexual impulses so that the apparent contradiction between evolution and emancipation is at the heart of the historical discourse to negate freedom. The discourse of this contradiction remains core to contemporary debates and ferocious culture wars that unfold loudly and destructively around the world today. This regressive contemporary contestation threatens even the modest gains that have been made for freedom.

In the area of sexual theory, the apparent contradiction between evolution and emancipation is crystallised in a problem known as *Darwin's paradox*. In observing the persistence of homosexuality in the human species, there is a paradox because the theory of evolution suggests that non-reproductive sexual attraction and behaviour would lead to less reproductive success, and so these traits would eventually die out. An overview of the historical discourse and development of theories around the paradox is provided by Milam (2021), who suggests there is growing research interest recently on the paradox in non-human species. A few main theories have emerged to explain the genetic persistence of homosexuality, including the kin altruism theory, the female fertility hypothesis and the alliance theory (outlined in Buss, 2016, p. 151). It is most striking that the research and discussion surrounding the paradox to date is entirely predicated not only on self-reported sexual orientation in humans, which ignores any unconscious element of sexual desire, but also an assumed *exclusive* orientation of either heterosexuality or homosexuality. Bisexuality does not feature as a concept in this research. This is amply demonstrated by Buss in his outline, which assumes the a priori exclusivity of sexual orientation, and by Prum (2017), whose novel thesis giving precedence to sexual selection rather than natural selection is unable to escape the assumption of exclusive sexual behaviour. More recently, however, Monk et al. (2019) have cautiously challenged the assumption of exclusivity in a highly technical study that presents research across a wide range of species in support of an alternative hypothesis for the evolution of same-sex sexual behaviour in animals. Their hypothesis is that "indiscriminate sexual behaviour, or sexual behaviour without sex-based mate identification resulting in the expression of both SSB [same-sex sexual behaviour] and DSB [different-sex sexual behaviour], is the most likely ancestral condition of sexually reproducing animals" and that

> the expression of both DSB and SSB, to varying degrees across individuals' lifetimes and across individuals in a population, may be the norm for most animal species, representing the legacy of an ancestral condition of indiscriminate sexual behaviour that remains either neutral or, in some contexts, advantageous.
>
> (p. 1623)

Stripped of technical jargon, Monk et al. are putting forward *a universal bisexuality thesis* in the evolutionary paradigm. Despite their cautious presentation sheathed in technicalities, this is a radical position that upends the consensus assumption of exclusive heterosexuality and homosexuality. Any paradox evaporates as soon as the discourse admits the indiscriminate sex of universal bisexuality in place of exclusive sexual behaviours. It is to Freud's credit that he recognised (and more than a century ago) not only a thesis of universal bisexuality but also its radical implications for evolutionary science and emancipation. While the purpose of my book is to reconstruct Freud's thesis of universal bisexuality, the outcome is a broader recognition that evolutionary research and debates can no longer rely on the presumption of self-reported and exclusive heterosexual or homosexual behaviour as the baseline for humans. Exclusivity is an a posteriori and provisional political nomination, not the destiny bequeathed by evolution.

Preliminary comments on the veracity of scientific discourse

Given the relativism of knowledge – there are no facts, only interpretations – an important cornerstone of my approach to methodology has been finding a way of determining the veracity of discourse, and especially discourse that describes itself as scientific. By *veracity*, I mean the accuracy and reliability of an interpretation. In order to assert and establish the veracity of scientific discourse, there is always an *appeal* to the truth of such a discourse – it *claims* to be true. For example, to assert the principles of evolution and emancipation is to appeal to the truth of these two principles. To make the matter clearer, and in recognition of the inherently contested and relative nature of truth, it is therefore better to call this appeal the *truth function* in discourse. In his "grand narrative" theory, Paul Ricoeur calls this truth function a "striving for truth" (1975, p. 218) and "the ambition of truth" in narratives (1983, p. 226, also 267 fn 1; see also 1984, pp. 156–7, 159, 162 fn 4; 1985, pp. 5–6). It seems to me that there are two main routes that can be taken to appeal to or establish the truth function in scientific discourse: an appeal to *authority* and an appeal to *reality*. Discourses may also deploy two other techniques to assert their claim to veracity, namely rhetoric and aesthetics. However, rhetoric and aesthetics are not strictly speaking components of science or truth.

Rhetoric should be restricted to the style of the presentation of an argument and refers to the way in which a claim for truth is laid out to the audience. Ideally, the style should be clear and logical to enable the audience to evaluate the argument. Unfortunately, rhetoric today has become much abused as a form of persuasion that appeals to emotions rather than logic, and as such has become purely the performance of political manipulation. This type of instrumentalised rhetoric is grotesque in politics, and certainly has no place in scientific discourse. The aesthetics of an argument are similarly located outside of its veracity, but beauty earns a place in my esteem by virtue of being disinterested in the argument's political value. There is therefore an aesthetic component in my methodology. This acknowledges my profound need to reflect and create beauty in the world, as well as construct a more attractive social reality founded on full emancipation.

This leaves authority and reality as the two principal methods to claim veracity in scientific discourse. The appeal to authority is the mainstay of academic discourse today. Something is claimed to be true because it is said by so-and-so, whose authority is evidenced by a host of higher degrees from and appointments to academic institutions in a mutually reinforcing and self-selecting circularity. Authority as the basis for veracity relies primarily on *tradition*, and so this methodology can be called the authority of the *magisterium*. Tradition is a convention, a body of received interpretations, and the authority granted by tradition is a type of licence. In the academic tradition and associated professional institutions, this licence bears witness to training; call it an academic or professional apprenticeship. At best, the magisterium's claim to truth relies on sustaining a previously asserted interpretation of reality through the transmission of tradition. At its worst, magisterium authority entails all the personal and systemic abuses that are inherent to training by guilds.

Thus, only the appeal to *empirical reality* remains as the basis for scientific veracity. Reality is far from simple in its scientific role, however, and half the battle in science is determining which aspects of reality are constructed by humans and which part of reality is actually empirical. At the best of times the line is difficult to determine, but especially in late modernity this is indisputably a complex problem because humans play an ever-greater and now dominant role in constructing, reconstructing and destroying reality, as the crisis of anthropogenic climate change demonstrates.

The way I picture science is as follows: there is a point of contact where the human constructions of reality and empirical reality intersect, or perhaps it is better to say the two realities brush up against each other. My approach is to establish a position – an outpost – balanced on this frontier zone as optimally as possible using the following methodological components and bearing in mind the practical limitations of method given the inherent relativism of knowledge. This simply affirms the provisionality and emergent nature of scientific knowledge.

In a fundamental manner, I eschew appeals to the authority of the magisterium. Inspired by the example of Roland Barthes (1967) and Michel Foucault (1969), I adopt an approach that I characterise as *sola scriptura*, which is Latin for: *only by the text*. This method dates back to the Protestant Reformation in Europe and embraces the individual responsibility of the scientist to consult the evidence, which is presented in the text. It eliminates the intermediation of the magisterium, which in turn implies a focus on the ideas rather than the personality or biography of the thinker. In a special way, this non-biographical approach requires an abstraction in the human sciences, away from the neo-Romantic obsession with the biography of individuals to an aggregation or composite view of knowledge. This is exemplified by thinking in systems rather than individual experience. Foregrounding the text requires a technique of *close reading*, where the text is the initial and sole focus of attentive and detailed engagement. Close reading also entails always going to the primary text. First read the primary authors themselves, and avoid summaries, paraphrases and appropriations of the primary theory by secondary writers. To understand Lacan, for example, don't waste time reading Žižek on Lacan, go to the source: Lacan's texts. To understand Freud, don't read Lacan on Freud or any of the other myriad derivatives, read Freud's texts.

It is important to note that I define the concept of text very broadly to mean not only the written scientific text in which findings are recorded but also the broad range of evidentiary fields that underpin and generate the written text. These evidentiary fields are the points of contact with empirical reality. Nevertheless, the written text retains a place of privilege in science by virtue of its suitability for the logical and systematic laying out of the argument, as well as the democracy of exchange and readership the written form offers and the durability it allows after the lifetime of its author. Finally, the text leads to a key component of the scientific method: repeatability. An interpretation is true if it holds up to repetition in its verification when measured against empirical reality. The truth – to the extent that such a term can be used – is not vested in the authority of the scientist but in the authority of empirical reality.

In practical terms, this methodology is a complex process in a field such as Freud's metapsychology, with its delicate interplay of empirical and constructed realities. It must be stated from the start that my embrace of Freud's work is not an appeal to his authority. Readers of this book may be surprised to find no biographical dimension to the examination and reconstruction of Freud's bisexuality thesis. I reject the concept of Freud-as-master as well as the idea that Freud-the-person somehow holds the trump card in an argument. This does not mean I position myself against Freud, however. Quite the opposite. While there is certainly a strong, even dominant, element in Freud's work of asserting his own authority, which some of his followers have taken as a licence for their own authoritarianism, there is the element of radical emancipation that Freud espoused, tied with a scientific honesty which is reflected in the recourse of his work to the empirical reality of biology. In Freud's work I have found reflected a revolutionary approach to received ideas and conventions and a willingness to embrace the provisional and emergent nature of knowledge that reveals a common purpose I share: to enhance the cause of emancipation, and to inspire people to pursue their own freedom and the freedom of their brothers and sisters on the basis that freedom is indivisible. My freedom cannot come at the cost of your bondage, and my bondage cannot be the price for your freedom.

In summary, my approach is not anti-authoritarian. It is the approach of the authority of empirical reality. This approach may seem odd and even uncomfortable at first to readers who come from the authoritarian guild tradition of universities and training institutions, but I place my faith in the curiosity of readers with a background in hermeneutic flexibility and a shared interest in universal emancipation.

System and instance

An important cornerstone of my understanding of textual reading is the distinction between system and instance, which I believe is well defined in the *Course in general linguistics* (1906–1911) by Ferdinand de Saussure. There is much epistemological value in the ideas of Saussure that has been overlooked, not only in his native field of linguistics but also more broadly in the human sciences, including this fundamental distinction between system and instance. The work published posthumously under the name of Ferdinand de Saussure is a composite principal text *Cours de linguistique générale* based on a series of lectures given by Saussure at the University of Geneva over several years, for which no written form was found to exist after his death in 1913. The text of the *Course* was compiled retrospectively by a group of his university colleagues drawn from student notes taken during the different lecture series and aimed to reproduce an approximation of the lectures. This principal text has been augmented by more student notes that came to light decades later, and later still the student notebooks were themselves supplemented in various published editions to the printed record of the principal text. Finally, and quite unexpectedly, this composite principal text is augmented eighty years after its publication by the discovery of papers on the topic attributed directly to Saussure and now published as *Écrits de linguistique générale* to distinguish them from but indicate their affinity to the *Course*. In consequence of this supremely fragmented and authorially unorthodox text, much intellectual endeavour surrounding the meaning and interpretation of the *Course* has devolved into elaborate attempts to divine what Saussure-the-person said or didn't say. Foremost in this field is the study by Harris (2001), which is exemplary of the general tortured scholarly relationship with and interpretation of the composite *Course* text. Given the sheer effort needed to understand the radical conceptual paradigm contained in the *Course*, much scholarship predictably regresses into interpretations appealing to Saussure's biography. Saussure's *Course* is undoubtedly a key paradigmatic text of high modernity, on a par with the work of Darwin, Nietzsche, Marx and Freud, but given the lack of authorial certitude, the interpretation of the *Course* has been especially prone to opportunistic appropriation by the likes of Lacan (1955–1956) and Derrida (1967).

The orphan history of the *Course* and the composite nature of the text are immaterial to the ideas contained in the *Course*, which inform an understanding of the structure of language. It does not matter if Saussure-the-person did or didn't say any of these ideas; the *Course* itself provides a solid and radical understanding of language, which is extremely valuable because language is an inescapable and central part of constructed human reality. The approach of relativism I espouse is profoundly influenced by the *Course*, and in Chapter 5 (pp. 133–42) I will return to the famous and central signifier-signified pairing from the *Course* (1906–1911, especially Part 1, pp. 65–78) to explore the relative basis of meaning in the clinical situation, but here I would like to explain the relevance of the *Course* for the distinction between system and instance.

The *Course* distinguishes between language as a system (*la langue*) and the individual spoken and written instances of language usage (*la parole*) (1906–1911, especially Introduction, Chapter 3 and 4, pp. 7–20). This distinction is important for determining and analysing the elements of a text because texts do not come into existence randomly at the whim of a particular author nor do they exist in isolation. Each text is the individual product of an overarching system. A text must therefore be analysed as an instance or expression of the rule-governed patterns of the system that produces the text. The significance of this distinction between system and instance also has a central paradigmatic value for the human sciences, with broad application, as a fundamental way of looking at textual structures beyond their immediate basis in language. For each instance (text) with a social dimension, such as an event in history, an economic or political action, or a sexual encounter, there is an underlying system that gives rise to and can account for this particular social instance. The langue/parole (system and instance) distinction has value as an analogy or metaphor that helps to sift and segment the myriad instances in the social evidentiary field into their various components, and from these into categories and relations. These components are the building blocks that are selected and combined in various ways to form the social field. Like language, any social field will have a limited and predictable number of components (a lexicon), and their selection and combination follow predictable patterns with a rule-like nature (syntax). This could be called a social grammar. The langue/parole distinction therefore also has methodological value as a way of segmenting social fields for analysis.

The perspective goes much further than analogy and methodology, however, because the straightforward ubiquity of the human language system as a universal social fact gives language the character of a template for all social systems. This formative aspect has profound implications, not least for the study of human mental formations and sexual expressions. Even if this higher order determinative aspect of langue is rejected and not adopted at the epistemological level of social research, the methodological value of the langue/parole distinction as analogy is sufficient to provide a useful approach to segmenting human behaviour (sexual and otherwise) into those aspects that are individual instances. Once the instances are sifted into segments, this segmentation can be used as a foundation for identifying and analysing the underlying system. The approach of rigorously distinguishing between system and instance is not only useful for its method of segmentation and analysis; it also allows for the exclusion of external and extraneous value judgements from the process of identifying and analysing instances. All instances are thus understood as instances within a system of relations, rather than characterised from outside the system as examples of nominated and privileged values, such as normality, pathology and so on. The focus is always on and determined by the underlying system and its component relations. The methodology of this book proceeds from this system and instance perspective, always seeking the system that underlies the more easily discernible instances.

In a profound and fundamental manner, Freud's theory of the unconscious follows this method as does his study of sexuality, where the systems of the unconscious and sexuality are the focus and not the countless individual instances articulated by these systems. Perhaps even more striking though is the clinical situation envisaged by Freud, where the analysand is essentially an instance of the greater system, and the role of psycho-*analysis*, shared by the analyst, is to analyse the instance in relation to the system in order to determine points where intervention is necessary to restore functionality. This specific aspect of clinical treatment in relation to Saussure's linguistics is explored in greater detail in Chapter 5.

In my method as much as Freud's, the system is the object of study. This underlines the importance of a non-biographical approach – the biography of scholars as much as the biography of analysands – and to see these individual case studies perhaps as a necessary basis for working through in treatment but an inadequate form of epistemological advance. This extends to my reading of Freud's work, where I am not interested in the paroles of his case studies, which were also of receding importance for Freud, but the langue that is the paradigm of Freud's thought.

Freud's methodology and epistemology

It is to his credit that Sigmund Freud recognised not only the distinction between instance and system but also the arbitrariness of constructed human reality when juxtaposed to the natural laws of evolution. Freud was part of the generation of scientists and scholars who emerged in the second half of the 19th century and came of age in the period after Darwin's (1859) publication of *Origin of species*, a group that includes the paradigmatic thinkers Nietzsche, Marx and Saussure, whose work navigates the contradiction between the inviolable laws of evolution and the constructed arbitrary conventions of human society. Their work has become the foundation for the modern discourse of freedom, and it is a bizarre situation today that these men have somehow become associated with the social constrictions they sought to escape. The unfairness of the contemporary consensus is challenged in the following pages with particular reference to the work of Freud, and the extremely radical nature of Freud's ideas will be recuperated and demonstrated for a new generation that is faced with navigating the apparent contradiction between evolution and emancipation. Freud's work is devoted to the investigation and analysis of the myriad social constructions that bear down on the individual and reproduce themselves in the mental world of humans. Freud's analysis, however, is always grounded in the empirical reality of evolution, and the resolutions he proposes to the puzzling contradiction are of supreme importance, not only for the specific details he discovers but also for the epistemological methods he employs.

Central to Freud's epistemology is a constant awareness of the structure of bifurcations and polarities in mental life brought about by the force field of evolution and emancipation that humans as both biological and social creatures must inhabit. These bifurcations and polarities are often read in a static manner, whereas they are at the heart of Freud's fluid mode of thinking in continuums between polarities. This in turn indicates his being attuned to the centrality of the dialectic in epistemology and method. Here in a nutshell is the radical structure of relativism in Freud's thinking, which he applies in a number of fields, including human sexuality.

There is no doubt that Freud's sexual theory is both radical and at the core of his entire project. His early work on sexuality culminates in the *Three essays on the theory of sexuality* (1905), which underwent ongoing revision over twenty years, and his sexual theory found further expansion and integration in virtually all of his other significant publications. Coinciding with the centenary of the first edition, Ethel Person (2005) provides an orthodox assessment of the *Three essays* and an overview of its subsequent reception in the main currents of psychoanalysis. More recent valuable insight into both the structure and history of Freud's sexual theory is offered in the editorial material accompanying Ulrike Kistner's English translation of the first edition of the *Three essays* (Freud, 1905a). Part of the significance of Kistner's translation, as cogently explained in her translator's note (2016), is the restoration of Freud's key dual terminology: *Geschlechts-* and *Sexual-* are used in the German but were replaced by a single term in James Strachey's *Standard edition*, namely *sexual*. Freud's two terms allow him to distinguish between two regimes of sexuality: reproductive (*der Geschlechtstrieb*) and non-reproductive (*der Sexualtrieb*). The genitals (*die Geschlechtsteile*) dominate in the reproductive regime while in the non-reproductive they do not play a primary role (lxxxi–iv).

This type of semantic dualism is crucial to Freud's sexual theory but also foregrounds some of the main dimensions of the value in his theory, namely the problem of *terminology* and the issue of *relativism*. While of lesser importance, the terminological aspect plays no small part in framing the more fundamental issues. In the historical and current discourse about gender and sexuality in general, the difficulty of agreeing on universal terminology is a leading indicator of the problem. This is illustrated by many examples, but some of the most notable include the core terminologies of socially constructed gender and sexuality that are the focus of this book.

The problem of terminology is in part a problem of language. Language functions by constructing meaning on the basis of convention. Human language is a conventional reference to an empirical reality, but empirical reality can never be translated into language. This is the problem of language as self-referential substitution (metaphor) and underpins the extreme relativism necessary to understand a second and more fundamental aspect in Freud's sexual theory, namely the question of a starting point or anchor when talking about sexuality. The first suggestion in the broader theory of sexuality as it developed in the 19th century on the basis of a far longer lineage in religious doctrine is the appeal to *normality*. Normality is charted on two plains: normality in the sense of physical and mental health as the opposite of pathology (or earlier formulations of pathology such as sin, degeneracy and so on) and sexual reproductive normality, where the act of gamete fertilisation is posited as the teleological goal of sexual relations.

Much of the hostility and misunderstanding surrounding Freud's sexual theory at the time of its publication and in subsequent decades rests on the apparently normative discourse used by Freud. There is the dimension of normal mental health versus pathology, which of course was the primary thrust of Freud's clinical interest. His discourse also navigates the terms normal and normality in relation to sexual reproduction. Although he repeatedly expresses a nuanced view of both pathology and reproductive normativity, his use of apparently normative terminology may appear to a casual reader to underpin his work, and this legacy of terminology is easily bequeathed to the theory – allowing for the types of wide-ranging repression and displacement that are so characteristic of ideology. However, a key example of Freud's careful formulation will show how his sexual theory is acutely aware of the problem surrounding the appeal to normativity:

> The final outcome of sexual development lies in what is known as the normal sexual life of the adult, in which the pursuit of pleasure comes under the sway of the reproductive function and in which the component instincts, under the primacy of a single erotogenic zone, form a firm organization directed towards a sexual aim attached to some extraneous sexual object.
>
> (Freud, 1905, p. 197)

It should be clear that this subtle and complex formulation (from 1915, the third edition of the *Three essays*) undermines the very normativity it may superficially appear to invoke. For a start, the sentence is couched in the phrase "what is known as", and this immediately cautions against regarding penis-vagina coitus (aim: pregnancy) as the normal sexual act. This kind of qualification occurs numerous times (for example, 1905, pp. 156, 172; 1906, p. 207), although here as elsewhere the *Standard edition* translation has obscured the actual phrase used by Freud: *das sogenannte normale Sexualleben*, which translates more closely as "the so-called normal sexual life", clearly without any suggestion of normative endorsement. Similarly, the English adjective "firm" does not do justice to the German original (*eine feste Organisation*), which might better be translated as a *fixed* organisation, to reflect the unbending rule introduced by the social construction of gender ideology. Where previously, in the infantile period, the instinctual search for pleasure ranged freely, it is now tamed and pressed into the service of the reproductive function – a subordination ("primacy") indicating exactly the hierarchy at work, since reproduction requires an extraneous complementary object, unlike masturbation, where the object is the self.

This short passage illustrates a clear understanding by Freud of the limits of using the nominal outcome of reproduction as the sole basis for understanding sexuality. Reproduction is insufficient in various ways. As Freud shows in the *Three essays*, sexual reproduction is just one of many components in the sexual act. The terms in the chain of signification are not only organised around reproduction. It is possible to have sexual relations – centred on pleasure, and without an external object – that do not conform to the teleological outcome of reproduction. This is the first radical epistemological break that Freud introduces parallel to and as a consequence of his discovery of the unconscious. While sexual reproduction may be the manifest outcome of sexual relations, the aim of the reproductive act – the genital act and the teleological result (fertilisation) – does not reveal the unconscious content for the parties involved nor does it explain the pleasure quotient.

To approach sexuality, it thus becomes necessary to look backwards, so to speak, from the outcome of sexual relations and examine the terms in the core biological relationship: man-woman-child. This means exploring how the relationship is structured; what the relative value is of each term; and in relation to which nomination or ideology each term is valued. The problem can be restated more clearly as follows: the terms in the series man-woman-child are differentiated from each other on the basis of two possibilities: biological sex or socially constructed gender. A widely circulating and generally accepted thesis is that the gender of a child is shaped by its social environment. However, the proposition actually says nothing, because the inverse proposition is equally true: the human social environment is shaped by gender. Which comes first? Does gender shape the social environment or does the social environment shape gender? There is no independent external anchor point. The argument is circular and therefore meaningless, and so it is useless for determining the relationship of value between the terms. Biological sex is certainly differentiated in an indisputably tangible manner, with the XX/XY chromosomes playing a (more-or-less) fixed part (give or take a few genetic exceptions), so surely biological sex offers an empirical, physical and non-circular basis for the investigation of sexuality. However, several riders present themselves immediately. For example, biological sex is really only differentiated at puberty. Before puberty, girls and boys carry the different XX/XY chromosomes, but they have immature genitals and reproductive organs that do not function for procreation. Any apparent differentiation before puberty is always in the social attribution of gender to the child, anticipating the physical changes to come at puberty and laying the foundation for this fixity. Furthermore, as Freud shows in the *Three essays*, there are pre-genital forms of sexual activity in children that are by definition non-reproductive because of the immaturity of the genitals and reproductive system before puberty. Similarly, it may be added, the biological functions required for procreation decline steadily with age following the sexual maturity introduced by puberty, and reproductive potential eventually ceases in adults even though their sexual activity can continue. This means that biological sex in the form of the mature and differentiated genitals is a necessary but insufficient element of differentiation. A further complication is uncovered by Freud: in adults there are non-genital (i.e. undifferentiated on the basis of biological sex) zones of the body that are used in an obviously sexual manner, and this behaviour is also found in children, in an infantile form. The mouth and lips (kissing – Freud, 1905, pp. 150–1) and the skin (touching and looking – 1905, pp. 156–7) are the typical examples in adult sexuality, but of course the infantile inventory is much wider and extends to autoerotism of the common zones, areas shared by the alimentary and excretory systems (mouth and lips: thumb-sucking and taking nourishment, 1905, pp. 179–83; anal zone and excretion, pp. 185–7; genital zone and urination, pp. 187–9; also 1905b, pp. 97–8). None of these zones are differentiated on the basis of biological sex, with the exception of the urethral orifice. Perhaps Freud's most surprising discovery in the series, however, is the fact that certain behaviour with no manifest reproductive or sexual value whatsoever may be the unconscious extension of sexual material, which has been repressed into the unconscious and displaced from the genitals and the manifest aim of reproduction. This unconscious material is core to his broader project. Thus he shows that even the physiological level of sexuality – biological sex – is a problem of relative value.

Freud's sexual theory responds to the problem of relative value via a number of sophisticated bifurcations. The first step is to analyse the sexual relation and to structure it into two components – the sexual object and the sexual aim (1905, pp. 135–6), based on the observation that reproduction is not universally the sexual aim, nor is the complementary biological sex always the sexual object. This structure fundamentally shifts the paradigm by retracing the nominal and evolutionary outcome (reproduction) back to the underlying impulse, the drive or aim. Evolution shows that the driving force is the teleology of reproduction (genital sexuality), but paradoxically this force must remain present in the non-reproductive aspects of sexual behaviour. This in turn can explain the aim-object divergences that take place. Freud (drawing on Weiseman's genetic theory) describes this as a twofold function:

> The individual [*das Individuum*] does actually carry on a twofold existence: one to serve his own purposes and the other as a link in a chain, which he serves against his will, or at least involuntarily. The individual himself regards sexuality as one of his own ends; whereas from another point of view he is an appendage to his germ-plasm, at whose disposal he puts his energies in return for a bonus of pleasure. He is the mortal vehicle of a (possibly) immortal substance – like the inheritor of an entailed property, who is only the temporary holder of an estate which survives him.
>
> (1914, p. 78, similar formulation repeated in 1915, pp. 124–5;
> 1917, pp. 413–4; and 1920, pp. 45–6)

In a brief but important note about the translation here, it is striking that Freud uses the grammatical neuter *das Individuum* in the original German; the translation in the *Standard edition* has taken great liberty by transposing the neuter noun into the masculine form in English, thereby effectively giving the impression that Freud excludes half the species. There are many such instances where the fullness of Freud's thoughts are flattened by the choice of the masculine in the English, and these situations then appear to lend support to the argument that Freud was a misogynist. This translation decision to use the masculine is understandable in the English stylistic context of the 1920s, when the original English translation was produced, but it reflects the practice in Anglo-American thinking at that time of reducing the species to the male, not Freud's position. By failing to restore the intent of the original grammatical neuter in such situations, the new *Revised standard edition* has missed an enormous opportunity to reflect more clearly Freud's nuanced thinking.

In this passage, the outcome of sexual reproduction is recognised as the result of the biological drive to reproduce the species. Reproduction is burdensome for both parties to the reproductive act, and so evolution has endowed it with hormonal and neurological elements, which in a broad sense can be called pleasurable. This then is the explanation for the observed divergence from the reproductive purpose: pleasure. Freud conceives of it as a component of the aim, which meanders away from the straight and narrow teleological road of reproduction and takes a path of its own. He further characterises this pleasure in two observable forms – active and passive – as well as in its own negation, unpleasure. So, on the basis of a fundamental biological drive with a clear foundation in the empirical reality of evolution, Freud is able to infer a set of three polarities (pleasure-unpleasure, activity-passivity and subject-object) that have developed out of the biological drive in order to manage it, and this management becomes the role of mental life. These polarities are introduced to the theory already in the *Three essays* (1905, pp. 198–9), where they serve as key concepts throughout this work, but they find a more detailed and concise definition in the paper on *Instincts and their vicissitudes* (1915, especially pp. 133–4; 140).

In Freud's formulation of the polarity of subject and object and activity and passivity, he is at pains to show that these poles are not intrinsically aligned with male and female (biological sex) or masculinity and femininity (gender). In multiple passages, from the earliest publications onwards, Freud repeatedly asserts the non-identity of the activity and passivity polarity with the biological sexes (1905, pp. 198, 219–20 fn 1; 1915, p. 133; 1917, p. 327; 1930, pp. 105–7 fn 2; 1931, pp. 235–9; 1933, pp. 113–4). The section in the *Three essays* on "The differentiation between men and women" (1905, pp. 219–21, and especially the long footnote added in 1915) is exemplary of his formulation:

> observation shows that in human beings pure masculinity or femininity is not to be found either in a psychological or a biological sense. Every individual on the contrary displays a mixture of the character-traits belonging to his own and to the opposite sex; and he shows a combination of activity and passivity whether or not these last character-traits tally with his biological ones.
>
> (1905, pp. 219–20 fn 1)

This reflects an awareness of the distinction between biological sex and socially constructed gender, for which in Freud's time a terminology or conceptual framework was absent (in this regard, see Kistner, 2016, pp. lxxxii–iii). In the absence of the terminology developed by feminists such as Gayle Rubin (1975) in the last fifty years, Freud sidesteps the equation of gender to biological sex by the inspired conceptualisation of activity and passivity. Freud's sexual theory is radical in this way and specifically avoids embracing the conventional discourse that reduces biological sex to the totality of what is now called gender. This polarity provides both an alternative terminology and a radical conceptual framework to analyse and understand gender. For Freud, the two behavioural trends contained in the polarity activity-passivity are responses to stimulation (from instincts within or stimulus without) and are not characteristics tied to the biological sex of either the subject or an external object. They are the two forms taken by the sexual aim (1905, p. 157; 1931, p. 240). Activity and passivity as a subject or object are found equally in both biological sexes. Initially after birth, the child is predominantly passive, but then activity comes to the fore during the stages of infantile sexuality. Infant activity is expressed by autoerotism and also in the active pursuit of pleasure, even if this is spatially limited at first. The libidinal instinct is always active in nature even when pursuing a passive aim (1905, p. 219; 1915, p. 122; 1933, p. 96), and Freud is quite clear on this matter: both boys and girls equally demonstrate this nascent trend of activity (1931, pp. 235–7). Guy Hocquenghem's view of the active "unsublimated anus" (1972, pp. 93–132) illustrates this libidinal instinct for activity beyond Freud's texts. By implication this unsublimated activity extends also to the vagina, along with the potency for pleasure of the male prostrate and anal orgasm, not considered by Freud.

Each of Freud's polarities can be seen to function as a continuum, each with its own dialectic, and then their interactions with each other and interrelation to biological development can be plotted systematically based on the biological force, which Freud calls the libido. He characterises each dialectic pair as follows: activity-passivity as the biological; subject-object as the real; and pleasure-unpleasure as the economic polarity (1915, p. 140). Foucault (1976) adopts these polarities and adapts them to the broader discursive context of his own historical project, aligning activity-passivity with knowledge and subject-object with power (p. 11). In effect, however, the subject-object pair must be defined as linguistic, at least initially, because it infers and reflects the constructed reality of language, which relies on the subject-(verb)-object syntax. For each of these three polarities, the dialectic dynamic emerges into mental life from the basis of the biological drive. Freud then tracks this backwards, starting at the child (the outcome of the cycle) to trace the winding path of the libido in relation to the straight teleological biology culminating in gamete fertilisation. This exemplifies the genealogical method.

In its broadest characterisation, Freud's epistemological method is "to obtain the most accurate knowledge of the nature and origin of these formerly unconscious psychical structures" (1905, p. 164). This approach looks backwards at the origins of the behaviour to uncover patterns, interrelations and deviations in order to explain the deviation as well as the origins before the deviation – quite literally to make conscious the unconscious material of an ideology. Although the content is different, Freud shares this methodology with Nietzsche and Marx. All three demonstrate what is virtually impossible: how to uncover an ideology while within that ideology. Freud's underlying use of nuance is symptomatic of the necessary contingency of this methodology, as are his frequent revisions and redirections. As much as the content he uncovers in the process, his genealogical method is the enduring strength of his epistemology. In principle, the work of the psychoanalyst with an analysand also follows the genealogical method but uncovers the genealogy of the individual rather than of the species. This can be understood as uncovering the individual in ideology, although equally the analyst is simultaneously exercising an interpellative role within this ideology, which serves to illustrate the extreme difficulty of uncovering ideology from the inside.

There is one further aspect of Freud's method that requires comment, namely his style:

> I am now prepared to hear you ask me scornfully whether our ego-psychology comes down to nothing more than taking commonly used abstractions literally and in a crude sense, and transforming them from concepts into things – by which not much would be gained. To this I would reply that in ego psychology it will be difficult to escape what is universally known; it will rather be a question of new ways of looking at things and new ways of arranging them than of new discoveries.

(Freud, 1933, p. 60)

At the start, it is important to distinguish between two general styles in Freud's work: the metaphorical and the empirical. Of course these two categories also apply more generally to all human epistemology. There are components of the theory that are clearly metaphorical constructs, which attempt to illuminate arrangements in the human construction of reality (or "psychological reality" as Freud terms this, 1921, p. 80), and then there are components that aspire to model empirical reality directly, in the scientific ambition to apprehend empirical reality. The distinction is only partly successful because even the empirical (physical and biological) components described in the theory are subsumed – by the act of making such a distinction, if not already previously in the material itself – into the model of constructed human reality, which is to understand this model as the creation of specific and extended metaphors. From the perspective of science, these metaphors are a bridge between empirical reality, which is always out of reach, and human understanding. An important example of these two categories is Freud's topographical and structural modelling of the mental apparatus. These two models are clearly metaphorical in nature, in particular the second model of the id, ego and superego. The models are metaphors for interpreting and understanding the more general and physical distinction between conscious and unconscious mental activity; these are empirical forms of mental activity that can be observed directly and somatically, as can the class of behaviour known as the instincts (or drives), all of which in turn informs Freud's observations. Another major example of the metaphoric style of Freud's work is presented by his sexual theory, with its tension between the reproductive and non-reproductive regimes. Here the metaphor of the Oedipus complex is obvious and widely known.

Psychoanalytic theory and (especially) clinical practice today have necessarily invested heavily in Freud's metaphors as a mode and model of differentiation from other schools of psychology, and for the differentiation of psychology from the other sciences. In my discussion, I am primarily interested in privileging the scientific ambitions of Freud's metaphors. My approach therefore is keenly aware of the pitfalls of taking the metaphors ("abstractions") literally – as is often done in Anglo-American scholarship – or extending the metaphors into inflationary constructs – as emerges conspicuously in the psychoanalytic tradition in France. Down the literal path lies the fetishism of concepts, whereas an over-investment in metaphors produces a proliferation of derivative abstractions under self-referencing authority. In principle, while it is necessary and unavoidable to metaphorise the scientific, it is also necessary to avoid literalising the metaphorical. At the very least, the distinction between the two domains must be kept clearly in view. Science can proceed to the frontier between metaphor and empirical reality and stare wistfully at the unreachable empirical territories beyond human access, but this frontier is the limit of the scientific endeavour no matter how much science may dream of incursions.

The following discussion is concerned with the human biological substrata and the structures of the subsequent mental activity that develop on and from this foundation under the influence of social forces. Although this approach entails an inevitable circularity of argument, my ambition remains to establish an invariable material factor (or factors) as the preliminary point for a discussion of human sexuality in the sense of Freud's "new ways of looking at things and new ways of arranging them". It must be emphasised again, however, that Freud and his texts are invoked in this book not by way of an appeal to their authority but simply as the progenitors of a paradigm, which my analysis and interpretation extend considerably.

Definitions and terminology

In precisely this sense of avoiding an under- or over-investment in metaphors, it is important to offer preliminary clarification on several terms and concepts that will be frequently encountered in the book, and to provide some initial definition. In most cases, my definitions function directly in relation to Freud's terminology and usage. Three central clusters of terms are addressed here in order to clarify them in advance of the main discussion: identity and identification; biological sex and gender; and sexual orientation. These definitions are further refined and expanded in the flow of the discussion in the book. Some contemporary terms or usages are explicitly excluded. An important such exclusion is the increasingly common colloquial meaning of *ego* and *narcissism* as an inflated valuation of the self. Ego and narcissism are used throughout in line with Freud's usage of these terms to mean the self, without express valuation.

Identity and identification

The concept of *identity* has become so commonplace in popular and academic discussions of sexuality today that the meaning of the term is most often taken for granted and given little further consideration. The prevailing explanation of identity is a sense of self: a self-identity in which each individual takes an active role defining their identity, now often in opposition and variation to some broader social norm or standard of identity. In much current discourse, identity is considered to entail a range of constructed personal and social spheres, ranging from sexual orientation to gender and broader intersections with race, class and nation. In this book, however, the word identity will not be encountered in this sense. The book instead relies fundamentally on the concept of *identification*, a process that is key to Freud's (1923) structural theory of the id, ego and superego. The concept of identification is complex and central to the reconstruction of Freud's bisexuality thesis; it is defined in Chapter 2 and examined in detail in Chapter 3. It is important to remember in the context of this book that identification is in no way analogous to or synonymous with identity.

Biological sex and gender

A fundamental aspect of the broad contemporary discourse around identity entails the recognition and definition of *gender*. It must be understood from the start that I regard gender as a fictional construct, with no basis in empirical reality. Gender is a purely social construct that serves specific economic and political interests. As such, it has no independent basis in reality outside of the social reality in which the concept arises and *circulates*. Consequently, I wish to make clear that I intentionally sidestep the circular discourse this term entails. Toril Moi's (1999) over-wrought study of the development of gender as a concept demonstrates by example the profitless circularity of deploying the term and the endless conceptual labyrinth entered when taking gender seriously, as if gender were actually an empirical reality. Scholars like Rubin (1975), Butler (1990) and Moi have chosen a poisoned chalice with their focus on and affirmation of gender. As an alternative expression, *social sex* has much to recommend it in a parallel to *biological sex* as a way to distinguish the psychological and physical dimensions. Unfortunately, social sex has not been taken up in the discourse as a term in this way, and so I tend to use the expression *socially constructed gender* or variations of this throughout to keep in mind the socially predicated aspects and contingency of the psychological representations of biological sex. In Chapter 5, it becomes strategic to use social sex as a neutral term in the discussion to avoid lapsing into gendered terms.

Socially constructed gender stands in contrast to the biological sex of individuals. While biological sex is itself increasingly contested in Gender Studies and Queer Theory, biological sex is tightly defined in this book as the combination of biological factors present in an individual and required to produce male or female gametes that in turn play the crucial role in sexual reproduction. This is the sense in which *male* and *female* are used by Freud, who presents these biological terms in contrast to other terms, such as *masculine* and *feminine* (or variations of these), to designate the social constructs that are today generally rendered under the umbrella concept of gender or variations such as gender identity or gender roles. In contemporary discourse, these terms today are so accepted there is little actual dissent about the nature of gender, and it is seen in a broadly positive light, with emphasis placed on social or individual gender construction, almost as if gender were a simple and uncomplicated consumer choice, and moreover a choice that can be adopted or changed at will. Contemporary debates give scarcely any consideration to the destructive and incarcerating nature of gender, focusing instead on the more obvious symptoms of gender, like inequality of the sexes, and putting forward proposals for reform conceptually limited to the symptoms. These debates ignore to their peril that gender is always constructed and has no objective basis in reality. An analysis and understanding of the intractable problem of gender is one of the aspects I aim to approach, albeit by specifically avoiding the pitfalls of contemporary debates around gender altogether.

As a phrase, *biological sex* is unfortunately cumbersome in English, which is possibly why the word gender has often been used loosely and in colloquial speech as a synonym for biological sex, even in much of the prevailing academic discourse. The point to remember throughout this book is that gender (masculine and feminine) must in no way be confused or conflated with biological sex (male and female) for the purposes of reconstructing Freud's bisexuality thesis. Freud's highly sophisticated usage of these terms (male and female, masculine and feminine) and especially the related polarity of active/passive are central to understanding his work; his usage has already been outlined above and is explored in further detail in Chapter 2 and broadly adopted throughout.

Sexual orientation: gay, lesbian, bisexual / trans / queer

More will be said about sexual orientation as the reconstruction of the bisexuality thesis unfolds, but it is important to understand that sexual orientation in the contemporary sense as a component of an individual's sexual behaviour and identity is fundamentally a social and political construct. Much of the discussion of sexual orientation today is premised on discreet categories, which is a reflection of the history of sexual orientation and emancipation but not of empirical reality. In no way can human sexual activity be classified in discreet and exclusive categories, as the well-known research of Kinsey et al. (1948, 1953) demonstrates beyond any doubt. Terms such as *gay* and *lesbian* are extremely specific to the development of sexual politics in the last hundred years, and these terms are excluded from the discussion of Freud's bisexuality thesis. To the extent that the term *bisexual* has similarly come to refer to an identity or sexual practice, this is also excluded. In addition, it must be made clear that the contemporary embrace of transgender is a complicated and conceptually untenable expansion of the already heavily encumbered category of sexual orientation. Such political expansion is fraught and tenuous. The use of the word or conceptual category of *queer* is also specifically avoided; queer is a relatively recent and equally contested political umbrella category of expansion that defies definition except by locking itself into a counter-defining relationship with entirely hypothetical norms or standards ("un-queer"), which are paradoxically affirmed in the process. To avoid confusion, the book utilises the now somewhat archaic terminology of *homosexual* and *heterosexual*, and bisexual is used in its collocation with this older lexicon. In all instances, these three terms are also useful because of their absence of marking the biological sex of an individual. They have the further utility of serving as adjectives describing both object and subject aspects of sexuality.

A final consideration is the degree to which any sexual desire is unconscious. It would be naïve to see sexuality only in terms of conscious self-recognition or in isolation from the social and economic conditions in which sexuality happens. This is true in the origins of the sexual self, as well as for later therapeutic interventions. That which can be observed is often a long way from what is going on below the surface for the individual and in the broader socio-economic context. This forces the question: Is there ever a scenario of two free and independent people engaged in the sexual act unencumbered by the past, the present and the future? Emancipation as such is never a state, always a process and goal.

Reference list

Barthes, R. (1967). The death of the author. Trans. by R. Howard and first published in the English version (not French) in *Aspen Magazine: The Minimalism Issue* (#5,6). New York: Roaring Fork Press.

Buss, D.M. (2016). *Evolutionary psychology: The new science of the mind* (5th ed.). London: Routledge.

Butler, J. (1990). *Gender trouble: Feminism and the subversion of identity*. New York: Routledge, 2006.

Darwin, C. (1859). *On the origin of species by means of natural selection or the preservation of favoured races in the struggle for life*. Oxford: Oxford University Press, 2008.

Deleuze, G. and Guattari, F. (1972). *Capitalisme et schizophrénie: L'anti-Œdipe*. Paris: Éditions de Minuit. Trans. by R. Hurley, M. Seem and H. Lane as *Anti-Oedipus: Capitalism and schizophrenia*. Minneapolis: University of Minnesota Press, 1983.

Deleuze, G. and Guattari, F. (1980). *Capitalisme et schizophrénie: Mille plateaux*. Paris: Éditions de Minuit. Trans. by B. Massumi as *A thousand plateaus: Capitalism and schizophrenia*. Minneapolis: University of Minnesota Press, 1987.

Derrida, J. (1967). *De la grammatologie*. Paris: Éditions de Minuit, 1967. Trans. by G. Spivak as *Of grammatology*. Baltimore & London: Johns Hopkins University Press, 1976.

Foucault, M. (1969). Qu'est-ce qu'un auteur? A seminar presented on 22 February at the *Société Française de Philosophie*, published version in *Société Française de Philosophie Bulletin*, 63(3), 73–104. A slightly modified version presented in 1970 at Buffalo University (USA), trans. by J. Harari and published as "What is an author?" in *Textual strategies: Perspectives in post-structuralist criticism*. Harari J.V., ed. Ithaca: Cornell University Press, 1979.

Foucault, M. (1976). *Histoire de la sexualité: La volonté de savoir*. Paris: Éditions Gallimard. Trans. by R. Hurley as *The history of sexuality. Volume 1: An introduction*. New York: Pantheon Books, 1978.

Freud, S. (1905). Three essays on the theory of sexuality. In J. Strachey, ed. and trans., *The standard edition of the complete psychological works of Sigmund Freud, 24 vols*. London: Hogarth Press, 1953–1974. 7:125–245.

Freud, S. (1905a). *Three essays on the theory of sexuality: The 1905 edition*. Trans. U. Kistner. London: Verso, 2016.

Freud, S. (1905b). Jokes and their relation to the unconscious. *Standard ed.*, 8:1–274.

Freud, S. (1906). My views on the part played by sexuality in the aetiology of the neuroses. *Standard ed.*, 7:269–79.

Freud, S. (1914). On narcissism. *Standard ed.*, 14:67–104.

Freud, S. (1915). Instincts and their vicissitudes. *Standard ed.*, 14:109–40.

Freud, S. (1917). Introductory lectures on psycho-analysis (Part III). *Standard ed.*, 16: 241–463.

Freud, S. (1920). Beyond the pleasure principle. *Standard ed.*, 18:1–63.

Freud, S. (1921). Group psychology and the analysis of the ego. *Standard ed.*, 18:65–143.

Freud, S. (1923). The ego and the id. *Standard ed.*, 19:1–66.

Freud, S. (1930). Civilization and its discontents. *Standard ed.*, 21:57–145.

Freud, S. (1931). Female sexuality. *Standard ed.*, 21:223–43.

Freud, S. (1933). New introductory lectures on psycho-analysis. *Standard ed.*, 22:1–182.

Harris, R. (2001). *Saussure and his interpreters*. Edinburgh: Edinburgh University Press.

Hocquenghem, G. (1972). *Le desir homosexuel*. Paris: Editions Universitaires. Trans. by D. Dangoor as *Homosexual desire*. Durham: Duke University Press, 1993.

Kinsey, A.C., Pomeroy, W.B. and Martin, C.E. (1948). *Sexual behavior in the human male*. Philadelphia: W.B. Saunders.

Kinsey, A.C. (1953). *Sexual behavior in the human female*. Philadelphia: W.B. Saunders.

Kistner, U. (2016). Translating the first edition of Freud's *Drei Abhandlungen zur Sexualtheorie*. In S. Freud, *Three essays on the theory of sexuality: The 1905 edition*. Trans. U. Kistner. London: Verso, 2016, pp. lxxvii–xc.

Lacan, J. (1955–1956). *Le Séminaire, Livre III – Les Psychoses*. Paris: Éditions du Seuil, 1981. Trans. by R. Grigg as *The seminar of Jacques Lacan: Book III: The psychoses 1955–1956*. New York: Norton, 1993.

Milam, E.L. (2021). The evolution of Darwinian sexualities. *BJHS Themes*, 6, 133–55.

Moi, T. 1999. *What is a woman? And other essays*. Oxford: Oxford University Press.

Monk, J.D., Giglio, E., Kamath, A., Lambert, M.R. and McDonough, C.E. (2019). An alternative hypothesis for the evolution of same-sex sexual behaviour in animals. *Nature Ecology & Evolution*, 3(12), 1622–31.

Nietzsche, F. (1885–87). *Sämtliche Werke Kritische Studienausgabe Band 12: Nachgelassene Fragmente 1885–1887*. Berlin: Walter de Gruyter & Co., 1967–77. Trans. by W. Kaufmann and R.J. Hollingdale as *The will to power*. New York: Vintage, 1968.

Person, E.S. (2005). As the wheel turns: A centennial reflection on Freud's *Three essays*. *Journal of the American Psychoanalytic Association*, 53(4), 1257–82.

Prum, R. (2017). *The evolution of beauty: How Darwin's forgotten theory of mate choice shapes the animal world – and us*. New York: Doubleday.

Ricoeur, P. (1975). *La métaphore vive*. Paris: Éditions du Seuil. Trans. by R. Czerny, K. McLaughlin and J. Costello as *The rule of metaphor*. Toronto: University of Toronto Press, 1977.

Ricoeur, P. (1983). *Temps et Récit, tome I – L'intrigue et le récit historique*. Paris: Éditions du Seuil. Trans. by K. McLaughlin and D. Pellauer as *Time and narrative – Volume 1*. Chicago: University of Chicago Press, 1984.

Ricoeur, P. (1984). *Temps et Récit, tome II – La configuration du temps dans le récit de fiction*. Paris: Éditions du Seuil. Trans. by K. McLaughlin and D. Pellauer as *Time and narrative – Volume 2*. Chicago: University of Chicago Press, 1985.

Ricoeur, P. (1985). *Temps et Récit, tome III – Le temps raconte*. Paris: Éditions du Seuil. Trans. by K. McLaughlin and D. Pellauer as *Time and narrative – Volume 3*. Chicago: University of Chicago Press, 1988.

Rubin, G. (1975). The traffic in women: Notes on the "political economy" of sex. In R.R. Reiter, *Toward an anthropology of women*. New York: Monthly Review Press.

Saussure, F. de. (i.1906–1911). Lectures delivered at the University of Geneva and published from auditors' notes by Charles Bally and Albert Sechehaye under the title *Cours de linguistique générale*. Paris: Payot, 1916. Trans. by W. Baskin as *Course in general linguistics*. New York: The Philosophical Society, 1959. Subsequently edited by Perry Meisel and Haun Saussy, New York: Columbia University Press, 2011; references are to this edition. Related unpublished manuscripts by Saussure discovered posthumously are published as *Écrits de linguistique générale*. Paris: Gallimard, 2002. Trans. by C. Sanders and M. Pires as *Writings in general linguistics*. Oxford: Oxford University Press, 2006.

Chapter 1

The de-radicalisation of Freud

It is curious that the most radical components of Freud's sexual theory should have been so rigorously and systematically repressed and displaced by the community of psychoanalysis and the broader practice of psychology. Sexual theory in general by its very character has always been fighting a rearguard action to defend its claims. Freud's sexual theory no less so, especially given the centrality of his views on sexuality to the broader framework of the epistemology of psychoanalysis he established. Freud himself was no doubt responsible in part for the suppression of his most radical ideas. His work is baroque, even labyrinthine in its development over many decades, and he reworked and extended ideas, sometimes shifting focus away from the more radical aspects. Freud's sexual theory often seems torn between a radical urge to expose the underlying sexual ("libidinal") forces at play in the human psyche and the necessary discursive restraint to communicate these novel findings to an inherently unadventurous audience. This urge, or will to truth, in Freud's texts is cloaked in a style of discourse that is part medico-scientific and part convention. The style can seem to give an oracular character to the discourse of Freud's texts, so that they lend themselves to a wide range of readings and interpretations. This reflects the undeniable and constant element in Freud's work of his radical hermeneutic openness, forging the paradigm that now bears his name, but it also opens the door to contrary readings and interpretations.

Freud's work still retained all the key aspects of its original radicalism right until his death, and it is his followers who have been at the heart of the subsequent project of repression and displacement of radicalism that has yet to be fully undone. In no area was Freud's radicalism more suppressed after his death than in his pioneering sexual theory. Scarcely had he died than his followers set about dismantling radical theoretical components, such as Freud's long-standing and central model of bisexuality as core to human sexuality, but the entire discourse in psychoanalysis around sexuality and gender became increasingly more repressive as it diverged from Freud's radical formulations, so that three decades after Freud's death Guy Hocquenghem accurately characterises post-Freudian psychoanalysis as "an institution of bourgeois society charged with controlling the libido" (1972, p. 77). Kenneth Lewes (1988, p. 142) is also scathing about developments after Freud's death, where "the simplification of sophisticated psychoanalytic ideas" produces

DOI: 10.4324/9781003498919-2

"cliché-mongering" (p. 141), "vulgarization" and "moral brutalisation" (p. 151). Lewes is strongly influenced by Herbert Marcuse's (1955) succinct materialist critique of revisionist psychoanalytic ideas in this early post-Freudian period; see especially Marcuse's "Epilogue", which highlights "the decline of theory in the revisionist schools" (p. 251) as the root cause of revisionist vulgarisation:

> in this process some of Freud's most decisive concepts (the relation between id and ego, the function of the unconscious, the scope and significance of sexuality) were redefined in such a way that their explosive connotations were all but eliminated.
>
> (p. 247)

In general, the clinical work of analysts became a process of helping their patients come to accept the most vulgar and stereotypical social conventions for gender and sexual roles. Feminists such as Juliet Mitchell (1974) and Gayle Rubin (1975) eloquently show the impact of the clinical profession in facilitating the constraint of female sexuality, while more recent studies have documented the history of and reasons for the repression of sexual theory in orthodox psychoanalysis in the classification and treatment of homosexuality as pathology (Bayer, 1981; Lewes, 1988; Isay, 1989; O'Connor & Ryan, 1993; Roudinesco, 2002; Fonagy, 2006; Drescher, 2008; Silverstein, 2008). A further significant example of the harsh conservatism of the psychoanalytic establishment is the automatic disqualification of homosexuals as analysts that persisted until quite recently (discussed at length by Roudinesco, 2002, pp. 11–2). Of course, this exclusion of alterity from psychoanalysis postponed the day of reckoning but made the reckoning much harder when it did arrive, and it is Freud's reputation which has suffered permanent damage.

There are many ways in which Freud's sexual theory has been misunderstood or poorly interpreted. One of the most pernicious and widespread errors is the common assumption that Freud's approach is prescriptive rather than descriptive. Readers stumble over the apparent appeal to normativity in Freud's style. English-speaking readers in particular easily forget that they are reading translations, which are by their very nature already a layer of interpretation. It is also often forgotten that Freud was writing and publishing at a time when the discourse around sexuality was vastly different. Much of the early 20th-century style and terminology has dropped out of fashion today, and some words or concepts now taken for granted did not yet exist, such as gender. No doubt, Freud was always working with one eye on establishing and maintaining his intellectual following, and this leads to some compromise and even obscurity in his formulations. There is also the consideration that Freud himself may not always have been fully conscious of the implications of his texts at the time he was writing or at later stages of revision. However, this is entirely consistent with his theory of the unconscious. Readers and interpreters of Freud are no less prone to approaching the texts along the paths of their own (unconscious) desires and conflicts. This would go some way to explaining the individual aspects of many de-radicalised readings of Freud's work.

In principle, Freud's work is de-radicalised along two main thrusts. In both approaches, Freud's consistently descriptive method and style are replaced by the erroneous assumption that his work is prescriptive. One approach commonly encountered is the post-Freudian introduction of pathology to the sexual theory, where Freud himself did not characterise a specific action or behaviour as pathological. This is clearly seen in the important example of homosexuality and, by extension, bisexuality. A second fundamental approach in post-Freudian interpretation is the vulgarisation of Freud's ideas, most often done via extremely reductionist readings that ignore or neglect the primary texts.

Freud on bisexuality

As a counterpoint to the discussion in this chapter of the de-radicalisation that followed after Freud's death, this opening section provides a summary of Freud's position on bisexuality. This is a brief overview to prepare the way for the discussion that follows in Chapter 2 (pp. 64–7), which returns in greater detail to Freud's manifest position on bisexuality. Today there is general consensus that Freud addressed bisexuality, and in a positive light, but many scholars speak about the vague nature of Freud's views on bisexuality, characterising it as an undeveloped and obscure theme in his work. This simply is not the case. From a purely factual perspective, this consensus view is incorrect. There are frequent manifest and unambiguous statements about bisexuality in Freud's work that leave little room for misunderstanding or misinterpretation. These statements by Freud show the two main ways in which he understands bisexuality: as bisexuality of the subject and towards the sexual object. A third, early view of bisexuality as the presence of both sexes in the same body was suggested by Wilhelm Fliess but was not seriously entertained by Freud.

Via the initial influence of Fliess (Freud, 1901, pp. 143–4; 1905, p. 143 fn, p. 147 fn; see also editor's introduction p. 127), Freud adopted and maintained a view of the centrality of bisexuality throughout the span of his work, and both components of Freud's standpoint – object-focused bisexuality and bisexuality of the subject – persist. He sees bisexuality as a disposition or characteristic expressed in the physical and mental structures of sexuality; this entails a form of radical relativism that extends firstly to the concept of a bisexual orientation in sexual object choice, and secondly to the bisexual nature of the sexual subject's intermingling of masculine and feminine characteristics. This in turn rests on Freud's understanding of masculine and feminine traits as not absolute values but characteristics that are entirely relative to each other, at best markers of the dualism or antithesis of activity and passivity (already discussed in the Introduction, pp. 18–19; see especially Freud, 1915), with the inherent co-occurrence of active and passive traits in both biological sexes (1905, p. 219, fn 1; 1913, p. 182; 1915, p. 134; 1919, p. 202; 1920, p. 171; 1925, pp. 250, 258; 1930, p. 106 fn; 1938, p. 188). For Freud, the libido itself is always active in nature, whether in men or women, and it oscillates freely between male and female objects (1905, p. 219; 1920, p. 158; 1921, p. 141;

1930, p. 106 fn; 1937, p. 244). Freud thus explicitly views bisexuality as a bedrock formation in both biological sexes (1905, p. 220; 1911, p. 46; 1912, p. 249; 1913, p. 182; 1920, p. 157; 1925, p. 258; 1930, p. 106 fn; 1937, p. 244), and this formation then generally develops under the pressure of socialisation into fixed gender and heterosexuality (1920, p. 171; 1930, pp. 104–5), with a manifest or repressed homosexual residue. Freud's most fully developed formulation of bisexuality is presented in *The ego and the id* (1923), but the intricate presentation in this text in fact entails two parallel theories of bisexuality, one encapsulated by the complete form of the Oedipus complex and the other by the bisexuality thesis. These two theories are examined in the next chapters (Chapters 2 and 3), where the bisexuality thesis is reconstructed in detail.

1940

Freud's explicit views on bisexuality are undoubtedly a central aspect of the radical paradigm of his sexual theory, and these views have suffered greatly from the history of subsequent de-radicalisation within psychoanalysis. There is a humorous comment by Deleuze and Guattari early in their monumental text that neatly sums up the dilemma: "Psychoanalysis is like the Russian Revolution; we don't know when it started going bad" (1972, p. 55). Yet there are key moments of inflection in this history of "going bad", and the starting point of the de-radicalisation is undeniably clustered around two publications in 1940, the year immediately after Freud's death. The first of these publications is the now infamous paper by Sandor Rado that ruthlessly discards the "deceptive concept of bisexuality" (1940, p. 467). The second paper, by Ruth Mack Brunswick (1940), is not as well known or referenced as Rado's text, but her contribution is perhaps the more insidious of the two because of the new element of pathology which she introduces to Freud's sexual theory.

Rado was a long-standing psychoanalyst with a close association to Freud but then, like so many of his colleagues before, he broke with Freud. Roazen (1995, 2002) attributes Rado's rift with Freud to a perceived slight over the reception of an earlier article published by Rado in the 1930s. In general, Roazen's personal-historical survey of Rado is hearsay thinly veiled as biography, and he offers no analysis of Rado's underlying theory that is of actual interest. Recourse to hearsay about Freud's personal life has little value as the basis for theoretical models.

Whatever the reasons for this breach with Freud, Rado continued to hold powerful and influential positions in the psychoanalytic establishment in the USA, where he directed training at two of the early and important New York psychoanalytic institutes. Through this influence, a direct line can be traced from Rado to the next generation of problematic psychoanalysts, like George Wiedeman, Charles Socarides, Robert Stoller, and the notorious Irving Bieber and his associates. Their unflinching commitment to curing the so-called pathology of homosexuality reflects an obsessive interest bordering on the pathological. It is clear that this new stance of elevating pathology to a central role in the sexual theory in the period after Freud echoes the general hardening of US and European social attitudes in the Cold War era after 1945, epitomised, for example, by the criminalisation of homosexuality in many jurisdictions, even in ostensibly progressive countries like France, where previously the liberties of the French Revolution had always been extended to homosexuals. This conservative outlook in the psychoanalytic establishment of the post-war decades persisted even after the broader generational social shifts that started in the 1960s and 1970s.

Quite how much influence can be attributed to one paper or even one person is speculation to say the least. However, Rado's paper does give some indication of the brazenness of opposition to Freud's radicalism that emerged from within the ranks of established and younger psychoanalysts. In recent years, Rado has received a more critical re-evaluation. Angelides (2001, pp. 78–82) and, in greater detail, Tontonoz (2017) examine the context and content of Rado's 1940 paper, although interestingly they both fail to consider Brunswick's text. Both Angelides and Tontonoz pay too much credence to Rado's argument. It is better to understand and treat Rado's paper as pure rhetorical posturing that aims to provide propaganda cover for the new conservative ideology taking root in the psychoanalytic movement after Freud's death. Rado's argument, such as it is, centres mainly on the pre-Freudian biological definition of bisexuality as the presence in one body of both biological sexes in nascent form, with one sex assuming a dominant role in the individual. Only the last part of Rado's paper refers directly to Freud's position on subject and object bisexuality; here Rado challenges head on and dismisses the complete form of the Oedipus complex (Rado, 1940, pp. 465–6) but with purely rhetorical flourishes and no actual engagement with Freud's position. The result is a broad ideological attack on homosexuality, relying on the basest appeals to heteronormativity in order to generate a vocabulary for the new bigotry of psychoanalysis going forward: Rado characterises homosexuality as "aberrant", a "morbid" sexual development and sexual stimulation, with "innate defects of the sexual action system". This type of language leaves only a small semantic step remaining from *defect* to full *pathology*, and that step is taken by Brunswick's paper. In contrast to Rado, however, Brunswick engages with Freud's position on subject bisexuality in a far more direct and concrete manner. She unites her hostility to Freud with an unsophisticated theoretical position that becomes the standard discourse surrounding pathology for psychoanalysis for the rest of the 20th century. Arguably, the reductionism of Brunswick's theoretical position still holds today, not simply as a manifest or latent residue in standard psychoanalytic theory but also and especially in the ways Freud's work is criticised and stereotyped by contemporary theorists of gender like Judith Butler.

Intertwined with a confused restatement of some of Freud's key concepts, Brunswick presents a reductionist formula based on the straightforward equation of biological sex and what is now termed gender. To this commonsensical equation she adds the unapologetic *prescriptive* register that is never found in Freud's work. Brunswick shows a distinct disregard for the nuances of Freud's relativism, not only in the central focus of her paper on the fixing of gender but also in the vulgar misrepresentation of Freud's theory of the Oedipus complex. The homosexual

portion of the complete (i.e. bisexual) series of the Oedipus complex is here characterised and defined as pathology. This is a total misrepresentation of Freud's theory
by Brunswick. It is here that homosexuality – and by extension bisexuality – as
pathology enters the post-Freudian lexicon, and in a stark manner that bears no
resemblance whatsoever to Freud's *descriptive* formulations of bisexuality and the
Oedipus complex. Brunswick's paper is often rambling and incomprehensible; it
is interesting that she frequently appears to anticipate the work of Lacan, both in
her strident style and her novel terminology. Brunswick also revives the seduction
theory (1940, pp. 306, 315), which Freud abandoned very early in his work.

In complete contrast to Freud, Brunswick relies on a crude normative equivalence of passivity to female and activity to male, and so her argument for bisexual
pathology runs along the lines of passivity in a man or activity in a woman as
straightforward pathology: "Normality demands that the boy give up his passive
wish for a child, and the girl her active wish" (pp. 309–10; see also pp. 299–301,
303–4, 316–9). Quite apart from the semantic confusion of what is meant by a
passive or active wish, Brunswick's approach relies on a number of obnoxious
stereotypes, such as: "In the normal girl it is essentially the passive strivings which
… are successfully transferred [from the mother] to the father in the oedipal phase,
and in adult life to the husband" (p. 303). However, the reliance on crude stereotypical sexual roles for men and women is only the first step down the path leading
to the far more serious conceptualisation of these stereotypical social roles as fixed
and tied immutably to biological sex in a supposedly correct and unpathological
outcome. Any other outcome, such as inverted or unfixed roles, is the pathology
Brunswick defines. She subverts Freud's own relativist formulations of active and
passive to serve up her clinical formula that goes on eminently to serve the rigid
social and medical conservatism of psychoanalysis after Freud's death. Worse still,
psychoanalysis thus defines for itself an entirely new and lucrative class of patients
to treat: the homosexual. There can be no talk of bisexuality after Rado and Brunswick, except by including bisexuality in the same clinical frame of homosexual
pathology.

Perhaps the most galling aspect of Brunswick's position is that she asserts her authority on these matters not on the basis of a textual reading of Freud's work but
purely on her earlier nebulous status as Freud's collaborator. This allows her to present herself in the role not simply of interpreting Freud but rather as bearing the true
meaning of the Freudian ideas in a way that Rado cannot claim, and so Brunswick's
paper becomes a far more forceful foundation for and illustration of the de-radicalised
pattern that took hold in the psychoanalytic establishment after Freud's death.

This is the point in the history of psychoanalysis at which bisexuality and homosexuality are formally repressed and pathologised, and Freud's sexual theory
is fully de-radicalised. It may not be an exact moment or the responsibility of one
individual, but this de-radicalised and pathologising view, based on the reduction
of biological sex to specific and fixed, supposedly characteristic male and female
roles and sexual orientations, opens the door to the next logical step in the progression, namely the creation of the term *gender* by John Money in the 1950s and its

widespread and uncritical adoption ever since. Money also added other notable derivative terms such as *gender roles* and *gender identity*, merely doubling down on the original reductionism to biological sex implicitly inflected with Brunswick's pathologising: "A boy knows how to do and say boy things, because he simultaneously recognizes girl things as unfitting for him to express, though requiring complementarity or reciprocity of reaction on his part – and vice versa for girls" (Money & Ehrhardt, 1972, pp. 245–6; see also chapter 8). Their breathtaking assumption of something self-evident, universal, fixed and inherent ("boy things", "girl things") in an outcome that – in its entirety – is socially constructed and culturally specific reflects a total absence of any understanding of the social processes and forces at work in manufacturing boys and girls.

From this origin in American social realism, gender as a term thus takes hold and remains the unchallenged conceptual principle at work in the standard diagnostic criteria until the changes in psychopathology classification commence in the early 1970s; and while those classifications have now been successfully contested, the reduction of biological sex to gender has enjoyed far longer staying power as a theoretical concept. This is due in no small part to similar work by Robert Stoller:

> Gender is the amount of masculinity or femininity found in a person, and, obviously, while there are mixtures of both in many humans, the normal male has a preponderance of masculinity and the normal female a preponderance of femininity.
>
> (1968, pp. 9–10)

This conflation is clearly evidenced by statements such as:

> A sex-linked genetic biological tendency toward masculinity in males and femininity in females works silently but effectively from fetal existence on, being overlaid after birth by the effects of environment, the biological and environmental influences working more or less in harmony to produce a preponderance of masculinity in men and of femininity in women.
>
> (p. 74)

Infused with unexamined stereotypes and underlying all use of the term gender is the original reduction of social identity to biological sex. This produces a quasi-religious belief in the sheer obviousness of gender, even today where the stereotypical dual gender model is under assault. There is a parallel process at work, similar to the pathologisation of homosexuality, where failure to affirm gender itself is pathologised. In the social construction of gender, the individual outcome today is less important than the imperative to adopt a gender, even if this entails sweeping realignment of physical realities. The pathologisation follows the same arbitrary axis as Brunswick's fixed conflation of active with male and passive with female.

The consequences of this de-radicalisation for psychoanalysis as a body of knowledge and a clinical profession are twofold. The first consequence is a broad rejection of Freud's views on bisexuality and homosexuality by the widest range of psychoanalytic traditions after his death. When confronted by the social and political emancipation sweeping through Europe and North America in the late 1960s and the 1970s, establishment psychoanalysts responded by further hardening their de-radicalised position, thereby losing the opportunity to reform from within. This process has been described by Bayer (1981), Lewes (1988), Isay (1989) and Drescher (2008), who all draw attention to the rearguard action fought by the psychoanalytic establishment. This hardening of positions led to Freud's reputation and his work becoming inseparably coupled with the conservatism of the post-Freudian psychoanalytic establishment. The second and more unfortunate consequence is therefore a lingering popular and scholarly linking of psychoanalysis in general and Freud in particular with the conservative forces that took hold in the 1950s, even as these forces have been gradually challenged and overturned since the 1970s. As a younger generation of psychoanalysts today confront the dark history and legacy of psychoanalysis and try to assert an allegiance with the newer popular psychologies of emancipation, they do this on the understanding that they must recant the perceived prejudices of Freud, and they jettison with great fanfare any lingering basis for close association with Freud's work. Hertzmann and Newbigin (2019, 2023) are recent examples of this penitent "post-heteronormative perspective"; they baselessly describe Freud as heteronormative and phallocentric, characterising and rejecting him as "the 'Darwinian' Freud, who equated heterosexuality with full maturity" (2019, p. 4). Taken to the extreme, this leads paradoxically to an increasingly more vocal form of Freudianism without Freud. Even at the centre of contemporary psychoanalysis, there is now a seemingly compulsory contrite affirmation of the near universal popular consensus that Freud was terribly conservative.

Freud vulgaris

All of these historical and contemporary psychoanalytic discourses rely on the vulgarisation of Freud's work and his ideas, and the vulgarisation that entered the psychoanalytic discourse in 1940 has flourished ever since. In more recent scholarship, it is possible to discern various influential publications that appear to inflect and drive the process of vulgarising Freud's theory, both from within and outside established psychoanalysis, reproducing the recognisable trends and turning them into a broad new orthodoxy reflecting a monolithic consensus. Briefly summarised, the characteristics of this vulgarisation are: reductionism; revisionism; oversimplification; a failure to consult the original Freudian texts; an emphasis on pathology; and a shallow reliance on received knowledge and broader social debates that have become a new form of orthodoxy. The following section is a survey of some significant examples of vulgarisation.

The survey focuses on the main thematic areas relevant to the de-radicalisation of Freud's sexual theory: sexuality in general, homosexuality and bisexuality; but a survey of this nature would be incomplete without considering the ways in which

Freud is now held up as the paragon of male prejudice against women. The survey also considers Freud's central trope of the Oedipus complex and how this has been warped in its reception. In a related vein, the survey explores the recuperative value of some recent studies that also propose a radical re-evaluation of Freud. The survey concludes by briefly considering aspects of a more stylistic nature, especially the way in which Freud's relativism has been ignored or vulgarised by the medico-realism of scholarship influenced by neuropsychology. This thematic survey is not intended to be exhaustive. It presents a selection of important examples of the ways Freud's theory has been vulgarised in recent scholarship so that the radical elements of his ideas have been expunged. While, in general, the selected authors and texts are prominent, they are not being singled out per se but merely serve as an index of the de-radicalisation of Freud.

The history of psychoanalysis has been characterised by a regular splitting of the discourse; some new offshoots go on to become part of the contemporary broad church of shared psychoanalytic thought and some join the wider assault on Freud's ideas. This process already commenced in Freud's life with figures like Carl Jung, and then quickened after Freud's death with new streams such as those initiated by Lacan. These traditions offer their own form of vulgarisation, in general also characterised by heteronormativity and the same pathologising of non-reproductive sexuality. See, for example, Roudinesco's (2002) spirited attempt to rehabilitate Lacan's homophobia. These offshoots of Freudianism are not considered in this survey, primarily because they drift too far away from many of the core components of Freud's theory. Some aspects of these breakaway theories, such as Lacan's (1955–1956) psychopathology and Deleuze and Guattari's (1972, 1980) schizoanalysis, are reviewed here briefly and investigated again in detail in Chapter 5 (pp. 158–60) in the context of clinical practices.

Sexuality in general and female sexuality

There is frequent and widespread vulgarisation of Freud's ideas about sexuality in general and female sexuality in particular. The vulgarisation is broadly based on the concept of normativity. The source of such normativity is always ascribed to Freud, but inevitably the normative view actually underlies the thinking of the particular scholar deploying the concept. It would be like shooting fish in a barrel to use the examples of homophobic and misogynistic psychoanalysts in good standing such as Wiedeman, Stoller, Bieber and of course Socarides, who never gave up his rearguard action to pathologise and then cure homosexuals. However, a far more significant example of the vulgarisation of Freud's ideas is provided by the work of Roy Schafer exactly because he presents himself as not homophobic and misogynistic but as an enlightened force in psychoanalysis. Two key texts by Schafer exemplify and bookend his work spanning multiple decades: "Problems in Freud's psychology of women" (1974) and "The evolution of my views on non-normative sexual practices" (1994). Schafer's work continues to enjoy high repute in mainstream psychoanalytic circles, indicated by the re-publication of his 1974 essay in 2019 on the august pages of the *Journal of the American Psychoanalytic Association*, along with glowing endorsements and a memorialisation (Fogel 2019; Balsam, Fogel & Harris 2019).

Although by no means the sole initiator of anti-Freud psychoanalysis, the work by Schafer plays a major role in crystallising the dogma that Freud is the embodiment of wicked patriarchy, and so Freud becomes a scapegoat to blame for all the wicked patriarchal mistakes of post-Freudian psychoanalysis. The general view that Freud's work embodies heteronormativity and endorses patriarchy is now fully entrenched in the academic and popular understanding of Freud. When making reference to Freud in contemporary discourse, it is accepted as an unquestioned truth that Freud is a norm-endorsing, women-hating homophobe. Schafer comes at a late stage in a long tradition of writing against Freud that started already in Freud's lifetime with the likes of Jung. The profound splintering of the Freudian epistemology has produced contemporary renderings and interpretations that often bear little resemblance to Freud's original formulations. In the early stages of this splintering process, it was relatively easy to trace the many breaks with Freud, but understanding the various genealogies today is like trying to discern the splinters in a greenstick fracture that heals and is routinely re-broken so many times the break-lines are a dense matrix becoming part of the bone itself. Nevertheless, Schafer's work stands out as a leading example of the trend of vulgarisation within mainstream psychoanalysis that still nominally claims a link to Freud as its progenitor.

The first striking aspect of Schafer's work is the multiplicity of erroneous interpretations of Freud's theory that Schafer introduces to psychoanalysis. Schafer's writing relies on extreme generalisation about Freud that borders on parody. This generalisation is characterised by sweeping statements regarding Freud's work that come with no or very little textual evidence from the actual primary texts. Schafer frequently becomes tied up in Freud's biography, and he tends to treat Freud as a figurehead of masculinity and fatherhood, which is interesting for all sorts of reasons, including Schafer's strident rhetorical style. By personalising Freud, Schafer seems to suggest that Freud is personally responsible for the faults in psychoanalysis. Schafer makes no attempt to contextualise Freud in Freud's own times, and so Schafer is blinded to the quite radical components of Freud's work when viewed in the context of the late 19th- and early 20th-century intellectual environment. He also misses the radical components because he approaches Freud's epistemology with a preset frame. While Schafer gives no credit to Freud, he paradoxically adopts psychoanalysis as the paradigm he desires, and Schafer's feelings towards Freud as a person (rather than a body of texts) betray his own rather complex love-hate investment. This shapes Schafer's ideas, which in places show promise, but he is so determined to reach his own predetermined targets that the work by Freud serves only as a negative foil.

The 1974 paper by Schafer criticises Freud's views on women, but in a piecemeal manner that focuses on three supposedly "major and representative problems" (p. 461). These are simply presented as a priori problems, with no attempt to establish the problematic or to approach Freud's texts in a systematic manner.

Freud is presented as simply wrong. The case is closed before it is even opened. Enter the self-styled feminist hero Schafer to the rescue. Schafer neither declares his own position frankly and coherently, nor does he attempt to show how his position is different to the position he ascribes to Freud. This is crucial to understanding the deeper currents at play: Schafer is at war with himself, with his own views on women. He sets Freud up as an opponent against which he, Schafer, can emerge victorious and also the champion of the politically correct pro-feminist camp of the 1970s. This is tragic because it reduces Freud to a villain and sets the stage for five more decades of anti-Freud discourse. It is even more tragic though, because Schafer completely misses all the liberating and productive aspects of Freud's work on sexuality and women.

In producing this parody of Freud, Schafer starts by making the assumption that Freud is being *prescriptive*. In this fundamental error, Schafer misses the entire point that Freud's work is simply *descriptive* of the situation as it presents itself. This frequent misunderstanding of Freud's position is not limited to Schafer but is a common thread in almost all the criticism of Freud that has been produced to date. This thread assumes that Freud is prescriptive and normative, and that his work endorses a highly conservative social outlook. Nothing could be further from the truth. In part, this misunderstanding is derived from a reliance on the English translation of Freud, where the nuances and irony of Freud's original phrases are sometimes lost. However, the translation aspect can only play a small role, and the monumental translation endeavour of James Strachey's *Standard edition* generally does as much justice to the original text as possible given that Strachey and the other translators were working in a specific time and context. In the scholarship of someone like Schafer, there is a deeper factor at work than a simplistic and literal reliance on the English translation. In so much scholarship on Freud, and not only that from the Anglo-American world, there seems to be a need to find a rigid, prescriptive and fixed certitude in Freud's work. Schafer appears unable to countenance the fluid, tentative and experimental approach that Freud adopts as default.

An inability to recognise Freud's subtleties may have something to do with the clinical background and orientation of much of the scholarship because clinicians have very different expectations compared to an investigator focused on the theoretical and metapsychological dimensions. Authors like Schafer are working professionally as clinicians rather than theorists. The work of clinicians reflects a need for clinical certainty, and no doubt there are aspects of Freud's texts that feed this need, such as Freud's case studies. There is also no doubt that Freud was trying to establish his paradigm on both a theoretical and a clinical basis, and this required some degree of disciplinary clinical protocol. Of course, Freud's collaborative and iterative approach was also assailed by the various schisms over the years, as well as the inevitable frustrations of some clinical outcomes and the grave disappointments of his times that beset him: the horror of the First World War and the subsequent destruction of (the illusion of) a common European culture. Despite all this, Freud consistently remained not only a clinician but also a theoretician, and his fundamental approach on both fronts was always to revise and re-examine. Freud's open-ended approach is the approach that Schafer must close in order to present his own closed views.

Some examples from Schafer's text will illustrate these points more clearly. The first section of the 1974 essay (starting p. 461) stumbles into all the points raised so far. Schafer seizes the term morality in the most literal sense of the word and uses it crudely as a stick to beat Freud. To start with, Schafer assumes that there is such a thing as morality in an objective, timeless and non-instrumental way. He then proceeds to wade into a swamp of confusion by equating Freud's position to morality in general, which in turn is simplistically equated to the superego. This involves passing random and arbitrary sweeping judgements on Freud's work, such as: "it follows that Freud may have drawn exactly the wrong conclusion from his theory" (p. 465). Schafer would surely be expected to provide a detailed series of examples supported by quotes to back up such a strong position against Freud, but he offers none. All he provides is a glancing reference to texts: "Can one be satisfied with Freud's related view that women are less objective, lucid, and acute in comprehension than men (1920)?" (p. 466). The rhetoric in such a statement is breathtaking: Freud's supposed view is taken for granted and the reader is simply invited to concur. No evidence for Freud's alleged prejudice against women is given except the *in toto* reference to the 1920 case of female homosexuality, with no further detail such as a page number or an actual quote. The problems with Freud's view are never laid out with evidence; they are simply presented as fact. Another example from the conclusion of this first section: "Freud, too, presented the world as phallocentric" (p. 467). The abrupt but sweeping and damming conclusion about Freud relies on the term phallocentric, but this term only enters the lexicon because of Freud's critical analysis of sexuality. To turn the word against Freud with no reflection on the term itself and no evidence of Freud's actual phallocentrism is so sloppy as to be pathetically amusing. The conclusion that Schafer has delivered is transparently self-serving. He makes this final statement as if it is a fact, whereas it is only the foundation for Schafer's grandiose project of signalling his own supposedly non-phallocentric virtue.

Introduced *deus ex machina* in the first section of Schafer's paper, Freud's phallocentrism is now taken as a fact beyond any shadow of doubt in the next section and used to appropriate such aspects of Freud that suit Schafer in the act of what he presents as his progressive rehabilitation of Freud. Essentially, the structure of Schafer's argument is that the phallocentrism, which he has attributed to Freud – and let it be added, with no evidence – blinded Freud to the value of his own theory. Schafer paradoxically states that Freud disregarded the consequences of his own revolutionary theory (p. 472), and Schafer thus reduces Freud to a mute precursor waiting for the profound insights of Schafer to intervene and rescue the theory. Schafer goes on to spend the second section in a breathtaking appropriation of Freud's sexual theory and the theory of the Oedipus complex, while at the same time he systematically diminishes Freud's fundamental role as the actual progenitor of these theories. This section ends with Schafer's astonishing claim that Freud neglected bisexuality (p. 477).

The third and final section of the paper is a gross misunderstanding of Freud's relativism, based on Schafer's wild and unsubstantiated assumption that Freud makes an irrevocable equation of active with masculine and passive with feminine. In this, Schafer is following a logic similar to Brunswick. Schafer actually turns Freud's relativism on its head, and he explicitly assumes that Freud is being prescriptive. Clearly, this is a misreading of Freud, but it doesn't stop Schafer from repeatedly using his erroneous reading as evidence of Freud's conservative and patriarchal position, which of course is again taken for granted by Schafer. All that Schafer really demonstrates here is his own belief in the fixity of the supposed equation of passive with feminine. The worst of Schafer's errors appears in this section in that he assumes Freud to mean masculine-feminine is the *biological* pair in Freud's conception: "Such statements [by Freud] suggest that all kinds of 'right' answers about sexual identity are being dictated by a pair of biological principles – the masculine and the feminine" (p. 479). Even a very cursory reading of Freud's texts shows this to be an obvious novice mistake by Schafer. For Freud, the biological fact is biological sex, the male-female pair, and the dualism of masculine-feminine is the socially constructed reality. More importantly, Schafer does not recognise that Freud is scrupulous to avoid making any general equivalence between the sets: male-female (biological sex), active-passive and masculine-feminine; and Schafer completely ignores Freud's view of the libido as always being active, with this activity specifically unrestricted to either the male or the female of the species. Schafer is simply reflecting the wholesale psychoanalytic adoption of Brunswick's original error as fact, although Schafer himself is oblivious of Brunswick's work and so mistakenly attributes the fault to Freud.

There is no doubt in Schafer's version that he is right and Freud is wrong. This uncritical self-confident view of Schafer becomes so widespread and accepted in psychoanalytic circles that Balsam (2013) and Fogel (2019, see especially pp. 495–6) gushingly present Schafer's work as some kind of pioneering progressive feminist liberation of psychoanalysis from the patriarchal oppression of Freud. More than this unqualified praise for Schafer, Balsam and Fogel's lack of any critical engagement reflects the continued self-contented vulgarisation of Freud in mainstream psychoanalysis today.

The second paper in this sequence by Schafer (1994) continues the vulgarisation of Freud and is also characterised by scant reference to and no close reading of Freud's texts. Once again, the paper starts from and is entirely predicated on Freud's alleged "phallocentric approach to the psychosexual development of both sexes" (p. 237), and once again Freud's phallocentrism is presented as an incontrovertible fact beyond any need of actual textual evidence. Schafer doubles down on his original positions in 1974 (which he restates here in a rambling paraphrase) and updates these with sprinkles of the vogue "postmodern" vocabulary of the 1990s. He now disavows what he calls Freud's binary form of thinking, but Schafer inherently continues in his own discourse to rely on binarism by replacing the terminology of Freud's polarities with the binary concept of normative and non-normative. Schafer thus renders Freud as normative and opens the road to the virtuous non-normativity of Schafer. He shows no restraint in the sweeping and unsubstantiated gross generalisations he makes about Freud. Here are some prime examples of the vulgarisation of Freud in Schafer's account: "Freud naturalized and moralized normative sexual practices" (p. 244); "Freud's idealizing of compulsory heterosexuality" (p. 246); "Freud was working in conformity with the moral and esthetic dictates of his culture, and so he was effectively using the language of that culture in a way that tended to fence us all in further" (p. 247); "I became aware that Freud's position did not hang together and that it included bias" (p. 250). Once again, no evidence is provided for these claims.

A concerning feature of both papers is Schafer's rejection of evolution as a basic biological reality. This is also a recurring theme in the general vulgarisation of Freud, premised on the frequent assumption that Freud's high regard for Darwin's theory of evolution somehow translates into a prescriptive endorsement of teleological heterosexuality. Freud's extremely nuanced position on the matter of sexuality in evolution is completely ignored, and Freud's scientific honesty is turned against him by scholars like Schafer, who rejects any kind of biological substrate to reality. The entire third section of Schafer's 1994 paper is a restatement of his breathtaking rejection in 1974 of evolution. When he rejected evolution in the earlier paper, Schafer vested all his claims in the concept of "social values", but this is an entirely circular strategy with no way out of the absurdity it creates, because all the "psychosexuality" material (1974, p. 471 and esp. p. 472) of social values is subject to its own internal prescriptive teleology. Now Schafer (1994) doubles down on his assumption that Freud is being socially prescriptive and, by Schafer's telling, Freud is idealising "compulsory heterosexuality" (p. 246), although Schafer fails to acknowledge that he is pilfering the concept from Adrienne Rich (1980). The main passage of Schafer's argument is worth quoting at length to show his breathtaking audacity and utter lack of reference to Freud's texts:

> Freud naturalized and moralized normative sexual practices. He did not see that he was making an unwarranted leap from biological theory to moral judgment when he assumed that development ought to culminate in reproductivity. Also, he did not see that he was making a moral judgment when he reasoned that, because development can proceed to reproductivity, it is only the reproductive heterosexual who is the mature, normal, healthy, fully developed person, the better off person, and so, by implication (which he would have consciously repudiated), the person who is a better sort of person than others who have developed differently. Once Freud idealized this form of development, other forms had to be seen as immature, unfortunately arrested, perhaps irremediably so.
>
> (Schafer, 1994, p. 244)

Since there is literally zero textual evidence for Schafer's sweeping claims against Freud, Schafer apparently explains the contradiction to Freud's actual words by the argument that all of this was happening for Freud on some sort of unconscious level: "He did not see ...", "he would have consciously repudiated". This strategy allows Schafer to attribute ideas to Freud that are simply not there and to avoid providing even a single reference to the textual origin of these wild claims. To pull off this rhetoric, Schafer must ignore major core Freudian concepts, such as the pleasure principle and infantile sexuality, as if Freud had never put pen to paper and was just some random and inarticulate analysand blathering in Schafer's rooms, leaving the arrogant and all-knowing analyst to decode at full speed.

This strategy positions Schafer both to reject Freud and to use Freud as a fixed point of orientation to negate. In response to the alleged prescriptions by Freud, Schafer engages in a game of producing his own alternate prescriptions, and he adopts the virtuous role of giving prescriptions which are better just because they are not Freud's. Schafer's treatment is to pick and choose which broad social elements from American life to keep or throw out. Judith Butler (1990) is top of the to-keep list (Schafer, 1994, p. 246); she is for Schafer the grand anti-Freud trump card. Since Freud is never actually being prescriptive, however, and never said or subscribed to any of the prescriptive formulas of compulsory heterosexuality Schafer attributes to him, Schafer's new prescription is an idiosyncratic mixture of Freud's ideas and their negation. The result is very shallow moralising and self-affirming rhetoric by Schafer.

There is a further curious aspect to Schafer's perspective. He uses the phrase "Freudian psychoanalysis" (1994, p. 239) to imply that there could be some other variety or varieties of psychoanalysis. While this may seem self-evident to some (Lacanians, Kleinians, etc.), it is rather like saying Christian Christianity or Marxist Marxism, as if there were some other variety of Christianity or Marxism that sprung from a different genesis. Psychoanalysis is Freudian because it is Freud's discovery and creation. Schafer's use of this phrase points to exactly the kind of appropriation of knowledge that he and others have pursued. Consciously or unconsciously, he is suggesting that there is another kind of psychoanalysis, a non-Freudian variety or, more precisely, a Schaferian psychoanalysis. This betrays a magisterium concept of knowledge based on intellectual authority vested in the individual rather than in the ideas themselves.

In all of this, Schafer is caught in a central paradox that afflicts so much of the Freudian tradition after Freud. Schafer both needs Freud's epistemology as a basis for the clinical profession and rejects this original epistemology in favour of what can only be described as manipulation and appropriation of Freud's theory. The outcome is nothing less than intellectual parricide and usurpation of the father's place performed on Freud in a frenzied and apparently unconscious re-enactment of the Sophoclean tragedy. Schafer is destroying Freud the wicked father in order to bring Schafer the virtuous son into full possession of the mother, the female body, which in this case is the body of Freudian knowledge Schafer is claiming for himself. That Schafer is actually writing about women and their sexuality is only one of the many tragic ironies of his texts. While he portrays himself as an ally to women, he offers them nothing except his own new male reign, in place of the wicked father he thinks he is overthrowing. The wickedness attributed to Freud's reign (patriarchal, heteronormative, phallocentric, etc.) is so known because

Schafer says it is thus, and because Freud is no longer present to defend himself against this slanderous appropriation. In effect, Schafer must by necessity glide superficially over the Freudian texts because they consistently prove him wrong in the claims he is making about Freud's theory. More generally, Schafer's little coup d'état demonstrates how the entire programme of vulgarising Freud has come to exist and operate: by usurping the name of Freud, by ignoring the texts of Freud, and by putting words into Freud's mouth.

This is not to suggest the opposite, that Freud should be uncritically canonised. With the benefit of historical perspective though, it is clear that Freud faced an uphill battle from the start, with some of the worst friction to his ideas coming from within the ranks of his own supporters. The usurpation of his epistemology during his life was only accelerated after his death, to produce the paradoxical Freud-without-Freud Freudianism of today. It is important to see the very vested interests of somebody like Schafer, not only in destroying Freud in the practical sense of making a name for himself at the cost of Freud, but also in the deeper psychological sense of working through his own Oedipal issues in the form of these two papers and the wider body of his work. This is true of all the Freud usurpers, from the original parricide by Jung to more recent Oedipal assaults by the likes of Lacan or Deleuze and Guattari.

Schafer's work is not only deeply flawed by his erroneous interpretations of Freud; it is also intellectually and psychologically dishonest in its portrayal of Freud's theory. Even worse, Schafer's work creates a shield for others, who appropriate the clinical tradition of Freud without its intellectual foundation. The hypocrisy of this Oedipal appropriation goes hand in hand with an intellectual laziness. It is no surprise then that the psychoanalytic tradition after Freud erected by practitioners such as Schafer is so overwhelmingly conservative and complicit with Oedipal reproduction. The outcome is entirely predictable though, since the justification for these usurpations of Father Freud is to turn him into this grotesque father figure. In their intellectual fantasies, these sons and daughters can then act out all their deepest Oedipal fantasies against the caricature father. The profound pity of these approaches is not only that they sacrifice Freud on the pyre of popular misconception; they also blind themselves to the very powerful and radical dimension of Brother Freud, the fraternal ally to all women and gay men and to any straight men who might actually be interested in breaking free from the reproduction of Oedipus and the concomitant reign of capital.

Homosexuality

It is by now well recognised that the invention of the category/term homosexual necessarily predated the invention of heterosexuality. The term homosexual was invented in 1869 by Karl Maria Kertbeny (Hocquenghem, 1972, p. 51), and the category defined in 1870 by Carl Friedrich Westphal (Foucault, 1976, p. 43; for more details on both, see Katz, 1995). Where before there were anatomical practices, now there is classification. The construction of homosexuality and heterosexuality as categories is a discourse of origination that functions by means of exclusion based on a presumed distinctiveness and exclusivity of sexual object. This is a negative and reactive definition, built on the one category being what the other is not. In reality, however, the presumed defining specificity does not exist, except as a fantasy of those who are making the definitions and using the terms. The absence of a universal or even general exclusivity of sexual object choice has been demonstrated repeatedly, perhaps most vividly by Kinsey et al. (1948, 1953). The definitions and categories therefore function purely as a socially constructed means of exclusion. What is more, the historical categorisation of homosexuality and heterosexuality not only exclude each other but also, and perhaps most importantly, the possibly of being both.

The invention of the category of homosexual as the necessary negative and counter-definition of the category heterosexual is only where the problem starts. The definition of the term homosexual has flourished and grown into a vast and complicated industry of contradictory and competing values, and it is no surprise that according to psychoanalysts the cause of homosexuality (for it must have an origin if it is to exist) can be a range of vastly contradictory factors, from an absent, meek or doting parent (of either sex) to an overbearing, dominant and caustic parent. In more recent scholarship, the logical solution to this terminological Tower of Babel is apparently to adopt the plural *homosexualities*, which only further compounds the problem. Heterosexuality, it appears, is not so well blessed by plurality. Nowhere in the field of sexuality has the absence of definition contained in an affirmative counter-term been more apparent than in the use of the word heterosexuality, which is precisely why it remains the problem that needs elucidating.

There is a small but charming anthology that was published in 1987 by the pioneering Gay Men's Press, titled *Heterosexuality* (edited by Gill Hanscombe and Martin Humphries), which operates on the strategy of inverting the counter-definition of heterosexuality and uses a heterophobic parody of homophobia to elucidate some of the obvious problems with heterosexuality as a category. An extract from the back cover:

Why are some people so stubbornly attracted to the opposite sex? What exactly is heterosexuality? What causes it? Is it a satisfactory lifestyle for the individual affected? Can it be cured? And why is it so often the subject of powerful irrational feelings? Questions like these have vexed lesbians and gay men from time immemorial. ... Produced by a team of acknowledged experts, each with long experience in this field of study, this book has an appeal for both specialist and general reader. Certain to become the established authority of its subject.

This purposeful foregrounding of the absurdity of these categories by *inversion* is also at the heart of the now seminal essay by Adrienne Rich (1980), built on the proposition of *compulsory heterosexuality*. Rich (2004) later described her impulse to write the essay as "turning the picture – the presumption of female heterosexuality – around to view it from different angles, a hazarding of unasked questions" (p. 9).

Once homosexuality and heterosexuality were defined as separate and exclusive categories, the next step was the transformation of homosexuality into a pathology, as already described above (pp. 30–2) in the discussion of the work by Brunswick. Faced with this new pathology, the psychoanalytic industry could energetically set about curing the homosexual. This reflects a deep contradiction in the psychoanalytic legacy. Freud's work spans two conflicting interests. On the one hand, there is a clear aspiration to establish a medical science and clinical practice. On the other, Freud was much more than a medical doctor, and his interests ranged freely over history, anthropology, art, literature and culture with an insatiable curiosity and unshakable confidence in secular European idealist philosophy. All of these interests feed into and enrich his work, and counter-balance the urge of the medical doctor to identify and cure illness. The result is that Freud's approach of a strong reliance on the medical language of pathology and cure is also always inflected by rigorous theoretical introspection. This balance is largely lost in the psychoanalytic tradition after Freud, and not only in the English-speaking world.

The dominance of the psychoanalytic movement by medical doctors during Freud's lifetime and especially after his death through the exclusion of lay analysts resulted in the rapid withering away of the non-medical leg of Freud's legacy and a concomitant dominance of psychoanalysis by the psychiatric discourse of pathology. For example, where Freud had relied on case studies in his early publications, these cease to play a central role in the later exposition of his ideas (all the cases are published by 1915, except for one in 1920), but the psychoanalytic discourse after his death becomes dominated once again by the clinical case study as the primary vehicle for developing psychoanalytic epistemology. Even today, the case study vignette is the gold standard necessary for publication in the gatekeeper academic and professional journals of the psychoanalytic establishment, and the absence of case studies in a submission (with the implied lack of formal training as an analyst) means almost certain exclusion from publication in their pages. More broadly, the prevalence of the case study shows that a background in medical training is still explicitly more valuable in the mainstream analytic context. In turn, the medical and academic institutions retain their monopoly on analyst training and certification. This state of affairs both reflects and is reflected in the economic imperative of the analyst as economic profession. If there is to be a medical profession with paying patients to attend, then there must be something pathological in these analysands to make them a patient, something to cure.

Homosexuality was an ideal candidate for a cure: a pathology so wonderfully refractory to curing, it is guaranteed to generate hundreds of hours of analysis. For decades, the psychoanalytic profession milked this economic gift that kept on giving. Furthermore, the goal of curing this pathology one homosexual at a time came with the full political backing of the broader society. Faced with the real alternative of criminalisation, it is no mystery that homosexuals lined up for analysis. There was never any consideration, let alone regulation, of the conflict of interest and appalling malpractice by these clinicians, because the homosexual patient was beyond the pale for society throughout most of the second half of the 20th century. If the much-vaunted psychoanalytic cure somehow still failed to produce the desired conversion, it was always the fault of the homosexual. The social shame heaped on homosexuality was matched by the utter shamelessness of psychoanalysts in good standing who profited financially and professionally from their relentless determination to cure the homosexual. Review essays from that era (e.g. Wiedeman, 1962, 1974; Wiedeman & Payne, 1977) provide a direct taste of this horrific dehumanising period in psychoanalysis, while Bieber and his colleagues' ten-year project of curing homosexuals (Bieber et al., 1962) richly exemplifies the psychoanalyst's mental terrorism against gay men, replete with the case-study-on-steroids. Without a shred of embarrassment, they confidently claim: "all psychoanalytic theories assume that adult homosexuality is psychopathologic" (p. 18), in complete repudiation of the psychoanalytic theories of a certain Sigmund Freud. Bieber of course was an avid follower of Rado. The horrific history of the homosexual pathology of psychoanalysis is now well documented (Bayer, 1981; Lewes, 1988; Isay, 1989; O'Connor & Ryan, 1993; Roudinesco, 2002; Fonagy, 2006; Drescher, 2008; Silverstein, 2008), but it is still Freud who is most often made to carry the blame, as if he is the one responsible for the legacy of this anti-homosexual discourse in the decades after his death. In a comparable fashion, the intellectual reputation of Nietzsche has never recovered from the abuse of Nietzsche's ideas many decades after his death by his sister and her Nationalist Socialist friends for their *Herrenvolk* propaganda in the 1930s, while Marx's multifaceted analyses and theories of capitalist production will forever be reduced to the simple association of his name with the absolutist dictatorships of Lenin and Stalin, and the failed communist experiments of the 20th century, long after Marx himself was dead and buried.

Bisexuality

Freud's consistently strong position on bisexuality as a fundamental and universal component of human sexuality has been undermined in two ways, so that confusion and ambiguity reign in the interpretation of this area of his work. Several studies explore (directly or tangentially) the development of ideas in Freud's texts relating to bisexuality, notably David (1975), Angelides (2001), Young-Bruehl (2001), Rapoport (2009, 2010, 2019), Heenen-Wolff (2010a, 2010b, 2011), Flanders et al. (2016), Perelberg (2018) and Gulati and Pauley (2019). Along one path, some studies treat bisexuality as a fully independent adult sexual orientation and focus. The other path is the confusion introduced by the term *psychic bisexuality*.

The lengthy history of bisexuality by Angelides (2001) is exemplary of the first category. Like so many of his contemporaries, Angelides approaches the topic of bisexuality with the erroneous assumption that bisexuality is a fully independent sexual orientation in adulthood. This may seem like a preordained conclusion given the current consensus in progressive circles that endorses and affirms a broad plurality of sexual orientations on the basis of dissonant and dissident categories of identities (e.g. LGBTQIA+ etc.), but bisexuality conceived of in this way rests upon and compounds the original sin of inventing separate and discrete hetero-sexual and homosexual categories in the 19th century. To be vaguely internally consistent, this approach by Angelides requires the paradoxical rejection of evolu-tionary principles. His misstep is based on the general assumption that any regard for evolution automatically translates into a prescriptive endorsement of teleologi-cal heterosexuality. This assumption is a cornerstone of much of the work vul-garising Freud's position on homosexuality and bisexuality. The argument against evolution by Angelides focuses on a few vulgarised versions of evolutionary theory that were used historically to justify a range of racist and misogynist ideologies, and because these are vaguely drawn from the discourse around Darwin's work, Angelides casts doubt on the entire paradigm of evolution. From this general posi-tion, Freud's theory with its Darwinian foundation is blatantly misconstrued as the model of "palpable heteronormativity" (Angelides, 2001, pp. 61–2).

Here Angelides is simply following the lead of Butler (1990) with her chrono-logically earlier vulgarised interpretation of Freud as heteronormative. Butler's mistakes in her argument are multiple, such as her incredibly loose and inaccu-rate adoption of the word *melancholia*, which comes from a transitional text by Freud (1917) and actually means *clinical depression* in English; her disorganised deployment of the word *gender* in ways implying a direct parallel term and con-cept in Freud's writing, which do not exist; and her introduction of an extraneous *homosexual taboo* (Butler, 1990, pp. 86–8) as something both different to and yet somehow also included in Freud's concept of the incest taboo. With such a lack of attention to detail in her argument, Butler must then rely on rhetoric in order to diminish Freud's brilliant relativism about masculine and feminine, and she is re-duced to mocking this relativism as Freud's "confusion" (Butler, 1990, pp. 81–2). Butler misinterprets the key word *disposition* in the *Standard edition* translation to mean *inherent characteristics*, whereas even a cursory reading of Freud's texts shows the word to indicate a specifically relational and constructed dimension key to relativism. For Freud, both masculine and feminine aspects are present together in the human subject, especially in the original form of activity and passivity, but in a ratio determined individually. It is exactly Freud's relativism that contrasts to and highlights Butler's desperate need for a fixed organisation of gender in her own argument, against which she can be seen to rebel. This leads Butler to the dramatic but illogical and unsubstantiated conclusion that "for Freud bisexuality is the coincidence of two heterosexual desires within a single psyche" (1990, p. 82). Butler is clearly unaware of the seminal text in this regard by Hocquenghem (1972; the English translation appeared in 1978), which implodes the concept of homo-sexual or heterosexual oriented desire, with Hocquenghem taking his lead directly from Freud: "Freud expresses the fact that … desire is fundamentally undifferenti-ated and ignorant of the distinction between homosexuality and heterosexuality" (Hocquenghem, 1972, p. 74). The claims Butler uses to buttress her rhetoric make little sense, reflecting the absence of any substance in her parricidal performance. Her "two heterosexual desires" in one mind argument rests on the concomitant argument of the complementarity of the two biological sexes, but in order to sustain this unsustainable view of bisexuality, and without realising or acknowledging she is doing this, Butler is in effect reverting to the old 19th-century theory of Karl Heinrich Ulrichs, which reduced homosexuality to "*anima muliebris virili corpore inclusa*" [a female brain trapped in a male body] (Ulrichs, 1868, p. v), a theory much in vogue again today, and now used as an underpinning not for homosexuality but for gender dysphoria. Freud dispenses with Ulrichs's argument already in the first edition of the *Three essays*, and he sums up the problem in a single sentence: "We do not know what characterizes a 'female brain'" (1905a, p. 8; 1905, p. 142; reiterated in 1920, p. 170). Butler wilfully ignores Freud's own articulated view, which favours a theory of universal bisexuality that develops and is arrested under social force into monosexual expression. This is why Freud points towards the need to explain not only the phenomenon of homosexuality but also heterosexuality. Butler's implicit reliance on and extension of Ulrichs can be summarised as follows: for Butler, bisexuality is the concurrence of a masculine and feminine essence trapped in a male body, or a feminine and masculine essence trapped in a female body. This apparently neat and logical argument may appeal to Butler and her followers, but it goes nowhere beyond empty essentialism; nor can there be any basis for attributing this essentialist logic to Freud.

Butler's rhetoric against Freud is taken over and extended by Angelides (2001) with the view that Freud adopts

a distinctive linear model of evolutionary psychosexual maturation. The 'normal' heterosexual child progresses along an evolutionary line from an immature and originary bisexual disposition passing through the (racialized) axis of identification to the apposite form of 'civilized', mature, genital sexuality.

(2001, p. 62)

Angelides provides no textual evidence from Freud's work for this incoherent argument, but how could he if it does not exist. Like Butler, Angelides's argument desires a Father Freud who is both rigidly prescriptive and heteronormative. When Angelides concludes (quite incorrectly) that "bisexuality was the central aporia of Freudian thought" (p. 54), he is merely reflecting his own aporia. Although without direct acknowledgement, Butler's argument of a heteronormative Freud is also deployed by Mader (2011) and used (independently of Angelides) to interpret Freud as representing a heteronormative evolutionary position.

The entire linear evolutionary model erroneously attributed to Freud's bisexuality theory by Butler, Angelides and Mader is then taken up from them verbatim by Rapoport (2009, 2010, 2019), and her influential transmissions of this mistaken interpretation in turn become the foundation for the more recent and much broader adoption and cementation of this vulgarised and de-radicalised consensus view of Freud as the master proponent of an outdated evolutionary heteronormative patriarchy. For example, the editors of a recent collection of essays take their lead from Rapoport to assert confidently that "Freud's 'polymorphous perversity' situates the attainment of a sexual subjectivity as a process with only one desired trajectory, heterosexuality" (Anderlini-D'Onofrio & Alexander, 2009, p. 209). Similarly Rapoport (2009) is the inspiration for the following very recent example of extreme vulgarisation:

> [Freud] believed that we are all born with both male and female bodies and brains, and this he hazily called bisexuality. These male and female parts of every one of us being in conflict, he surmised, was key to understanding human psychology. Related to this idea, Freud considered bisexuality to be a primordial state of being that people should grow out of, as they resolve the push and pull of the male and female forces within themselves. This meant that he believed that we are all bisexual as children and so bisexuality is a childish, immature sexuality. Freud also considered bisexual desires in adulthood to be fantastic or impossible, and linked bisexuality with hysteria.
>
> (Shaw, 2022, pp. 34–5)

Admittedly this text is aimed at a mass audience, with no pretence of rigour or scientific aspiration, but it is nevertheless an influential example of the way this crude view of Freud has become popularised based on vulgar psychoanalytic presentations of Freud's work.

Psychic bisexuality

The term *psychic bisexuality* (or sometimes *psychical bisexuality*) is now widely used in psychoanalytic discourse, though its origin and definition are obscure. While it appears to carry the certainty and assurance of other Freudian neologisms, Freud himself never used the term, although he briefly used a somewhat similar phrase – psychical hermaphroditism (1905, 1920) – but in a limited and exploratory sense, which he quickly dropped. A universal characteristic of the usage of the term psychic bisexuality in psychoanalytic discourse is the consistent failure to provide a definition, or to explore the genealogy of the term. In the only glossary entry I found for the term in any source, it is confidently attributed to Freud: "Freud progressively elaborated his views on psychic bisexuality" (Perelberg, 2018, p. 277), but the gloss goes no further than this bland sweeping claim and provides no reference to Freud's work beyond a vague mention of the Fliess correspondence. Gulati and Pauley (2019) come closest to offering a specific though imprecise definition: "the *sum total of gender and erotic representations present in the human unconscious*" (p. 115, emphasis in the original). The passage seems to define psychic bisexuality as an *unconscious* bisexuality, although to mean this, the definition implicitly combines all mental representation of sexuality, including the subject aspect of bisexuality ("gender") with object bisexuality ("erotic"). This is so broad as to be meaningless and would be synonymous with Freud's *libido*. The authors fail to explain any further. It is also not clear if the definition encompasses all unconscious sexual representations in each human or is suggesting some kind of aggregate and collective human unconscious in the style of Jung. The paper is distracted by extensive biographical speculations, especially regarding Freud's own *literal* object bisexuality and Lacan's homophobia. They attribute their definition of psychic bisexuality to Blechner (2015), but he does not mention the concept at all. Instead his paper proposes an entirely new term for subject bisexuality, namely *bigenderism*, though Blechner is clearly ignorant of Stoller's (1975) far earlier and identical neologism, which Christian David (1975, p. 724) equates with *bisexualité psychique* (psychic bisexuality).

From my own reading, it seems a tentative origin, for the term is to be found in an oblique reference in a letter to Fliess (Letter (145), 7 August 1901, Freud, 1887–1902b, pp. 333–5), where Freud distinguishes between the biological and mental aspects of bisexuality as two parallel themes in a book-length collaboration with Fliess he is proposing. The word in the German original is *psychisch* ("Den psychischen Aspekt der Bisexualität ...") (Freud, 1887–1902a, p. 359), which the older English translation renders as the *mental* aspect of bisexuality but Masson translates as the *psychical* aspect of bisexuality (Freud, 1887–1904, p. 448). From this humble origin, the term has grown into an unwieldy empire of signification, especially in the Francophone world. In an obvious way, the term serves as code, as a *passepartout* in the psychoanalytic community. Whatever limitless and undefined manifest content the term might represent, it also allows scholars to slip vague formulations and indeterminate ideas past readers. As such, it is much abused in psychoanalytic scholarship, and many uncertainties are passed over by the use of an apparently authoritative technical term.

André Green (1973) offers an early use of the term in French, but without definition. The earliest generalised usage in French appears to be at a conference on the theme of psychic bisexuality in Paris in 1975, organised by the Société Psychanalytique de Paris, especially in the lengthy framing presentation by Christian David. This text (David, 1975) offers a wide-ranging report that traces Freud's views of bisexuality and also examines later psychoanalytic work on the theme. Given that in this study David is to a great extent initiating the term, it would be too much to expect a concise definition of how it is used. He addresses a definition of psychic bisexuality variously (pp. 721–9), e.g. he attributes the following definition to Freud (without providing any actual reference):

> Par bisexualité psychique, qu'il [Freud] appelle aussi hermaphrodisme psychique, il désignait la coexistence chez un même être humain de dispositions et de traits masculins et féminins influant sur le choix d'objet aussi bien que sur toute la personnalité, quoiqu'il eût reconnu la relative dépendance de ces données entre elles comme par rapport aux caractères sexuels somatiques.
>
> (p. 723)

> [By psychic bisexuality, which he also calls psychic hermaphroditism, Freud designated the coexistence in the same human being of masculine and feminine dispositions and traits influencing the choice of object and the entire personality,

although he recognised the relative dependence of these factors on each other as well as on somatic sexual characteristics. (my translation)]

David is of course putting words in Freud's mouth; this represents merely an interpretation of Freud's ideas based on David's rough paraphrase and summary of various texts by Freud. Unfortunately, David goes on to ignore exactly the "relative dependence of these factors", probably because he frequently relies on Stoller's work. It is thus no surprise that David then embraces Stoller's neologism "bigenderality" as an appropriate synonym for psychic bisexuality. From this strategy, it is possible to deduce David's definition as follows: the coexistence of masculine and feminine aspects, a double gender identity (p. 724). In this definition, David is explicitly following Stoller by making a fixed equation of masculine with activity, and feminine with passivity. Both David and Stoller do this in contradistinction to Freud, who repeatedly warns against such simplistic reductionism and literalism. Logically, there is no way to support such a definition. It relies on a series of socially constructed stereotypes, which are obnoxious at best and harmful at worst. Furthermore, this linear conflation is weak as a definition because it relies on other undefined (and indefinable) concepts, such as gender, masculine, feminine. Clearly David's usage has in mind subject bisexuality, but his text repeatedly elides this with object bisexuality. Despite his overall imprecision, the broad range of David's seminal text, especially the bibliography (pp. 846–56), stands out.

The first appearance of the term found in circulation in English is a paper "On psychic bisexuality" by Henry Smith (2002), but the title is misleading, and the phrase is not the focus. Smith does not mention David's work, although he uses the phrase in a similar way to suggest "the observation of mixed masculine and feminine traits in all individuals" (p. 552); Smith in fact advocates for replacing the term psychic bisexuality with the concept of gender (p. 553). Since its fairly recent introduction, the phrase has been taken up surprisingly widely so that psychic bisexuality is now completely naturalised as a standard term attributed to Freud in a prominent guide to reading Freud's work (Quinodoz, 2004) and serves as the main theme of essays and collections (Perelberg, 2018; Yumatov, 2019).

In the literal sense of how the term seems to be typically used, the phrase gestures towards the psychological reality of sexual identity (and especially self-defined identity) constructed from the biological reality of the sexual drive. In this sense, the phrase appears to serve as a Freudian-sounding catchall term for bisexual *subjectivity* (i.e. subject bisexuality) within the current context of discussions around gender. It suggests two genders in one body instead of just one, like Butler's "two heterosexual desires" idea of bisexuality outlined above. The word gender was not available to Freud and does not appear in his texts. Freud instead uses the terms masculine/feminine and active/passive, but in a guarded manner to mean the socially constructed representation of biological sex. The conclusion must be that contemporary psychoanalytic discourse uses the phrase psychic bisexuality, albeit inconsistently, to mean an individual's social subjectivity constructed around some degree of exhibiting both masculine and feminine stereotypical characteristics.

This definition is not only a lazy workaround to avoid addressing the complexity of socially constructed gender; it also sidesteps Freud's radical relativism and allows the discourse to adopt a register that sounds scientific. In effect, however, the term facilitates confusion in the discourse, which selectively and indiscriminately tends to encompass both subject and object bisexuality to suit the theme of a particular author. One final observation about the inadequacy of the concept of psychic bisexuality: the scholars who use this phrase never seem to extend their consideration to an implicit psychic heterosexuality or homosexuality.

The Oedipus complex

Freud's theory of the Oedipus complex is a crucial focus point for the reconstruction of the bisexuality thesis in the next two chapters (Chapter 2 and 3), so the goal here is not to explore the theory of the Oedipus complex in any detail but to show briefly some of the main ways in which this theory has been vulgarised.

There has been much recent scholarship focused on the Oedipus complex, indicating that it remains central in psychoanalytic theory and practice. The frequent ways in which this key theory has been abused include first and foremost a range of strategies that simply diminish the centrality of the Oedipus complex in Freud's work or reduce its meaning to Freud's early outline of the simple form while ignoring or neglecting his later and final version of the complete form. Invariably, these approaches are paired with a strong emphasis on biological sex, which is also often confused with gender. Other vulgarised approaches include literalising the discussion of the Oedipus complex, especially by focusing on Sophocles's dramatic text. A related approach to literalism is to invest heavily in personifying the discussion by linking it to Freud's (auto)biography and speculating about the development of his thinking. Some studies do recognise that the Sophoclean drama should be understood in a more metaphorical manner but then take the opposite approach to literalism and introduce a range of entirely new metaphors. Needless to say, there is also always a proliferation of clinical case studies to fall back on whenever the Oedipus complex is examined. Finally, perhaps the most significant but overlooked form of vulgarisation is to disregard the constitutive link of the Oedipus complex to Freud's structural theory of the mental apparatus. It must always be remembered that the Oedipus complex and the structural theory come together as two sides of the same coin, namely the 1923 text *The ego and the id*.

Few studies pay any attention to bisexuality in relation to the Oedipus complex, except briefly in passing as reference to a theorised preoedipal state of primitive or immature sexuality. In broader debates over the last two decades around sexuality and gender, and especially since the emergence and ascendancy of Queer Studies, I would have expected a strong focus on Freud's elaboration of the "more complete" Oedipus complex (1923, p. 33) as a way to accommodate contemporary interest around a multiplicity of sexual identities and behaviours. Surprisingly, this has not been the case. Or perhaps this is unsurprising, given the general antipathy towards Freud's theory from outside mainstream psychoanalysis.

Lewes (1988, pp. 76–89) provides perhaps the most sympathetic and comprehensive interpretation of the full form of the Oedipus complex by elaborating his famous twelve outcomes of the Oedipus complex (summarised in his table: 1988, p. 83) but, even after this fascinating engagement with plurality, Lewes still manages to miss the link between the Oedipus complex and the formation of the ego and superego. This may be because he has not understood the child's process of parental identification, or perhaps it is simply because he maintains the long-standing emphasis in psychoanalysis on the difference in biological sex of the parents, as if the difference were always apparent to the child from the start of its life. This is an entirely understandable and common error appearing consistently throughout the psychoanalytic literature on the Oedipus complex, resulting from an inadequate and partial reading of Freud's theory. On some basic level, and even with his comprehensive explication of the Oedipus complex, Lewes still regards Freud as heteronormative (p. 93), so in turn there may be a residue of this heteronormative expectation in Lewes's own interpretation.

Initially, Deleuze and Guattari recognise the complete form of the Oedipus complex (1972, p. 51), but on this occasion they conclude that Freud links the negative (homosexual) component to the period of infantile sexuality, in their view, thus bringing the infantile period into the ambit of the Oedipus complex, and they slip back to focus explicitly on only the simple form and adopt the idea that Freud is being prescriptive (p. 59). After this single mention, the homosexual side of the full complex is not directly considered again in the first volume of *Anti-Oedipus*, although it does seem to hover in the background and reappear in other aspects of the negation that Deleuze and Guattari pursue. The second volume of their work (Deleuze & Guattari, 1980) has no reference to the full form. Even though the Oedipus complex is a central focus of Hocquenghem's (1972) work, he similarly fails to consider the full form and entirely disregards Freud's 1923 text. Although Green (1973) recognises the bisexuality of the complete form, he sees this as a subject bisexuality of masculine and feminine, and he concludes that one will always dominate and conceal the other (p. 161). In this he follows the consensus that gender equates biological sex, built on Stoller (1968) and Money's (Money & Ehrhardt, 1972) concept of gender. David (1975, pp. 769–79) characterises the complete form using the idea of a double Oedipus triangulation ("*la double triangulation oedipienne*", p. 771); while he recognises the importance of this for subject bisexuality, his interpretation is hamstrung by the imprecision of psychic bisexuality as an emerging term in the French tradition.

More recent iterations that neglect the complete form of the Oedipus complex include Fear (2016), who never considers the complete form, and Hartke (2016), who mentions the complete form only once. Perelberg (2015) ignores the complete form and, reflecting the persistent influence of Melanie Klein's work, dismisses the Freudian evidence for an undifferentiated parental function in the infantile period and instead introduces the concept of the paternal function. Barratt (2019) likewise ignores the complete form; he fully transforms the emphasis on differentiated biological sex into a maternal and paternal function, and then insists that the paternal function is the one that delivers prohibition. Butler (1990, p. 81) already paves the way to this sloppy conflation of biological sex and gender with her insistence on a cross-identified masculinity-threatening "feminine superego" as the outcome of the homosexual component of the complete form of the Oedipus complex. In this way, Butler demonstrates her misreading of Freud's complete form, which she also wrongly believes Freud rejected. Angelides (2001, pp. 54–61) recognises but is unable to understand the complete form, perhaps because his paraphrase is pre-framed by his open hostility to Freud's ideas.

Heenen-Wolff (2011) appears to be the first scholar since Lewes (1988) to return to fully understanding the complete form of the Oedipus complex, but her short paper addresses a range of unrelated themes (e.g. gay parenthood) and does not consider the full implications of Freud's 1923 text for bisexuality. Picking up on Heenen-Wolff's study, Yumatov (2019) also recognises the complete form but then misses the meaning of this by conflating the period of the Oedipus complex with an earlier period which he terms "early Oedipal" (p. 62). This blinds his work to the possibility of any identification entirely prior to the Oedipus complex (i.e. preoedipal) and reduces early identification to the complete form. Pederson (2015) embraces the full form of the Oedipus complex and its bisexual consequences, although the ensuing and extensive discussion from a clinical perspective is inflected by exigent use of the term psychic bisexuality. Flanders et al. (2016) touch on the complete form briefly but fail to realise the importance of this, even for their primary focus on Freud's theory of homosexuality. Similarly, Kakar and Narayanan (2023, p. 38) briefly recognise the potential of the full form of the Oedipus complex for explaining bisexuality, but then neglect to develop this argument and shift their focus to aspects of cultural difference and Indian mythologies. This directs their work towards a literal view of the Oedipus complex as the Sophoclean text and therefore a culture-specific myth.

The approach of literalism regarding the Sophoclean dramatic text is best exemplified by Zepf et al. (2014) and Smadja (2017). Along with Perelberg (2015) and Fear (2016), they reflect an inexplicable conviction that the ancient drama somehow holds the key to understanding Freud's theory of the Oedipus complex, when clearly Freud is simply using Sophocles's text as a moniker, a hook on which to hang his emerging ideas around the theme of the child's sexual development. The vast majority of these studies also tend to merge the biography of Freud unquestioningly with the theory of the Oedipus complex – though it is not clear how this biographical link advances the theory.

It seems a small step, albeit in the opposite direction, from literalising the Oedipus complex to offering a proliferation of new metaphors, such as the monumental figurative labours of Deleuze and Guattari (1972, 1980) resulting in their proposal for a *schizoanalysis* clinical method (this is considered in Chapter 5, pp. 158–60). The far more modest project of a non-oedipal psychoanalysis ("pathoanalysis") by Van Haute and Geyskens (2012) is based on case studies, especially a very narrow reading of Freud's *Psychogenesis of a case of homosexuality in a woman* (1920). With this limited gesture to Freud, Van Haute and Geyskens produce an entire book about bisexuality and the Oedipus complex that does not once reference *The ego and the id* (1923) or mention the complete form. A grossly incomplete scrutiny of Freud's work culminates in their peculiar claim: "In this case study [1920] Freud comes up against the boundaries of the psychogenetic Oedipal model he developed in previous years; he also returns to bisexuality for the last time" (Van Haute & Geyskens, 2012, pp. 78–9). While the psychogenetic worth of the Oedipus model can be debated, Freud's 1920 text is far from the last in which he addresses bisexuality. Given their standing as renowned Freudian scholars, it seems unlikely that the authors could make such an obvious mistake, and perhaps this sentence is actually a translation error in the English. Presumably the authors mean to say that Freud's 1920 case is the last case study in which Freud returns to bisexuality, although this too hardly needs stating, since the 1920 case is the last of Freud's published case studies. Van Haute and Geyskens's focus then veers off from Freud to Lacan's compound metaphors, which they blend with a number of other cultural artefacts in a fresh series of case study demonstrations. As is well known, Lacan's version of the Oedipus complex abandons Freud's model for a neo-Kantian restatement that embraces the paternal function and also famously ignores Freud's complete form, which is not suited to Lacan's stark homophobic worldview. Presumably the only benefit of this pivot to Lacan by Van Haute and Geyskens is to access additional case studies from the prolific Lacan, since Freud's ran out in 1920.

Other approaches to Freud's radicalism

Before concluding this review, it is worth considering some recent approaches that claim to discover or renew radical aspects in Freud's work. A prominent example is Barnaby Barratt's (2016) *Radical psychoanalysis*. Barratt argues that the radical element of the Freudian legacy is not Freud's theory, especially after 1914, but rather the clinical practices Freud developed in his early clinical work, particularly "free-associative discourse". Paradoxically, Barratt argues that Freud turns away from his own radicalism by his growing embrace of theory. Instead of a deeper engagement with Freud's theory, Barratt's version of back-to-Freud is to focus on Freud's clinical method and to disparage Freud's theory. This strategy produces a practice Barratt calls *workplay*: "a method of working-and-playing with the lived experience of our self-consciousness" (p. 10). When a method veers into the solipsistic realm of solitary lived experience, predictably it has no choice but to fall back on metaphysics. Barratt's method offers the consolations of metaphysics in abundance, from Love – with a capital L – will conquer suffering, to authenticity and truthfulness (p. 12). Along the way the text embraces a patchwork of (mostly) existentialist philosophy culled from sources as disparate as Lacan, Derrida, Marx and Adorno, but the underlying message of this "healing science of Love in psychoanalysis" sounds far closer to the Judeo-Christian tradition than any radical praxis. Barratt's characterisation of Freud's structural model as "a highly problematic recentering of the subject both by its biological idealism in the monadological depiction of innate drive forces and by providing a model of the ego organization that invites the subsequent assertion of a conflict-free sphere of its functioning" (p. 37) is mistaken in so many respects, not least by the assumption that the ego organisation is conflict free. The opposite is in fact the case, and Freud's structural model certainly has no centre or centring effect. Barratt's (2016) strong endorsement of his own new praxis in place of Freud's theory is rendered incoherent in a later text (Barratt, 2019) when he returns full force to adopt once again the later theory of Freud that was supposedly left in the dust by Barratt's 2016 methodology. Without a blush of explanation, Barratt climbs back on board the Oedipus train with great enthusiasm. While consistency is not necessarily a prerequisite in itself, the impression Barratt's radical psychoanalysis leaves is a fundamental inability to harmonise theory and clinical practice. It is also not clear how any radical Freudian praxis could ever be entertained without recognising Freud's radical theory.

The preference for clinical practice over theory and the neglect of the radical aspects of Freud's theory are two common and recurrent features in recent revisionist approaches by a new generation of psychoanalysts whose work foregrounds praxis. Examples include the contributors to Domenici and Lesser (1995), Fonagy et al. (2006), Perelberg (2018), Evzonas and Ayouch (2020), Ashtor (2021) and Evzonas (2021, 2022). Such reformism attempts to proliferate discourses of sexuality, precisely in the sense of the "great sexual sermon" that Foucault (1976) cautions against, but these clinical reforms are also always premised on accepting the popular assumption that Freud himself has nothing radical to offer today. The present revisionist trend of rehabilitating psychoanalytic discourse via the emphasis on diversity in clinical practice, especially in the direction of currently fashionable trans-affirmative and intersectional themes, commences by apologising penitently for Freud's (alleged) antagonism to marginal identities of any variety. Evzonas (2020, 2021) innovatively characterises these proliferations as *trans-epistemological*, and this kind of epistemological fluidity underpins his most recent work (2023), which refreshingly explores the reflexive position of the analyst. The discursive proliferation comes full circle in Ashtor (2021), like the snake eating its tail. Such revisionism risks becoming an ungainly rush merely to broaden the appeal of psychoanalytic discourse for the purposes of an expanded clinical practice; it toys with the discursive limits of assimilation and intelligibility posed by marginality while assiduously avoiding the original radical implications of Freud's sexual theory, which erase the very concept of marginal identity, even if marginality could be viewed simply as a statistical measure against some supposedly central stereotype.

Solms's error

There is one remaining form of vulgarisation to mention, namely the relatively recent and rather strange forced marriage of psychoanalysis to neuropsychology. The flamboyant aspiration to *realism* in neuropsychology today stands in diametrical contrast to Freud's metaphors and to the relativism that is inescapable in human constructs of reality, so the union seems unlikely and doomed from the start. It is not at all clear how neuropsychology became so mixed up in Freud's intellectual legacy, nor how one of the major current proponents of neuropsychology should have come to oversee the revision of the translation of Freud's work into English. Indeed, neuropsychology seems the least likely qualification for such a vast job of navigating and re-transposing Freud's metaphors. To revive a few early speculative neuropsychological papers abandoned by Freud and to use these to claim Freud for neuroscience is to misunderstand entirely Freud's epistemological project.

For a neuroscientist with a scalpel, everything is a brain for vivisection. The frontier of scientific knowledge is crudely overstepped by surgical incursion, in a failure to understand that knowledge can only ever be a metaphor. As an extreme form of literalism, neuropsychology has the ambition of mapping something it vaguely calls *the mind* onto the physical brain. To do this, neuropsychologists have simply resurrected the mediaeval religious *soul* in the guise of the mind, and they then rely on the false dichotomy of mind and body to make an equally false separation and equivalence of body and brain to thus present mind and brain as separate entities. It is a literal attempt to reverse-translate language into reality, with the absolute hubris to presume that such a negation is not also a metaphor.

Freud uses the most poignant metaphors to emphasise the impossibility of any ambition to pinpoint the boundary between the components of the mental apparatus or to establish the location of the mental in the physical. He frequently adopts images of political geography (realms, regions, provinces) to characterise the interlinked nature of the mental apparatus. In Lecture 31 (1933), this is presented as an extended metaphor of the mind that evokes the multicultural regions and peoples of the former Austro-Hungarian Empire. The partition between regions or cultures is never neat or clear-cut; "there is less orderliness and more mixing, ... Germans, Magyars and Slovaks live interspersed all over" (pp. 72–3). Later in the lecture, the region image is revived and then transformed into the trope of modern art:

> In thinking of this division of the personality into an ego, a super-ego and an id, you will not, of course, have pictured sharp frontiers like the artificial ones drawn in political geography. We cannot do justice to the characteristics of the mind by linear outlines like those in a drawing or in primitive painting, but rather by areas of colour melting into one another as they are presented by modern artists. After making the separation we must allow what we have separated to merge together once more.
>
> (p. 79)

In contrast to the ambitions of neuropsychology, Freud's model of the mental apparatus is explicitly holistic and integrative in understanding that the physical frontier of phenomena like mind, brain and consciousness cannot be drawn with a scalpel. The brain is an integral and inseparable component of the body: this integrity is precisely the meaning of the metaphor *the mind*. Beyond the obvious literal external frontiers of the body, like the skin or the senses, it is impossible to determine precisely where any physical or mental element begins and ends in its physiology and function. On closer examination, the frontiers of the body are everywhere and include such diffuse and internal sites as the respiratory system, the digestive tract and the immune system. Even these literal frontiers of the body are not impermeable or permanent. Each body was once literally part of and dependant on another body. After birth, the human body is still entirely immersed in and bound to empirical reality. The body relies on constant exchanges with the broader physical and natural environment for survival, even though people don't often consciously think of themselves in this way. Neurosurgical experiments and vivisections on the brain are like a crude trick showing the dead frog's leg move in response to an electric current, and they do nothing to explain (or even describe) the fundamental inter-reliance and remarkable plasticity and redundancy of the neural structures as integral parts of the human body or, in turn, the utter infant-like dependency of the human body as part of a broad non-human environment. Who dares say with conviction where the mind begins or ends? The glossy neuropsychology photographs of brain sections are a high-resolution tomography equivalent of Charcot's 19th-century *leçon clinique* spectacle. Besides, human consciousness is not the unique and apex miracle that neuropsychologists like to imagine. If only they could drop the scalpel for a moment and come to understand that the true miracle is life itself, which only has meaning in relation to its negation: non-life.

A recent neuropsychological essay (Solms, 2023) trumpets its vulgarisation of Freud in the title: "Freud's error". This is brilliant rhetoric – the scholarly equivalent of digital media clickbait – because the essay itself has no new content and simply recycles a string of previously published material, as Solms at least admits in the first paragraph. From the start, however, the title also trumpets the conflicted relationship of neuropsychology with Freud's metaphors. It is no surprise that Freud's metaphors will be seen as errors by scholars who deny the basic metaphorical nature of knowledge. The neuropsychological jargon is simply garb for more of the same pedestrian rivalry with the intellectual father already seen in the work of Schafer and Butler. I am always left wondering why someone like Solms is so madly keen on Freud if his only interest is to slay Freud's theory. In actual fact, the error here is on the part of Solms, who misunderstands Freud's metaphorical use of the word *surface* (of the mental apparatus) to mean a *literal* part of the brain, and then compounds this error by failing to see Freud's wry sarcasm directed towards the neural anatomy of his time. In part, Solms's error is also the result of his lingering attachment to Freud's first topography, which has more superficial affinity to the stark world of neuropsychology. Finally, Solms is only splitting hairs between consciousness and attention in order to repeat the grand literalist neural speculations from his earlier publications and present them as truth. To make oversimplified claims of irrefutable empirical knowledge with such an unabashed excess of self-confidence regarding a phenomenon so complicated and metaphorical, so elusive and recalcitrant to detection by scans and vivisection as consciousness, is the error of literalism that Freud succinctly avoids.

Reference list

Please note: References follow the system of historical layering, with a distinction between source texts and access texts. If the source date is different to the access date, page references are always for the access text, but the reference year is that of the source text. For more in this regard, please see the comment on historical layering in the Introduction, p. 5.

Anderlini-D'Onofrio, S. and Alexander, J. (2009). Introduction to the special issue: Bisexuality and queer theory: Intersections, diversions, and connections. *Journal of Bisexuality*, 9(3–4), 197–212. Reprinted in *Bisexuality and queer theory: Intersections, connections and challenges*. London: Routledge, 2012.

Angelides, S. (2001). *A history of bisexuality*. Chicago: University of Chicago Press.

Ashtor, G. (2021). *Homo psyche: On queer theory and erotophobia*. New York: Fordham University Press.

Balsam, R.H. (2013). Appreciating difference: Roy Schafer on psychoanalysis and women. *The Psychoanalytic Quarterly*, 82(1), 23–38.

Balsam, R.H., Fogel, G.I. and Harris, A. (2019). Roy Schafer, 1922–2018. *Journal of the American Psychoanalytic Association*, 67(3), 487–93.

Barratt, B.B. (2016). *Radical psychoanalysis: An essay on free-associative praxis*. London: Routledge.

Barratt, B.B. (2019). Oedipality and oedipal complexes reconsidered: On the incest taboo as key to the universality of the human condition. *The International Journal of Psychoanalysis*, 100(1), 7–31.

Bayer, R. (1981). *Homosexuality and American psychiatry: The politics of diagnosis*. Princeton: Princeton University Press, 1987.

Bieber, I., Bieber, T.B., Dain, H.J., Dince, P.R., Drellich, M.G., Grand, H.G., Gundlach, R.H., Kremer, M.W., Rifkin, A.H. and Wilbur, C.B. (1962). *Homosexuality: A psychoanalytic study*. New York: Basic Books.

Blechner, M.J. (2015). Bigenderism and bisexuality. *Contemporary Psychoanalysis*, 51(3), 503–22.

Brunswick, R.M. (1940). The preoedipal phase of the libido development. *The Psychoanalytic Quarterly*, 9(2), 293–319.

Butler, J. (1990). *Gender trouble: Feminism and the subversion of identity*. New York: Routledge, 2006.

David, C. (1975). La bisexualité psychique, rapport du xxxve Congrès des psychanalystes de langues romanes. *Revue française de psychanalyse*, 39(5–6), 695–856.

Deleuze, G. and Guattari, F. (1972). *Capitalisme et schizophrénie: L'anti-Œdipe*. Paris: Éditions de Minuit. Trans. by R. Hurley, M. Seem and H. Lane as *Anti-Oedipus: Capitalism and schizophrenia*. Minneapolis: University of Minnesota Press, 1983.

Deleuze, G. and Guattari, F. (1980). *Capitalisme et schizophrénie: Mille plateaux*. Paris: Éditions de Minuit. Trans. by B. Massumi as *A thousand plateaus: Capitalism and schizophrenia*. Minneapolis: University of Minnesota Press, 1987.

Domenici, T. and Lesser, R.C. (1995). *Disorienting sexuality: Psychoanalytic reappraisals of sexual identities*. New York: Routledge.

Drescher, J. (2008). A history of homosexuality and organized psychoanalysis. *Journal of The American Academy of Psychoanalysis and Dynamic Psychiatry*, 36(3), 443–60.

Evzonas, N. (2020). Prologue: Queering and decolonizing psychoanalysis. *Psychoanalytic Inquiry*, 40(8), 571–8.

Evzonas, N. (2021). Trans* becomings and countertransference volume 1: A contemporary perspective from France. Special issue of *Psychoanalytic Review*, 108(4).

Evzonas, N. (2022). Trans* becomings and countertransference Volume 2: An international perspective. Special issue of *Psychoanalytic Review*, 109(3).

Evzonas, N. (2023). *Devenirs trans de l'analyste*. Paris: Presses Universitaires de France / Humensis.

Evzonas, N. and Ayouch, T. (2020). Sexualities, gender, class, and race: A psychoanalytic view from France. Special issue of *Psychoanalytic Inquiry*, 40(8).

Fear, R.M. (2016). *The Oedipus complex: Solutions or resolutions?* London: Routledge.

Flanders, S., Ladame, F., Carlsberg, A., Heymanns, P., Naziri, D. and Panitz, D. (2016). On the subject of homosexuality: What Freud said. *The International Journal of Psychoanalysis*, 97(3), 933–50.

Fogel, G.I. (2019). Introduction: Roy Schafer's "Problems in Freud's psychology of women". *Journal of the American Psychoanalytic Association*, 67(3), 495–502.

Fonagy, P. (2006). Psychosexuality and psychoanalysis: An overview. In P. Fonagy, R. Krause and M. Leuzinger-Bohleber, eds., *Identity, gender, and sexuality 150 years after Freud*. London: International Psychoanalytical Association.

Fonagy, P., Krause, R. and Leuzinger-Bohleber, M. (2006). *Identity, gender, and sexuality 150 years after Freud*. London: International Psychoanalytical Association.

Foucault, M. (1976). *Histoire de la sexualité: La volonté de savoir*. Paris: Éditions Gallimard. Trans. by R. Hurley as *The history of sexuality. Volume 1: An introduction*. New York: Pantheon Books, 1978.

Freud, S. (1887–1902a). Letter (145) to Wilhelm Fliess. In M. Bonaparte, A. Freud and E. Kris, eds., *Aus den Anfangen der Psychoanalyse: Briefe an Wilhelm Fliess, Abhandlungen und Notizen aus den Jahren 1887–1902*. London: Imago, 1950.

Freud, S. (1887–1902b). Letter (145) to Wilhelm Fliess. In M. Bonaparte, A. Freud and E. Kris, eds.; E. Mosbacher and J. Strachey, trans., *The origins of psycho-analysis. Letters to Wilhelm Fliess, drafts and notes: 1887–1902*. New York: Basic Books, 1954.

Freud, S. (1887–1904). Letter (145) to Wilhelm Fliess. In J.M. Masson, ed. and trans., *The complete letters of Sigmund Freud to Wilhelm Fliess, 1887–1904*. Cambridge: Harvard University Press, 1985.

Freud, S. (1901). The psychopathology of everyday life. In J. Strachey, ed. and trans., *The standard edition of the complete psychological works of Sigmund Freud, 24 vols*. London: Hogarth Press, 1953–1974. 6.

Freud, S. (1905). Three essays on the theory of sexuality. *Standard ed.*, 7:125–245.

Freud, S. (1905a). *Three essays on the theory of sexuality*. Trans. U. Kistner. London: Verso, 2016.

Freud, S. (1911). Psycho-analytic notes on an autobiographical account of a case of paranoia (dementia paranoides). *Standard ed.*, 12:1–82.

Freud, S. (1912). Contributions to a discussion on masturbation. *Standard ed.*, 12:239–54.

Freud, S. (1913). The claims of psycho-analysis to scientific interest. *Standard ed.*, 13:163–90.

Freud, S. (1915). Instincts and their vicissitudes. *Standard ed.*, 14:109–40.

Freud, S. (1917). Mourning and melancholia. *Standard ed.*, 14:237–58.

Freud, S. (1919). "A child is being beaten": A contribution to the study of the origin of sexual perversions. *Standard ed.*, 17:175–204.

Freud, S. (1920). The psychogenesis of a case of homosexuality in a woman. *Standard ed.*, 18:147–72.

Freud, S. (1921). Group psychology and the analysis of the ego. *Standard ed.*, 18:65–143.

Freud, S. (1923). The ego and the id. *Standard ed.*, 19:1–66.

Freud, S. (1925). Some psychical consequences of the anatomical distinction between the sexes. *Standard ed.*, 19:241–58.

Freud, S. (1930). Civilization and its discontents. *Standard ed.*, 21:57–145.

Freud, S. (1933). New introductory lectures on psycho-analysis. *Standard ed.*, 22:1–182.

Freud, S. (1937). Analysis terminable and interminable. *Standard ed.*, 23:209–53.

Freud, S. (1938). An outline of psycho-analysis. *Standard ed.*, 23:139–207.

Green, A. (1973). Le genre neutre, pp. 251–62 in *Bisexualité et la différence des sexes: Nouvelle Revue de Psychanalyse*, 7. Paris: Gallimard. Also in *Narcissisme de vie: Narcissism de mort*. Paris: Minuit, 1983, pp. 208–21. Trans. by A. Weller as "The neuter gender". In *Life narcissism, death narcissism*. London: Free Association Books, 2001, pp. 158–69.

Gulati, R. and Pauley, D. (2019). The half embrace of psychic bisexuality. *Journal of the American Psychoanalytic Association*, 67(1), 97–121.

Hanscombe, G. and Humphries, M. (1987). *Heterosexuality*. London: Gay Men's Press.

Hartke, R. (2016). The Oedipus complex: A confrontation at the central cross-roads of psychoanalysis. *International Journal of Psychoanalysis*, 97(3), 893–913.

Heenen-Wolff, S. (2010a). Sexualität, Bisexualität und Homosexualität in der freudschen Psychoanalyse. *Texte*, 30, 65–81.

Heenen-Wolff, S. (2010b). *La bisexualité chez Freud*. In S. Heenen-Wolff, *Homosexualités et stigmatisation: bisexualité, homosexualité, homoparentalité: nouvelles approaches*. PUF: Paris, 41–65.

Heenen-Wolff, S. (2011). Infantile bisexuality and the "complete oedipal complex": Freudian views on heterosexuality and homosexuality. *The International Journal of Psychoanalysis*, 92(5), 1209–20.

Hertzmann, L. and Newbigin, J. (2019). *Sexuality and gender now: Moving beyond heteronormativity*. London: Routledge.

Hertzmann, L. and Newbigin, J. (2023). *Psychoanalysis and homosexuality: A contemporary introduction*. London: Routledge.

Hocquenghem, G. (1972). *Le desir homosexuel*. Paris: Editions Universitaires. Trans. by D. Dangoor as *Homosexual desire*. Durham: Duke University Press, 1993.

Isay, R.A. (1989). *Being homosexual: gay men and their development*. New York: Farrar, Straus, Giroux.

Kakar, S. and Narayanan, A. (2023). The capacious Freud. In F. Busch and D. Delgado, *The ego and the id 100 years later*. London: Routledge

Katz, J. (1995). *The invention of heterosexuality*. Harmondsworth: Penguin.

Kinsey, A.C., Pomeroy, W.B. and Martin, C.E. (1948). *Sexual behavior in the human male*. Philadelphia: W.B. Saunders.

Kinsey, A.C., Pomeroy, W.B. and Martin, C.E. (1953). *Sexual behavior in the human female*. Philadelphia: W.B. Saunders.

Lacan, J. (1955–1956). *Le Séminaire, Livre III – Les Psychoses*. Paris: Éditions du Seuil, 1981. Trans. by R. Grigg as *The seminar of Jacques Lacan: Book III: The psychoses 1955–1956*. New York: Norton, 1993.

Lewes, K. (1988). *The psychoanalytic theory of male homosexuality*. New York: Simon and Schuster.

Mader, M.B. (2011). *Sleights of reason: Norm, bisexuality, development*. Albany: State University of New York Press.

Marcuse, H. (1955). *Eros and civilization: A philosophical inquiry into Freud*. Boston: Beacon Press.

Mitchell, J. (1974). *Psychoanalysis and feminism: Freud, Reich, Laing, and women.* New York: Pantheon Books.

Money, J. and Ehrhardt, A. (1972). *Man and woman, boy and girl: The differentiation and dimorphism of gender identity from conception to maturity.* Baltimore: Johns Hopkins University Press.

O'Connor, N. and Ryan, J. (1993). *Wild desires and mistaken identities: Lesbianism and psychoanalysis.* London: Virago.

Pederson, T.C. (2015). *The economics of libido: Psychic bisexuality, the superego, and the centrality of the Oedipus complex.* London: Routledge.

Perelberg, R.J. (2015). *Murdered father: Dead father – Revisiting the Oedipus complex.* London: Routledge and The New Library of Psychoanalysis.

Perelberg, R.J. (2018). *Psychic bisexuality: A British-French dialogue.* London: Routledge.

Quinodoz, J. (2004). *Lire Freud: Découverte chronologique de l'œuvre de Freud.* Presses Universitaires de France. Trans. by D. Alcorn as *Reading Freud: A chronological exploration of Freud's writings.* London: Routledge, 2005.

Rado, S. (1940). A critical examination of the concept of bisexuality. *Psychosomatic Medicine, 2,* 459–67.

Rapoport, E. (2009). Bisexuality in psychoanalytic theory: Interpreting the resistance. *Journal of Bisexuality,* 9(3–4), 279–95.

Rapoport, E. (2010). Bisexuality: The undead (m)other of psychoanalysis. *Culture & Society,* 15(1), 70–83.

Rapoport, E. (2019). *From Psychoanalytic Bisexuality to Bisexual Psychoanalysis: Desiring in the Real.* London: Routledge.

Rich, A. (1980). Compulsory heterosexuality and lesbian existence. *Signs,* 5(4), 631–60.

Rich, A. (2004). Reflections on "compulsory heterosexuality". *Journal of Women's History,* 16(1), 9–11.

Roazen, P. (1995). *Heresy: Sandor Rado and the psychoanalytic movement.* Northvale, NJ: Aronson.

Roazen, P. (2002). *The trauma of Freud: Controversies in psychoanalysis.* New Brunswick: Transaction Publishers.

Roudinesco, É. (2002). Psychanalyse et homosexualité: réflexions sur le désir pervers, l'injure et la fonction paternelle. *Cliniques méditerranéennes,* 65(1), 7–34. There appears to be an English translation of this interview [Psychoanalysis and homosexuality: Reflections on the perverse desire, insult and the paternal function] in *Journal of European Psychoanalysis,* 15.

Rubin, G. (1975). The traffic in women: Notes on the "political economy" of sex. In R.R. Reiter, *Toward an anthropology of women.* New York: Monthly Review Press.

Schafer, R. (1974). Problems in Freud's psychology of women. *Journal of the American Psychoanalytic Association,* 22(3), 459–85. Republished in 2019 as Problems in Freud's psychology of women. *Journal of the American Psychoanalytic Association,* 67(3), 503–26.

Schafer, R. (1994). The evolution of my views on nonnormative sexual practices. In *Tradition and change in psychoanalysis.* New York: Karnac Books, 1997. Also reproduced in Domenici, T. and Lesser, R.C. (1995). *Disorienting sexuality: Psychoanalytic reappraisals of sexual identities.* New York: Routledge.

Shaw, J. (2022). *Bi – The hidden culture, history, and science of bisexuality.* New York: Harry N. Abrams.

Silverstein, C. (2008). Are you saying homosexuality is normal? *Journal of Gay & Lesbian Mental Health,* 12(3), 277–87.

Smadja, É. (2017). *The Oedipus complex: Focus of the psychoanalysis-Anthropology Debate*. London: Routledge.

Smith, H.F. (2002). On psychic bisexuality. *The Psychoanalytic Quarterly*, 71(3), 549–58.

Solms, M. (2023). Freud's error. In F. Busch and D. Delgado, *The ego and the id 100 years later*. London: Routledge.

Stoller, R.J. (1968). *Sex and gender: The development of masculinity and femininity*. New York: Science House; London: Routledge, 1994.

Stoller, R.J. (1975). *Sex and gender, Volume II: The transsexual experiment*. New York: Jason Aronson.

Tontonoz, M. (2017). Sandor Rado, American psychoanalysis, and the question of bisexuality. *History of Psychology*, 20(3), 263–89.

Ulrichs, K.H. (1868). *Forschungen über das Räthsel der mannmännlichen Liebe. Vol VII. Memnon. Die Geschlechtsnatur des mannliebenden Urnings. Eine naturwissenschaftliche Darstellung*. Schleiz: C. Hübscher'sche Buchhandlung (Hugo Heyn).

Van Haute, P. and Geyskens, T. (2012). *A non-oedipal psychoanalysis? A clinical anthropology of hysteria in the works of Freud and Lacan*. Trans. into English by J. Kok. Leuven: Leuven University Press.

Wiedeman, G.H. (1962). Survey of psychoanalytic literature on overt male homosexuality. *Journal of the American Psychoanalytic Association*, 10, 386–409.

Wiedeman, G.H. (1974). Homosexuality: A survey. *Journal of the American Psychoanalytic Association*, 22, 651–96.

Wiedeman, G.H. and Payne, E.C. (1977). Panel report: Psychoanalytic treatment of male homosexuality. *Journal of the American Psychoanalytic Association*, 25, 183–99.

Young-Bruehl, E. (2001). Are human beings "by Nature" bisexual? *Studies in Gender and Sexuality*, 2(3), 179–213.

Yumatov, R. (2019). Bisexuality and its vicissitudes: A psychoanalytic exploration. In P. Ellerman and K. Kleinman, *The Plumsock papers: Giving new analysts a voice*. New York: IPBooks, pp. 35–87.

Zepf, S., Zepf, F.D., Ullrich, B. and Seel, D. (2014). *Oedipus and the Oedipus complex: A revision*. London: Routledge.

Chapter 2

Reconstructing the bisexuality thesis I

The Oedipus complex

Freud's early insights into sexuality from the *Three essays* (1905) culminating in the theory of the Oedipus complex (1923) are the best-known aspects of his enduring theory of sexuality but, in parallel and less explicitly developed, Freud suggests and sketches an alternative and quite radical theory of universal bisexuality in humans. This chapter lays out in detail Freud's bisexuality thesis and also contrasts it to his better-known Oedipus theory. By way of introducing this core section of the book, the following aspects must be kept in mind. Firstly, there are in fact two discrete bisexuality theories in Freud's work. One theory emerges clearly and distinctly as part of the theory of the Oedipus complex, namely in the complete form of the complex as it is elaborated in *The ego and the id* (1923). The other bisexuality theory put forward by Freud is far more dispersed and was never presented in detail. It is this alternative theory that is the focus of the following reconstruction, and for clarity in the discussion it is referred to throughout as Freud's *bisexuality thesis*. To be clear though, Freud never uses this term, and certain aspects of the reconstructed theory rely on work not directly produced by Freud. For reasons that will be explained, the bisexuality of the complete Oedipus complex is referred to as Freud's *rivalry thesis*, in order to distinguish it from the bisexuality thesis.

Secondly, for the reconstruction of the bisexuality thesis, this chapter must be read in conjunction with the following chapter because the bisexuality thesis has important implications for the structural theory of the mental apparatus, as it is presented in *The ego and the id*. There is a constitutive link between the Oedipus complex and Freud's structural theory of the mental apparatus. The Oedipus complex and the structural theory are two sides of the same coin, and the bisexuality thesis emerges from a different way of looking at the structural theory. This acknowledges and reaffirms the centrality of the complete form of the Oedipus complex in Freud's work. In turn, the complete form removes the emphasis from the biological sex of the child and the parents. The only extent to which biological sex plays a role is the manner in which the Oedipus complex is the mechanism that leads to a fixed mental representation of biological sex in the social constructs of masculinity and femininity (i.e. gender). In this regard, the terminology discussion in the Introduction (pp. 22–3) must be kept in mind. The Oedipus myth and its specific staging in Sophocles's dramatic text are merely a metaphor and deserve no focus; no new

DOI: 10.4324/9781003498919-3

metaphors will be added either. There is also nothing to be gained in personifying the discussion, and no link is made to Freud's own (auto)biography.

This chapter starts by reprising Freud's explicit position on bisexuality in his texts that was already sketched at the start of the previous chapter (pp. 29–30). This review is followed by an overview of Freud's general theory of sexuality, with the specific focus on how this relates to bisexuality. It is obvious that the theory of the Oedipus complex is a fundamental component of Freud's theory of sexuality, so much so that it has come to represent the main model of psychosexual development for the psychoanalytic tradition. The theory of the Oedipus complex not only obscures Freud's bisexuality thesis in his writings; it is the contention of the following reconstruction that Freud's bisexuality thesis stands in a dialectical relationship to the theory of the Oedipus complex, both in the theoretical descriptions and in the manner in which the child itself emerges into adulthood. This dialectic is so significant that it can be seen to initiate a further form of bisexuality, which emerges from a dialectical synthesis of Freud's two theses. This will be discussed in later chapters.

The reconstruction of Freud's bisexuality thesis is built from a close reading of several texts by Freud, especially *Three essays on the theory of sexuality* (1905), *Group psychology and the analysis of the ego* (1921) and *The ego and the id* (1923). There is one sentence in particular in *The ego and the id* that is the springboard for reconstructing a thesis in Freud's work built around bisexuality rather than the Oedipus complex. While scholars broadly recognise the general importance of *The ego and the id* (e.g. most recently in Busch & Delgado, 2023), they have used this text solely to reinforce the centrality of the Oedipus complex to Freud's sexual theory. Some of these studies even quote the paragraph containing the crucial sentence in *The ego and the id* but without recognising its significance (David, 1975, p. 772; Lewes, 1988, p. 81; Butler, 1990, p. 80; Garber, 1995, p. 183; Angelides, 2001, p. 58; Heenen-Wolff, 2011, p. 1216; Flanders et al., 2016, pp. 936–7; Yumatov, 2019, p. 63; Kakar & Narayanan, 2023, p. 38), thereby missing what is perhaps the most important clue in Freud's discussion of bisexuality.

Freud's explicit position on bisexuality

In addition to *The ego and id* that is the focus of the discussion in the rest of this chapter, it is worth reviewing the central instances of Freud's explicit position on bisexuality in his texts. The prevailing consensus is that Freud maintained a vague position on bisexuality as a fundamental component of human sexuality. This is a typical example: "The most significant relevant consistency in Freud's thinking about homosexuality lies in the assumption, never proven or very thoroughly explained, that every individual is endowed with an innate bisexuality which is both biological and psychological in its foundations" (Flanders et al., 2016, p. 934). Deleuze and Guattari also unquestioningly join this consensus: "Freud had a concept at his disposal ... : the concept of bisexuality; and it was not by chance that he was never able or never wanted to give this concept the analytical position and extension it required" (1972, p. 60).

This consensus view has caused much confusion and ambiguity in the interpretation of bisexuality in Freud's work. However, Freud makes frequent manifest and unambiguous statements about bisexuality that leave little room for misunderstanding or misinterpretation. He thus explicitly views bisexuality as a foundational or bedrock formation in both biological sexes, and this formation then generally develops under the pressure of socialisation into a fixed state of sexual orientation and gender, although it is important to note that Freud does not use the words orientation or gender, which are more recent terms. A simple chronological survey of his statements about bisexuality (1905, p. 220; 1911, p. 46; 1912, p. 249; 1913, p. 182; 1920, pp. 157–8, 171; 1925a, p. 258; 1930, pp. 104–5, 106 fn; 1937, p. 244; 1938, p. 188) shows the consistency of this view over his lifetime. As an easy gloss, it is possible to summarise that there are two main ways in which Freud understands bisexuality: as *subject bisexuality* and *object bisexuality*. By subject bisexuality, Freud means the fluidity of a subject's action and character traits unfixed to biological sex:

> in human beings pure masculinity or femininity is not to be found either in a psychological or biological sense. Every individual on the contrary displays a mixture of the character-traits belonging to his own and the opposite sex; and he shows a combination of activity and passivity whether or not these last character-traits tally with his biological ones.
> (1905, p. 219, fn 1; see similar formulations 1913, p. 182; 1915a, p. 134; 1919, p. 202; 1920, p. 171; 1925a, pp. 250, 258; 1930, p. 106 fn)

This fluidity in turn rests on Freud's understanding of masculine and feminine traits as not absolute values but entirely relative to each other, at best markers of the dualism or antithesis of activity and passivity (see especially Freud, 1915a), as already discussed in the Introduction (pp. 18–19).

Freud's understanding of object bisexuality is similarly fluid: "In all of us, throughout life, the libido normally oscillates between male and female objects" (1920, p. 158; see similar formulations 1905, pp. 145, the 1915 fn; 1911, p. 46; 1912, p. 249; 1925a, p. 250; 1930, p. 106 fn; 1937, p. 244; 1938, p. 188). In no manner could such statements ever be interpreted as heteronormative, and these words of Freud still sound radical today. It is essential also to emphasise again that there is no teleology or inevitability in Freud's view of sexual development, and to remember always that he is only describing what he observes, never with the ambition or hubris to imagine he is in a position to prescribe a certain outcome of individual or species sexual development.

As radical and pioneering as they are, however, Freud's explicit statements about human bisexuality are extremely meagre when measured quantitatively in proportion to the total volumes of his immense written output in the *Standard edition*. For a topic that is clearly and persistently close to his heart, his manifest comments remain a catalogue of scattered statements about bisexuality apparently devoid of a comprehensive theoretical development, and it must be conceded that there is not enough sustained material in these manifest statements to develop a theory of bisexuality per se. It is valid to wonder about an explanation for this apparent gap in Freud's sexual theory. One plausible explanation is that the sheer magnitude of the consequences of a theory of universal human bisexuality could be enough to dissuade its pursuit, especially in the socio-political context of the first half of the 20th century. Freud had endured headwind enough from the hostile reception of his general sexual theory put forward in the *Three essays*, and for this reason perhaps he permanently postponed a direct and full exposition of bisexuality to avoid greater public and professional resistance.

Another explanation for Freud's apparent hesitation to be more outspoken on the topic of bisexuality, as well as for the absence of a book-length study on the theory of bisexuality by Freud, is suggested in details from Freud's letters to Wilhelm Fliess and by the context of the deterioration and eventual termination of their friendship. While I am principally opposed to biographical speculation, it does seem valuable briefly to mention these details that emerge from the correspondence, but with the caveat that Freud wished his letters to Fliess to be destroyed and had indeed himself destroyed the letters he received from Fliess, so that even the limited and posthumously published letters available today give only one side of the exchange.

In the first edition of the *Three essays*, Freud openly acknowledges Fliess as the source of his interest in bisexuality:

> Since I have become acquainted with the notion of bisexuality through Wilhelm Fliess I have regarded it as the decisive factor, and without taking bisexuality into account I think it would scarcely be possible to arrive at an understanding of the sexual manifestations that are actually to be observed in men and women.
> (1905, p. 220; 1905a, p. 71)

In Freud's letters to Fliess (1887–1902), there is frequent mention of bisexuality (letter (52) of 6 December 1896, p. 179; letter (81) of 4 January 1898, p. 242; letter (85) of 15 March 1898, pp. 247–8; letter (113) of 1 August 1899, p. 289; letter (141) of 30 January 1901, pp. 326–7), giving an indication of the direction of their discussion. This culminates in the letter (145) of 7 August 1901 (pp. 334–5), where Freud states he is planning to write a book on the topic of bisexuality, and he solicits Fliess's collaboration. This is the first and only mention by Freud of such a project, and it takes place directly prior to their falling out (letter (146) of 19 September 1901, pp. 337). Three years later, and long after the friendship between Freud and Fliess had come to an end, there are two further letters (only in Masson's edition: Freud, 1887–1904) with comments of interest that indicate Freud held back on addressing bisexuality in the *Three essays* (1905) out of deference to Fliess.

> At present I am finishing "Three Essays on the Theory of Sexuality", in which I avoid the topic of bisexuality as far as possible. At two places I cannot do so: in the explanation of sexual inversion there I go as far as the literature permits ...;

furthermore, when I mention the homosexual current in neurotics. There I plan to add a note that I had been prepared for the necessity of this finding by certain remarks of yours. Or you may want to propose a comparable formulation to me. The rest deals with infantile sexual life and the components of the sexual drives.

(Freud, 1887–1904, letter of 23 July 1904, pp. 464–5)

The last of the letters to Fliess (of 27 July 1904, pp. 466–8) confirms this sense of Freud postponing a direct and focused discussion of bisexuality in deference to Fliess, and Freud again solicits Fliess's concurrence with the scattered references to bisexuality in the *Three essays*:

I trust you will still be so kind as to help me out of my present predicament by reading the remarks on bisexuality in the proofs of my just completed "Essays on the Theory of Sexuality" and changing them to your satisfaction. It would be easier to postpone publication until you have surrendered your [book on bisexual] biology to the public. But I do not know when this will be. You will scarcely hurry for my sake. In the meantime I can do nothing, not even finish the *Jokes*, which in a crucial point is partially based on the theory of sexuality. I also do not gain anything by waiting for your publication, because then I could not possibly avoid the topic of bisexuality, as I do now; I would have to take a stand and eventually prepare new works. On the other hand, there is so little of bisexuality or of other things I have borrowed from you in what I say, that I can do justice to your share in a few remarks. I must only be sure that you agree with them and do not find grounds in them for reproaches later on.

(Freud, 1887–1904, pp. 467–8)

By avoiding a comprehensive theory of bisexuality, Freud is clearly at pains not to overstep a perceived intellectual boundary introduced by Fliess or cause further friction between the two men. There is an impression too of the lingering loss of an important friendship that seems to hang over Freud's theory of bisexuality like a pall.

Freud's sexual theory in overview

It is valuable to take a step back and briefly review Freud's general sexual theory, starting from the framework laid down in the *Three essays on the theory of sexuality* (1905) and then augmented by his later theory of the Oedipus mechanism. This is presented here as an ontogenesis of the individual's libidinal development.

To understand Freud's sexual theory fully, it is necessary to commence with the distinctions and bifurcations Freud introduces to the discussion of sexuality. The first formulation of a bifurcation offered by Freud is in the now-familiar and basic distinction he makes at the start of the *Three essays* between the sexual *aim* ("the act towards which the instinct tends") and the sexual *object* ("the person from whom sexual attraction proceeds") (1905, pp. 135–36; described in more detail

1915a, pp. 122–3). The sexual aim is thereafter presented as a mix of two components: reproductive (*der Geschlechtstrieb*) and non-reproductive (*der Sexualtrieb*) sexual *regimes*; this term, introduced by Kistner (2016, p. lxxxi), is adopted below.

The development of Freud's ideas about sexual aims in this two-regime distinction must be seen especially in the context of his novel observations about pre-pubertal ("infantile") sexuality. In the development of his ideas about sexual aims after the *Three essays*, Freud adds several reformulations. In essence these modifications are refinements of the initial two-regime dualism, based on the idea that non-reproductive *emotional ties* form part of the libidinal relationship between people. In some degree, these modifications are a response to Freud's introduction of the concept of the Oedipus complex, which was not part of the original formulation of sexual theory in the first edition of the *Three essays* (1905). In general, however, the two-regime distinction also accords with the principles of evolution.

While Freud doesn't reference the theory of evolution directly in this regard, a differentiated view of sexuality that also encompasses emotional ties instead of purely reproductive relations makes sense in an evolutionary understanding of sexual reproduction. Sexual reproduction of the species is technically possible on the basis solely of the sexual reproductive act. In many animal species, especially those with short gestation and maturation spans and/or high rates of reproductive success, a genital/gamete-focused reproductive regime is often the extent of sexual reproduction. In some species, however, survival rates are significantly enhanced by post-natal parental care, which in turn is a function of longer duration bonds between the parents and between parents and offspring. These bonds of caring and nurturing attachment are presumably what give rise to the non-reproductive sexual regime and, more broadly, the social group.

The description of the non-reproductive sexual aim is developed by Freud in a reworking of the initial object/aim dualism that results in a further distinction between directly sexual object ties (attachments, investments) called *object cathexis* (*die Objektbesetzung, die Besetzung*) and *identification* (*die Identifizierung*), the internalisation of aspects of the external object. This distinction is first encountered in *On narcissism* (Freud, 1914) as a distinction between object cathexis (necessary for sexual relations) and affectionate attachment. In *Group psychology and the analysis of the ego* (1921), this distinction evolves into the phrases: directly sexual aims and inhibited aims; and then soon after in *The ego and the id* (1923, p. 32) the mechanism is developed comprehensively so that the inhibited sexual aim is now expressly called identification. The identification mechanism is first presented in *Mourning and melancholia* (1917), but that paper is more concerned with the function of identification in the process of grief and depression and serves as a pre-study of sorts for the concept of identification, which Freud revives with far greater ambition in 1921 and 1923. In *The ego and the id* (1923, p. 32), Freud comprehensively describes object cathexis and the subsequent identification after the loss of the object as the crucial mechanism that produces the ego and the superego out of the id: once an object is lost to cathexis, a residue of the object is internalised and reproduced in the mental apparatus as an identification. The object may simply become lost to the subject, where loss is the withdrawal and absence of the object, or the object may be lost due to a prohibition or inhibition of the object. The object cathexis -> loss -> identification mechanism is also important for the reconstruction of the bisexuality thesis. The genealogy of the concept of identification in Freud's thinking is examined in detail in the next chapter (Chapter 3), to reveal the existence of a special type of *primary identification* at the heart of the bisexuality thesis. In turn, this primary identification is significant for a full understanding of Freud's structural theory of the mental apparatus.

Taking these two refined sets (subject and object; reproductive and non-reproductive sexual aims), it is thus possible to summarise the sexual act as follows. There are two parties to the sexual act, the sexual subject and object, and two classes of sexual aims, which are resolved finally as two classes of subject-object bond, with a direct or indirect sexual aspect and some measure of duration in the attachment. In a range of combinations, the subject has various sexual convolutions open to it under the cohabitation of the two regimes: a sexual object of either biological sex and a sexual aim that is focused on reproduction and/or non-reproduction. It is important to consider here that the infantile period is not *objectless*, as is so often maintained in the literature. For Freud, autoerotism clearly demonstrates that the infant does have an object in its own body. These aims generate a bond (temporary or more lasting) between sexual subject and object that is dominated by genital sexual satisfaction or more diffuse identification. Very early on, Freud expresses this multiplicity of the sexual situation in a now famous formulation: "I am accustoming myself to regarding every sexual act as an event between four individuals" (letter (113) to Fliess dated 1 August 1899, p. 289; quoted in the editor's footnote in Freud 1923, p. 33 fn). It is only twenty-four years later in *The ego and the id* that Freud fully explains the four parties, and this serves as the frame for reconstructing the bisexuality thesis in this chapter.

Some general comments have already been made regarding terminology in the Introduction (pp. 22–4). The terms bisexual, heterosexual and homosexual are used here not in the sense of contemporary debates about *self-identity* but as the conventional descriptive terms historically and currently in use for the libidinal relationship of a sexual subject and a sexual object on the basis of biological sex. In fact, it will be seen that the discussion – taking its lead from Freud himself – erases the distinction of bisexual, heterosexual and homosexual as they are used today to designate separate and discrete identities. This is not least the consequence of Freud employing activity and passivity (outlined in the Introduction, p. 18–19). The social construction of gender is not considered here in any detail, except to the extent that a fixed gender is one of the outcomes of the Oedipus complex. The terms inhibition, prohibition and injunction are used in the simple sense of an exogenous force or intervention (the mechanisms of shame and rivalry) to prevent a sexual aim, while the term repression refers to the endogenous or internalised effect of this inhibition, which Freud describes as "turning something away, and keeping it at a distance, from the conscious" (1915b, p. 147). This is a simplification of the external-internal dynamic (e.g. Freud, 1915a, pp. 119, 134) for purposes of the main focus of the discussion.

If these dualistic components and combinations are now considered together, they illustrate both the history of any individual's sexuality as well as the underlying inherent state of human bisexuality. A picture emerges of the multifarious coexistence of sexual object choices and subject positions, which operate in a polyvalent field of socially inscribed inhibitions and repressions. The following schema (Figure 2.1) offers a summary overview and interpretation of Freud's stages in the emergence and development of the sexual instinct: infantile, latency, genital and the Oedipus complex (whether at ages 3–5 or at puberty is immaterial for this simplified outline) and the various outcomes in adult sexuality. Picture a graphic illustration of this development from the perspective of the sexual subject with a focus on the sexual aim: let the x axis represent the reproductive regime (R) and the y axis the non-reproductive regime (N). Each axis has a potential binary value of 1 or 0, with 1 being the full activation of the regime and 0 being its non-activation. To start with, a straightforward binary situation is used for ease of illustration; in effect a more complex fractional situation of partial activation and non-activation/inhibition applies in the form of a continuum, but this is not vital to the initial analysis. In keeping with an agnostic view of biological sex (in line with subject bisexuality), the graph is equally valid irrespective of the biological sex of the subject. This graph produces four quadrants:

The sexual instinct develops in an anti-clockwise movement from quadrant A in the infantile period to B during latency and then into C in puberty and/or D in maturity. In A and B (i.e. before puberty) there can be no actual reproduction, only the autoerotism, object relations and identifications of the infantile period (for both, R=0). In B there is no sexual activity under either regime (N0R0) – this corresponds to the latency period of inhibition and repression, where the libidinal instinct is repeatedly restrained in its aim and redirected from its object. In C, the reproductive regime comes to the fore in puberty as the libidinal instinct is partially released from inhibition, but reproduction clearly does not require the full release of the concomitant non-reproductive regime (N0R1), which only features in D when both regimes coexist fully (N1R1).

This corresponds broadly to an explanation for the genesis of both the predominance of heterosexuality and a fixing of gender. Two forces are brought to bear

	1		
Quadrant A N1R0		Quadrant D N1R1	
0		x = Reproductive axis	1
Quadrant B N0R0		Quadrant C N0R1	
	0	y = Non-reproductive axis	

Figure 2.1 Development of the sexual instinct

on the child: shame and rivalry. These forces inhibit and deflect the child's libido. Freud often uses the image of a river to illustrate this: the libidinal current is obstructed, even dammed, and then channelled in a new, morally structured direction; for example:

> It is during this period of total or only partial latency that are built up the mental forces which are later to impede the course of the sexual instinct and, like dams, restrict its flow – disgust, feelings of shame and the claims of aesthetic and moral ideals.
>
> (1905, p. 177; the river and dam image is repeated frequently, here only references for 1905: p. 162, 170, 178, 191, 232, 237)

Shame (quadrant A + B) is the earlier of the two inhibitory forces and predates the rivalry that is introduced in the Oedipus complex (quadrant C). For Freud, shame is a compound of mental force (shame-disgust-morality, but also fear, pain and anxiety – all indicated for simplicity in this discussion by the term shame) that opposes the sexual instinct (1905, pp. 157, 159, 161–2, 164, 177–8, 191–2, 219, 231; 1908, p. 171; 1910, p. 45; 1925b, p. 37; 1926, pp. 210–1). The role of shame is the devaluation and inhibition of the infantile narcissism and pleasure. Shame is imposed on the genitals and other zones of shame, and these zones never lose their shamefulness. They are enshrouded by the productive injunction and the allure of unobtainable satisfaction. This is only further compounded by the rigidity of the Oedipus complex constructed on the basis of parental rivalry. If anything, the Oedipus complex must undo some of this earlier shame to differentiate and rehabilitate the genitals (especially the aroused and erect penis, 1905, p. 222) for reproductive intercourse. The real mystery of sex is that the libido survives shame at all: "The sexual instinct goes to astonishing lengths in successfully overriding the resistances of shame, disgust, horror or pain" (1905, p. 161).

While shame is the mechanism of the earliest infantile period and never fully recedes in force, the mechanism of rivalry is the novel and defining feature of the Oedipus complex and the key element to understanding the complex. From the perspective of the child, the rivalry in the Oedipus complex is the rivalry of seeking one's own subjectivity through the external object path. It is immaterial that a child should desire the parent of the same or the opposite sex; the essential outcome of rivalry is that the child of either sex is forced to concede the central subject position to the parent, and hence negotiate its own subjectivity from the starting position of being the object of the parent. For the child, the core outcome is solidification as an object that confirms and affirms the narcissism and subjectivity of the parents. In essence, this means an affirmation of the broad social hierarchies established by the mechanism of rivalry. For sexual theory, the most obvious and pernicious of these is the simple social hierarchy built on the foundation of biological sex. There is a solidification of activity and passivity that overrides the previous fluid coexistence of both in each child. Taking the form of gender and flowing from the Oedipus complex, activity becomes a privilege traditionally apportioned to biological males – of course always conditional on their obedience and cooperation, pursuant to the threat of castration, i.e. reduction to biological female and the concomitant loss of active privilege. The masculinity and femininity (i.e. gender) subsequent to the Oedipus complex are both substitutes for the original fluid and universal infantile activity which children of both sexes enjoy. Masculinity and femininity are the products of the rivalry of the Oedipus complex and become fixed at this time in their alignment with biological sex. Gender is thus socially and psychologically manufactured by a solidification of the polarity of subject-object and active-passive. The psychosocial fixity of gender combines with the rehabilitation of the reproductive regime of male-female sexual intercourse by its partial release from the blanket shame over all sexuality to provide the general social valorisation of heterosexuality that still dominates society today. This limited form of rehabilitated sexual activity enjoys social approval while all other sexual impulses remain subject to shame. Rivalry cements the social approval of heterosexuality by the construction and fixity of gender. The valorisation of reproductive sexual relations within the stricture of a fixed system of gender explains "the exclusive sexual interest felt by men for women". In the last hundred years, quadrant D has become a contested terrain in some jurisdictions where the reproductive and non-reproductive regimes (N1R1) coexist. This is the terrain of adult bisexuality within the Oedipus mechanism.

Of interest now is how this development relates more broadly to infantile bisexuality and the Oedipus mechanism. Beyond the biological aspect of the binary immaturity or maturity of the genitals, it is hard to specify with certainty the chronological sequence of the two regimes of the sexual instinct, and the proposition is assumed that they coexist initially in a less differentiated form with one developing out of the other in the same way that the libidinal instinct itself develops out of the self-preservation instinct, and the ego out of the id. It is indisputable that the non-reproductive regime is present and has predominance at the start, if for no other reason than the immaturity of the genitals. The way this graphic perspective encompasses the sexual object illustrates the matter of bisexuality. The sexual object under the reproductive regime is indisputably the complementary biological sex. However, the reproductive regime is a late stage of the development of the sexual instinct, predated by the infantile stage and the non-reproductive regime, and it is here in quadrant A that the sexual subject and its object relations are initially and fundamentally fashioned. There can be no question of the object being the complementary biological sex at this early stage, because the infant has no conception yet of differentiated biological sex. This encapsulates the important second component of Freud's understanding of bisexuality as the sexual subject's intermingling of active and passive characteristics before the solidification of these characteristics into socially determined masculine and feminine roles aligned to the genital zone. This is Freud's view in 1905 and also later, but this view becomes more complicated and contradictory after he introduces and develops the idea of the Oedipus complex. His various attempts to explain the infant's initial bisexual orientation – as subject and towards the sexual object for the genesis of the later sexual regimes – all run aground on the Oedipus complex, and he has to revert to the circularity of biological and social roles (child, mother, father) to explain the sexual object of the infant. The same problem haunts his theory of the genesis of homosexuality, which undergoes several (ultimately unsatisfactory) permutations. The negation of the Oedipus complex brings Freud's thesis of bisexuality into the centre of the discussion.

The negation of the Oedipus complex

It says much of the theoretical resourcefulness of Freud's model of the Oedipus complex that it can accommodate a very diverse range of outcomes which go beyond straightforward exclusive heterosexuality and fixed gender – although this diversity is exactly what has been repressed and pathologised by psychoanalytic discourse until quite recently. The broad rejection of Freud's theory in Gender and Queer Studies for the extraneous and erroneous reason of his supposed heteronormativity has deprived this now dominant scholarly field of the heuristic value of Freud's Oedipus complex (1923, p. 33) as a model of sexual multiplicity untrammelled by social identities and gender.

The following discussion eschews new metaphors or literalism about the Greek myth and concentrates instead on Freud's own sketch of the Oedipus complex in *The ego and the id* (1923). As the title suggests, the focus of this important text is the tripartite structure of the mental apparatus, but Freud is clear that this structure is established on the foundation of the libidinal theory. Part three of *The ego and the id* on the superego is of particular significance for his elaboration of the Oedipus mechanism and his simultaneous recognition of its negation. However, his emergent and dense outline has caused much confusion, and the radical view he puts forward is somewhat obscured, partly by his own tentative expression and partly because the formulation in 1923 makes no sense without an inter-textual understanding of another text, *Group psychology and the analysis of the ego* (1921), which in turn is also famously dense. Even the title of the 1921 work shows some of the inter- and extra-textual conflict underlying the tentative formulations of this most radical recognition. The 1921 paper also stands out for being Freud's only major foray into the field of group psychology, and this leads to considerations of other influences Freud was unwilling or unable to recognise.

The challenge in understanding the Oedipus complex is that it straddles and unites the bifurcated reproductive and non-reproductive regimes to bring about "a certain degree of synthesis" (Freud, 1921, p. 112; discussed at length pp. 134–43), which essentially means the Oedipus complex defeats bisexuality. In dialectic terms, the Oedipus complex *negates* bisexuality. This is to say that there are two forces at work against each other in a dialectic movement; Freud points to this himself: "The whole subject [of the Oedipus complex] is so complicated .... The intricacy of the problem is due to two factors: the triangular character of the Oedipus situation and the constitutional bisexuality of each individual" (1923, p. 31).

The two dialectic elements are thus the triangular situation and constitutional bisexuality. They are best elucidated by a close reading of Freud's texts. A detailed reading opens up new ways of looking at the two elements and shows how they emerge as two competing theses: the thesis of rivalry and the thesis of bisexuality. It is assumed that readers are familiar with the 1921 and 1923 texts, but some crucial passages are quoted in the flow of the analysis. Two later texts are relevant to the Oedipus complex (1924, 1925a). Coming after *The ego and the id*, they attempt to merge or at least to harmonise the two theses, bisexuality with rivalry. By the time this material is presented again in Lecture 31 of the *New introductory lectures* (1933, pp. 57–80), the absence of any mention of rivalry in Freud's description is striking.

Freud starts with the organisation and components of the triangular situation in the simple form of the Oedipus complex. The three parts of the triangle (1923, pp. 31–2) are the child with an object cathexis to the mother and identification with the father. In the case of a male child:

> These two relationships proceed side by side, until the boy's sexual wishes in regard to his mother become more intense and his father is perceived as an obstacle to them; from this the Oedipus complex originates. His identification with his father then takes on a hostile colouring and changes into a wish to get rid of his father in order to take his place with his mother.
>
> (p. 32)

This is the rivalry at the heart of the Oedipus complex. It is not simply the difference in the type of bond with each parent but the factor of one relationship being perceived as an obstacle to the other, resulting in the element of hostility and the wish to eliminate the obstacle. The outcome is the fixing (*die Festigung, festlegen*) of the masculine character of the boy and *mutatis mutandis* the fixing of her feminine character for the girl. In contemporary language, this is the social construction of gender by giving it a fixed value (the parents) and tying this in equivalence to biological sex.

In the very next paragraph (p. 32) the structural theory around identification strikes the reef of the Oedipus complex: there is recognition that the sequence of identification described in this Oedipus process does not proceed according to the initial outline of identification (p. 29) in the formation of the ego, i.e. where identification is the residue in the ego of a previous and now lost object cathexis. For this definition of identification to remain valid would mean the boy first had to develop an object cathexis to his father, which is subsequently sublimated into identification with the father. For a moment, this paradoxical identification is set aside, and the text returns to the usual structural identification, which can and does also take place in the Oedipus complex, e.g. a girl may go on to form an identification with her father, instead of with her mother. This has significant implications for the social fixing of masculinity (boys) or femininity (girls) in the Oedipus complex, and an apparently illogical and contradictory situation arises of identification with both parents. This can only be resolved by reverting to subject bisexuality: "It would appear, therefore, that in both sexes the relative strength of the masculine and feminine sexual dispositions is what determines whether the outcome of the Oedipus situation shall be an identification with the father or with the mother" (p. 33). In other words, here is the genesis of subject bisexuality. "This is one of the ways in which bisexuality takes a hand in the subsequent vicissitudes of the Oedipus complex. The other way is even more important" (p. 33). The other way – object bisexuality – is then laid out in "the more complete Oedipus complex, which is twofold, positive and negative, and *is due to the bisexuality originally present in children*" (p. 33, emphasis added). Freud indicates that the complete Oedipus complex is actually the general case: "In my opinion it is advisable in general ... to assume the existence of the complete Oedipus complex" (p. 33). He nails his colours to the mast in favour of a schema that explains not only subject bisexuality but also bisexuality towards the object.

In a brilliant reworking of the simple Oedipus complex into the more complete form, Freud then lays out this schema, producing

> a series with the normal positive Oedipus complex at one end and the inverted negative one at the other, while its intermediate members exhibit the complete form [German = *die Mittelglieder die vollständige Form*] with one or other of its two components preponderating.
>
> (p. 34)

The schema of this series becomes instantly recognisable as a continuum.

Before moving on to examine the continuum in more detail, it is useful to address head on the apparently normative connotation of the adjectives used here: normal, inverted; positive, negative. In the context not only of Freud's work generally but also the inclusive focus of this specific passage, there is no evidence that Freud is using these terms in a prescriptive or teleological sense. It seems self-evident that the two pairs are deployed here in the sense of a relativisation, to indicate the two end points on the axis of the continuum being proposed. At one end is the outcome that produces exclusive heterosexuality and at the other exclusive homosexuality. Given Freud's opinion that most people fall somewhere in the spectrum between these poles, the terminology clearly has little normative intention or value. Further support for this interpretation is given by the rest of the description of the complete form and the link Freud makes to the formation of the superego from the identification with the parents.

> At the dissolution of the Oedipus complex the four trends of which it consists will group themselves in such a way as to produce a father-identification and a mother-identification. The father-identification will preserve the object-relation to the mother which belonged to the positive complex and will at the same time replace the object-relation to the father which belonged to the inverted complex: and the same will be true, *mutatis mutandis*, of the mother-identification. The relative intensity of the identifications in any individual will reflect the preponderance in him of one or other of the two sexual dispositions.

> *The broad general outcome of the sexual phase dominated by the Oedipus complex may, therefore, be taken to be the forming of a precipitate in the ego, consisting of these two identifications in some way united with each other. This modification of the ego retains its special position; it confronts the other contents of the ego as an ego ideal or super-ego.*

(p. 34, emphasis in original)

Three aspects stand out in this passage. First, the formula applies to any individual, i.e. it is not specific to the boy or girl child. Second, there are four trends, namely bisexuality of the subject (identifications with parents) and object (object relations with parents); the relative intensity of these trends in each person determines the individual outcome. This confirms the non-normative nature of the terminology used here. Third, and this is the point made in the second paragraph with emphasis, the most common outcome is the bisexual one: a united identification of the four trends. This precipitate or united *parental identification* leads to the formation of the superego.

The radical idea of the bisexual continuum in the complete Oedipus complex that Freud presents in *The ego and the id* is not new in his work, however. A continuum structure is already present in Freud's thinking in the *Three essays*, where he variously speaks about a *series*: the "connected series" (p. 138) to show that there is a homosexual range rather than a single phenomenon of homosexuality; and an "aetiological" or "complemental series" of constitutional and accidental factors giving rise to individual sexual development (pp. 239–40). Perhaps most significantly, in the footnote added in 1915 (1905, pp. 145–6), Freud is clearly suggesting a continuum of both subject bisexuality ("the occurrence in the subject of a mixture of sexual characters") and object bisexuality ("freedom to range equally over male and female objects"). This is an exact pre-study for the continuum of the Oedipus complex in its full form (1923).

Perceptive readers will instantly recognise the schema of Freud's 1905 and 1923 continuums in a different and later but equally radical continuum, the one proposed by Kinsey et al. (1948, 1953) based on their now famous survey results: a continuum of sexual behaviour where "the world is not to be divided into sheep and goats. Not all things are black nor all things white" (Kinsey et al., 1948, p. 639). Astonishingly, neither of the Kinsey reports (Kinsey et al. 1948, 1953) makes the link or relates the Kinsey continuum to Freud's (1923 and 1905) formulation. Lewes (1988) discusses the Kinsey reports extensively and dedicates a whole chapter to a comprehensive review of the reception of the reports, showing clearly that Kinsey "did not receive an adequate response from the psychoanalytic community" (p. 138), which at the time and subsequently was generally distinguished by widespread indifference to non-analytic ideas and special hostility to progressive views of sexuality. Even Lewes, however, with his very comprehensive analysis of the complete form of the Oedipus complex (1988, pp. 76–89) fails to connect his interpretation to Freud's suggestion of a continuum of sexual behaviour in 1923 or to Kinsey's survey findings in 1948. Hocquenghem (1972) expands on the sexual continuum perspective, which he derives from Kinsey (not Freud), and presents the following cogent summary of the implications of a continuum for object bisexuality:

> There is no subdivision of desire into homosexuality and heterosexuality. Properly speaking, desire is no more homosexual than heterosexual. Desire emerges in a multiple form, whose components are only divisible *a posteriori*, according to how we manipulate it. Just like heterosexual desire, homosexual desire is an arbitrarily frozen frame in an unbroken and polyvocal flux.
>
> (pp. 49–50)

Despite his otherwise extensive engagement with Freud's work, Hocquenghem's impressive interpretation fails to link his own conclusion with Freud's continuum, but the reason is easy to explain: Hocquenghem (1972) does not once consider Freud's *The ego and the id*.

By my reading of *The ego and the id*, the Oedipus complex in its full form reflects a fluid subject and object bisexuality at the heart of Freud's thinking. The world of sexual behaviour is a spectacular "unbroken and polyvocal flux" in which sexuality in its uninhibited, unsublimated form is fully bisexual and ultimately the outcome of personal dispositions and individual relations of desire. Unfortunately, this happy perspective is not the end of the story. The bisexuality of the more complete Oedipus complex is scuttled by one crucial aspect in Freud's (1923) account of the complex that has been touched on only briefly so far: *rivalry*. The triangular relations of the Oedipus complex, even in the more complete form, are not only structured around the polyvocal flux of the libido; they contain the important and inescapable component of rivalry. The next paragraph on p. 34 goes on to highlight the special character of the superego: it is built on a double character of precept (be like the parent) and prohibition (at the same time there are parental prerogatives not open to the child). This is the character of rivalry:

> The super-ego is, however, not simply a residue of the earliest object-choices of the id; it also represents an energetic reaction-formation against those choices. Its relation to the ego is not exhausted by the precept: 'You *ought to be* like this (like your father).' It also comprises the prohibition: 'You *may not be* like this (like your father) – that is, you may not do all that he does; some things are his prerogative.' This double aspect of the ego ideal derives from the fact that the ego ideal had the task of repressing the Oedipus complex; indeed, it is to that revolutionary event that it owes its existence.
>
> (p. 34)

This aspect of rivalry is cogently summarised by Laplanche and Pontalis (1967, p. 286) in their structural overview of the Oedipus complex, where the triangular elements, stripped of biological sex, are "constituted by the child, the child's natural object and the bearer of the Law". Ignore the word "natural", which is an unfortunate regression to the simple form of the Oedipus complex by Laplanche and Pontalis and not immediately relevant here; the question of what or who the "natural object" is remains an open one, as Freud himself indicates in the more complete schema, and is determined individually. It is the prohibition or injunction ("the Law") that brings about rivalry, not the biological sex of the object per se. The injunction is typically portrayed in two ways: around an awareness of biological sex and the subsequent threat or fear of castration, as a specific neutralisation and stasis caused by rivalry; or as a more general incest taboo, which also creates a universal stasis of relations.

The exact nature of the injunction will become apparent in the discussion in Chapter 3, but injunction and the fixity introduced by injunction are, without a doubt, critical to understanding the Oedipus complex. Injunction is the fulcrum of Freud's rivalry thesis; but then, without warning, in the last sentence of the paragraph outlining the complete Oedipus complex in *The ego and the id*, Freud suddenly throws this essential component of rivalry into question:

> It may even be that the ambivalence displayed in the relations to the parents should be attributed entirely to bisexuality and that it is not, as I have represented above [in describing the Oedipus complex], developed out of identification in consequence of rivalry.

> (1923, p. 33)

It is this key sentence that reveals Freud's alternative thesis constructed on bisexuality, without rivalry.

The most striking aspect of the formulation in this sentence is the use of the subjunctive mood: "*It may even be*" ... "*should be*"; but this aspect is easily overlooked because the subjunctive is hardly noticeable in English, where it plays a less recognisable and less significant role in style and usage. English no longer has specific verb inflections that make the subjunctive stand out, and the subjunctive in English is more situational and contextual. Vestiges of the subjunctive in English are found in apparently commonplace statements like: it may rain tomorrow. This banality is underlined by the variability and interchangeability of such statements: it could, it might, it may rain tomorrow. Languages like German and French, however, typically give far stronger weight to the subjunctive, which is used to signal the potential for novel speculation without firm commitment. The subjunctive in German and French is further strengthened and its usage sustained over time by being instantly and unmistakably recognisable in the specificity of the verb conjugation. In addition, the subjunctive in German is used to express the exaggerated degree of politeness and civility common in Germanic middle-class society. In a conservative culture with strict moral values and a high intolerance of errors, such as the Germanic cultures of central Europe, the utility of a speculative mood like the subjunctive is even clearer. In combination with the tentativeness and theoretical speculation allowed by the subjunctive, this polite vagueness can cushion or couch a potentially transgressive or even radical idea.

Reading with this in mind, the note of novel speculation introduced by the opening phrase "*It may even be ...*" ("Es könnte auch sein ...") is further reinforced by the second subjunctive verb *"should be"* ("wäre"). The content of the statement is clearly signalling a daring, speculative idea that breaks sharply with the model of the Oedipus complex outlined up to this point in the chapter: *"It may even be that the ambivalence displayed in the relations to the parents should be attributed entirely to bisexuality and that it is not, as I have represented above, developed out of identification in consequence of rivalry"*. The original German sentence in full reads: "Es *könnte* auch sein, daß die im Elternverhältnis konstatierte Ambivalenz durchaus auf die Bisexualität zu beziehen *wäre* und nicht, wie ich es vorhin dargestellt, durch die Rivalitätseinstellungaus der identifizierung entwickelt *würde*" (p. 301, emphasis added to show subjunctive verbs). There is a third instance of the subjunctive ("würde"), which is left out entirely in the English, and this lends further support to the suggestion of an alternative theory. A better translation would read: It may even be that the ambivalence displayed in the relations to the parents should be attributed entirely to bisexuality and that it *would* not *develop* out of identification in consequence of rivalry, as I have represented above.

As mentioned previously, several studies of the Oedipus complex have quoted the paragraph containing this crucial sentence but without recognising its significance, thereby missing this important clue in Freud's discussion of bisexuality. Butler (1990, p. 80) and Flanders et al., (2016, pp. 936–7) fundamentally misunderstand rivalry and ambivalence to be synonyms. Angelides (2001) reflects his own uncertainty in the bland comment that "Freud here attempts to cover all bases and to defer the question of bisexuality's meaning" (p. 58), while Garber (1995) simply quotes the passage in a jumble of references to Freud with no further comment or analysis (p. 183). David (1975) sees in this passage the basis for a distinction between psychic bisexuality and something he calls "constitutional" bisexuality (p. 772), presumably a hangover from the confusion around hermaphrodism introduced via Fliess. While Heenen-Wolff (2011) recognises the importance of the complete form of the Oedipus complex for bisexuality, she goes no further than linking this passage to the complete form (p. 1216; same formulation in Heenen-Wolff, 2016, pp. 142–3), similar to the approach of Lewes (1988, p. 81). For a brief moment, Kakar and Narayanan (2023, p. 38) appear alert to Freud's curious formulation in this sentence, but then they are blinded by their culturalist focus and also assume Freud is simply making reference to the more complete Oedipus complex. Yumatov (2019) conflates the period of the Oedipus complex with an earlier period which he terms "early Oedipal" (p. 62). This pre-empts any possibility of an identification that is entirely prior to the Oedipus complex (i.e. preoedipal) and thus reduces all identifications to the form defined by the rivalry of the Oedipus complex.

Laplanche and Pontalis (1967) are the only authors to recognise – albeit indirectly – the potential in this paragraph for an opposing thesis:

> The description of the complex in its complete form allows Freud to elucidate ambivalence towards the father (in the case of the little boy) in terms of the play of heterosexual and homosexual components, instead of making it simply the result of a situation of rivalry.
>
> (p. 284)

In this brief suggestion, Laplanche and Pontalis are correct in noticing the word *ambivalence* is not a synonym for hostility and rivalry, but they do not make the obvious and logical connection to a potential and entirely different thesis based solely on bisexuality and the absence of rivalry. After this sentence, they do not return to the possibility that Freud was proposing an alternative to rivalry, and the remainder of their discussion of the Oedipus complex assumes that both rivalry and the Oedipus complex are universal. They then move on to a technical discussion of the Oedipus complex in relation to biological sex, which implicitly returns to the simple form of the complex. Biological sex is clearly not the issue in Freud's complete form, and their backwards shift in focus to the simple form leads Laplanche and Pontalis to overlook the possibility of an alternative thesis. To support their interpretation that rivalry is universal, Laplanche and Pontalis discuss the idea of a *preoedipal* phase, which they suggest was first introduced in the paper by Brunswick (1940), but in fact Freud already uses the concept in his 1931 paper on female sexuality. However, proposing the idea of a preoedipal phase does not address or resolve the presence of two theses in Freud's conceptualisation; in fact, the way a preoedipal phase is addressed by subsequent authors like Melanie Klein and Jacques Lacan precludes the possibility of an alternative because they simply transpose the rivalry of the Oedipus complex to an earlier age.

The epistemological and heuristic need for a preoedipal phase is self-evident, not only in the psychoanalytic theory after Freud that reinforces the rivalry thesis but also for Freud's own formulation of the underlying categories of object cathexis and identification. The early life of a child is a critical time in its development, where all the object cathexes and identifications that play a role later on must surely be laid down structurally if they are to be laid down at all. Psychoanalytic theory after Freud simply digs the hole deeper by insisting on the presence of the Oedipal triangle in what is then inaccurately termed a preoedipal phase. Logically, it cannot thus be preoedipal but is simply an early manifestation of the rivalry triangle. This strategy introduces more problems than it solves, with much emphasis on the biological sex of the child and the parents, and, of course, that great Lacanian endowment to the theory, the phallus (symbolic or otherwise).

It is clear, and Freud himself emphasises this in *The ego and the id*, that for the child there is a substantial and significant early period (here Freud calls it the *prehistory* of the child, p. 31) in which a distinction between biological sex is not possible: "before a child has arrived at definite knowledge of the difference between the sexes, the lack of a penis, it does not distinguish in value between its father and its mother" (1923, p. 31 fn 1). The use of terms such as father/mother based on their biological sex is an artificial and *a posteriori* rhetorical device to underpin the rivalry thesis. Freud is responsible for much of the confusion surrounding the Oedipus complex by regularly ignoring his own advice that "it would be safer to say 'the parents'" (p. 31 fn 1) rather than mother or father. Of course, it is difficult to know exactly when such a differentiated awareness of biological sex arises for the child. In general though, much is gained for understanding the bisexuality thesis if Freud's texts are read with this suggestion constantly in mind: There is an early preoedipal period, and one of the characteristics of this period is the absence of an awareness of the difference between the sexes, i.e. the lack of a penis. The child does not distinguish in value between its father and its mother (i.e. male and female caregivers) and also the child does not distinguish itself as male or female. This specific characteristic of the preoedipal period is a vital part of the reading matrix in the chapters to come.

There can be no doubt that a period before the distinction of biological sex by the child is possible, and this is also the period in which the earliest object cathexes and identifications are laid down. This precludes biological sex as the basis for rivalry in the form of castration/envy in the way it is traditionally defined for the Oedipus complex. If the element of injunction takes the form of the father, as it does in the commonly cited simple Oedipus model, this would only be possible "after a child has arrived at definite knowledge of the difference between the sexes". In other words, rivalry and castration can only be linked to the Oedipus complex at a later age. The other argument for the rivalry thesis at this early age is via the introduction of conflict by way of a general, symbolic injunction ("the Law") bereft of biological sex. This primal law can only take the form of a universal incest taboo. However, the taboo cannot be reserved for heterosexual incest, because this runs into the same problem of timing. The rivalry thesis thus stands or falls on the universality of the incest taboo, yet a universal incest taboo turns straight into an argument *for* the bisexuality thesis: it is not necessary to prohibit something that does not exist. This is the crux of my argument, and it leads into the next chapters. The issue of rivalry, prohibition and taboo will be examined in detail in Chapter 4, but, first, the next step in reconstructing the bisexuality thesis is taken in Chapter 3.

Reference list

Please note: References follow the system of historical layering, with a distinction between source texts and access texts. If the source date is different to the access date, page references are always for the access text, but the reference year is that of the source text. For more in this regard, please see the comment on historical layering in the Introduction, p. 5.

Angelides, S. (2001). *A history of bisexuality*. Chicago: University of Chicago Press.
Brunswick, R.M. (1940). The preoedipal phase of the libido development. *The Psychoanalytic Quarterly*, 9(2), 293–319.
Busch, F. and Delgado, N. (2023). *The ego and the id 100 years later*. London: Routledge.
Butler, J. (1990). *Gender trouble: Feminism and the subversion of identity*. New York: Routledge, 2006.
David, C. (1975). La bisexualité psychique, rapport du xxxve Congrès des psychanalystes de langues romanes. *Revue française de psychanalyse*, 39(5–6), 695–856.
Deleuze, G. and Guattari, F. (1972). *Capitalisme et schizophrénie: L'anti-Œdipe* Paris: Éditions de Minuit. Trans. by R. Hurley, M. Seem and H. Lane as *Anti-Oedipus: Capitalism and schizophrenia*. Minneapolis: University of Minnesota Press, 1983.

Flanders, S., Ladame, F., Carlsberg, A., Heymanns, P., Naziri, D. and Panitz, D. (2016). On the subject of homosexuality: What Freud said. *The International Journal of Psychoanalysis*, 97(3), 933–50.

Freud, S. (1887–1902). Letters to Wilhelm Fliess. In M. Bonaparte, A. Freud and E. Kris, eds.; E. Mosbacher and J. Strachey, trans., *The origins of psycho-analysis: Letters to Wilhelm Fliess, drafts and notes: 1887–1902*. New York: Basic Books, 1954.

Freud, S. (1887–1904). Letters to Wilhelm Fliess. In J.M. Masson, ed. and trans., *The complete letters of Sigmund Freud to Wilhelm Fliess, 1887–1904*. Cambridge: Harvard University Press, 1985.

Freud, S. (1905). Three essays on the theory of sexuality. In J. Strachey, ed. and trans., *The standard edition of the complete psychological works of Sigmund Freud, 24 vols*. London: Hogarth Press, 1953–1974. 7:125–245.

Freud, S. (1905a). *Three essays on the theory of sexuality*. Trans. U. Kistner. London: Verso, 2016.

Freud, S. (1908). Character and anal erotism. *Standard ed.*, 9:167–75.

Freud, S. (1910). Five lectures on psycho-analysis. *Standard ed.*, 11:1–55.

Freud, S. (1911). Psycho-analytic notes on an autobiographical account of a case of paranoia (dementia paranoides). *Standard ed.*, 12:1–82.

Freud, S. (1912). Contributions to a discussion on masturbation. *Standard ed.*, 12:239–54.

Freud, S. (1913). The claims of psycho-analysis to scientific interest. *Standard ed.*, 13: 163–90.

Freud, S. (1914). On narcissism. *Standard ed.*, 14:67–104.

Freud, S. (1915a). Instincts and their vicissitudes. *Standard ed.*, 14:109–40.

Freud, S. (1915b). Repression. *Standard ed.*, 14:141–58.

Freud, S. (1917). Mourning and melancholia. *Standard ed.*, 14:237–58.

Freud, S. (1919). 'A child is being beaten': a contribution to the study of the origin of sexual perversions. *Standard ed.*, 17:175–204.

Freud, S. (1920). The psychogenesis of a case of homosexuality in a woman. *Standard ed.*, 18:147–72.

Freud, S. (1921). Group psychology and the analysis of the ego. *Standard ed.*, 18:65–143.

Freud, S. (1923). The ego and the id. *Standard ed.*, 19:1–66. References to the German are to volume 3 of the *Studienausgabe: Psychologie des Unbewußten*. Frankfurt am Main: Fischer Verlag, 1975.

Freud, S. (1924). The dissolution of the Oedipus complex. *Standard ed.*, 19:173–79.

Freud, S. (1925a). Some psychical consequences of the anatomical distinction between the sexes. *Standard ed.*, 19:241–58.

Freud, S. (1925b). An autobiographical study. *Standard ed.*, 20:1–74.

Freud, S. (1926). The question of lay analysis. *Standard ed.*, 20:177–258.

Freud, S. (1930). Civilization and its discontents. *Standard ed.*, 21:57–145.

Freud, S. (1931). Female sexuality. *Standard ed.*, 21:223–43.

Freud, S. (1933). New introductory lectures on psycho-analysis. *Standard ed.*, 22:1–182.

Freud, S. (1937). Analysis terminable and interminable. *Standard ed.*, 23:209–53.

Freud, S. (1938). An outline of psycho-analysis. *Standard ed.*, 23:139–207.

Garber, M. (1995). *Vice versa: Bisexuality and the eroticism of everyday life*. New York: Simon & Schuster.

Heenen-Wolff, S. (2011). Infantile bisexuality and the "complete oedipal complex": Freudian views on heterosexuality and homosexuality. *The International Journal of Psychoanalysis*, 92(5), 1209–20.

Heenen-Wolff, S. (2016). Die "genitale" Sexualität – Versuch der Dekonstruktion eines normativen psychoanalytischen Konzepts. *Journal für Psychoanalyse*, 57, 2016, 133–49.

Hocquenghem, G. (1972). *Le desir homosexuel*. Paris: Editions Universitaires. Trans. by D. Dangoor as *Homosexual desire*. Durham: Duke University Press, 1993.

Kakar, S. and Narayanan, A. (2023). The capacious Freud. In F. Busch and N. Delgado, *The ego and the id 100 years later*. London: Routledge.

Kinsey, A.C., Pomeroy, W.B. and Martin, C.E. (1948). *Sexual behavior in the human male*. Philadelphia: W.B. Saunders.

Kinsey, A.C. (1953). *Sexual behavior in the human female*. Philadelphia: W.B. Saunders.

Kistner, U. (2016). Translating the first edition of Freud's *Drei Abhandlungen zur Sexualtheorie*. In S. Freud (1905a). *Three essays on the theory of sexuality*. Trans. U. Kistner. London: Verso, 2016, pp. lxxvii–xc.

Laplanche, J. and Pontalis, J-B. (1967). *Vocabulaire de la psychanalyse*. Paris: Presses Universitaires de France. Trans. by D. Nicholson-Smith as *The language of psychoanalysis*. London: Hogarth Press, 1973.

Lewes, K. (1988). *The psychoanalytic theory of male homosexuality*. New York: Simon & Schuster.

Yumatov, R. (2019). Bisexuality and its vicissitudes: A psychoanalytic exploration. In P. Ellerman and K. Kleinman, *The Plumsock papers: Giving new analysts a voice*. New York: IPBooks.

Chapter 3

Reconstructing the bisexuality thesis II

Primary identification

The previous chapter has shown a central difficulty in reconstructing the bisexuality thesis. While Freud sketches the Oedipus complex and the rivalry thesis in detail over many decades (as described in the previous chapter) so that they become core to orthodox psychoanalytic thinking, nowhere in his work does he explain the bisexuality thesis in a manifest or detailed form. His radical proposal of a bisexuality thesis is offered in the most tentative of subjunctive terms: "It may even be ..." (*Es könnte auch sein ...*). The thesis is hidden and obscured and has to be reconstructed from multiple textual instances. Like the key sentence in *The ego and the id*, however, the thesis is hidden in plain sight so that those looking for it will not have far to search.

The thesis of bisexuality as an alternate and parallel theory to the Oedipus complex is not simply the bisexual, polyvocal modification of the Oedipus complex in the sense of a continuum. The bisexuality thesis rests on the supposition of an early type of libidinal relationship that is unmediated by rivalry or injunction. Restated: the bisexuality thesis supposes an object identification unmediated by rivalry or injunction but still in conformity with the defining structural parameters of object cathexis followed by loss and the mental internalisation of the object as identification. Any investigation or discussion of a preoedipal phase is predicated on this supposition, in one form or another, and the argument will either show rivalry is ever-present (i.e. provide support for the Oedipus complex being extended further back to commence in infancy) or provide the material to flesh out the bisexuality thesis fully. As the previous chapter has shown, the axis of the bisexuality thesis is therefore a form of early and primary identification before the Oedipus complex.

The bisexuality thesis and primary identification

Both the rivalry and bisexuality theses rest upon and must contend with the distinction between object cathexis and identification, in which object cathexis takes place first and is followed by loss of the object and then identification with the lost object later. This sequence is so central and unalterable that it forms the foundation for elaborating the structural theory of the ego and superego in the third section of *The ego and the id*. Nevertheless, even a cursory reading of this text shows the

DOI: 10.4324/9781003498919-4

curious matter of some early identifications apparently arising independently of an object cathexis: "These identifications are not what we should have expected, since they do not introduce the abandoned object into the ego" (1923, p. 32). Freud thus signals that there is another form of identification, which appears to exist without a preceding object cathexis, and that this is somehow crucial to the bisexuality thesis. "It is this complicating element introduced by bisexuality that makes it so difficult to obtain a clear view of the facts in connection with the earliest object-choices and identifications, and still more difficult to describe them intelligibly" (p. 33).

Freud's first proposal for a solution is a fudge: "At the very beginning, in the individual's primitive oral phase, object-cathexis and identification are no doubt indistinguishable from each other" (p. 29). Although this brief explanation doesn't satisfy Freud here and he moves on, it reflects and anticipates the argument I am putting forward. The editor's footnote in this passage referencing *Group psychology and the analysis of the ego* (1921) is perceptive of the inter-textuality in this regard, but more of that in a moment. In the 1923 elaboration of the formation of the ego and superego, Freud then circles back to this problem. At this point of the discussion, it can humorously be characterised as the problem of the *immaculate identification*. This reflects the nature of an identification that appears to arise without an initial object relation. The paragraph is so important and so dense; it is worth quoting and examining in full:

> But, whatever the character's later capacity for resisting the influences of abandoned object-cathexes may turn out to be, the effects of the first identifications made in earliest childhood will be general and lasting. This leads us back to the origin of the ego ideal; for behind it there lies hidden an individual's first and most important identification, his identification with the father in his own personal prehistory. This is apparently not in the first instance the consequence or outcome of an object-cathexis; it is a direct and immediate identification and takes place earlier than any object-cathexis. But the object-choices belonging to the first sexual period and relating to the father and mother seem normally to find their outcome in an identification of this kind, and would thus reinforce the primary one.
>
> (1923, p. 31)

An initial reading of this paragraph appears to place the emphasis on an apparent *father identification*, but recall that this is where the term *father* is disclaimed by Freud in the footnote to this page (fn 2, p. 31; this critical aspect has already been highlighted previously in Chapter 2, pp. 80–1). Here Freud indicates that he concentrates on the father only to "simplify my presentation"; in effect, however, this has complicated the reception because scholars have tended to fixate on Freud's use of the male child as the example, and this often leads to a fixation in the scholarship on the simple form of the Oedipus complex. In order to obtain the full picture, *father* must always be replaced in the hypothesis with *the parents*; and the full *continuum* form of the Oedipus complex must be kept in mind.

This paragraph makes clear the supposition of an initial identification that is not the consequence of parent object cathexis: "it is a direct and immediate identification and takes place earlier than any object-cathexis". This would seem to suggest the identification with the parent is already a secondary identification that takes the place of an earlier identification. For Freud, this early identification is still somehow linked to the parents, but he does not go into any detail other than to say that later object cathexes with the parents follow and reinforce the model of this initial identification. There the paragraph ends on a most ungraceful translation, which completely hides the only occasion Freud ever uses the expression *primary identification*: the phrase "the primary identification" should have been deployed in the translation, instead of "the primary one". The German original is unambiguous: *die primäre Identifizierung*. It is significant and revealing to note that the new *Revised standard edition* does not take the opportunity to correct this translation oversight, and the text retains the original English: "the primary one". This only confirms a persistent blind spot around the phrase primary identification bequeathed by Freud. The phrase is not used by Freud before or after this single instance in 1923. Leaving aside questions of whether or not it was the translation's intention to obscure this phrase, Freud himself demonstrates a great reluctance even in the German to adopt fully what seems to be the obvious phrase for a form of identification which precedes any object cathexis. This reluctance might even be a kind of resistance given the linguistic convolutions needed to frame the concept in his work without using the actual phrase. As the two editorial footnotes (p. 31 fn 2 and p. 32 fn 2) indicate, the concept of a form of primary identification is not new in 1923 and dates back at least to *Group psychology* (1921), although the expression *primary identification* is not used in that text. In fact the concept in various forms and with different names predates even the 1921 iteration, as the following archaeological survey shows. The original source for this concept is surprising and unexpected.

Genealogy of the term primary identification

Given Freud's almost assiduous avoidance of the term primary identification, it has not received much attention in psychoanalytic scholarship. To the extent that primary identification does arise in discussion, the implicit subject cathexis (an apparent objectlessness) of primary identification has caused much confusion. Zepf and Hartmann (2005) provide a brief historical survey of usage of the term primary identification, but they fail to establish the actual origin of the term. They seek to resolve the confusion by way of developing a model of a simultaneous, undifferentiated state and process, implicitly following Laplanche (1970, pp. 66–84) in the view of the ego as both origin and agency. This in turn finds extensive but diffuse expression in metaphors of a monadic (e.g. Béla Grunberger) or anti-monadic/dyadic (e.g. Laplanche) state-process, with a concomitant reliance on the preoedipal period as either a dress rehearsal for the Oedipus complex or a revival of the seduction theory, respectively. Much of the discussion in the psychoanalytic literature about identification seems to centre on the mechanism itself (splitting hairs about introjection, etc.), and there is a general obliviousness to the concept of primary identification. Where the term does crop up, there seems to be a consensus that primary identification relates to identification with the father. Compton (1985, p. 228) attributes the expression primary identification to Freud but provides no reference. Lewes (1988) uses the expression four times (pp. 78, 80, 84, 202) but without fully demonstrating what he means, essentially because he is still working on the basis of differentiated mother and father positions; he uses the term without any definition or consideration, and he seems to take it over as meaning *father identification* from a too literal reading of Freud (1923, p. 31). Bondi (1994) considers the term in the same way but, in contrast to Lewes, assumes primary identification to be a *mother identification.*

Freud's apparent reluctance to use the term primary identification does not mean the concept is absent in his formulations in 1921 and 1923 – as already discussed above – but primary identification also appears in similarly indirect formulations in 1921 and in earlier texts. These lend support to the bisexuality theses, though not always in an explicit or obvious manner. While not calling it primary identification in *Group psychology*, this is clearly what Freud has in mind when he discusses the concept in section 7, which opens: "Identification is known to psycho-analysis as the earliest expression of an emotional tie with another person" (1921, p. 105). This formulation is repeated (p. 107) and contrasted with a second form of identification, the more familiar regressive "substitute for a libidinal object tie" via introjection of the lost sexual object into the ego (p. 108). A third form of identification is explored that is linked to group formation, where a common sexual object leads to a shared group identification. In principle, however, the description of identification follows the same formula for the identification mechanism in *The ego and the id*, with the same inability to capture the essence of the very first identification. The way of sidestepping the immaculate identification problem in *Group psychology* is twofold. First, Freud suggests early identification has an ambivalent character in itself, i.e. it is not introduced by loss, and secondly, he uses the ploy (revived and then rejected in *The ego and the id*) of suggesting the two early types of bonds – object cathexis and identification – coexist (1921, p. 105). Of interest here is the suggestion that the two early types of bonds come together, and their confluence is the Oedipus complex. This is a rough draft suggestive of the more complete form of the complex developed in *The ego and the id*. Although the description of the Oedipus complex in 1921 is still the simple form, even here the more complete outcome is anticipated (pp. 105–6).

While Freud's outline does not always distinguish clearly, there are two kinds of identification at stake here. This is shown by two important if subtle clarifications regarding "early identification" in this text. Firstly, the objects of the two early types of emotional ties – cathexis and identification – are distinguished by biological sex in this early outline of the Oedipus complex, which is still the simple form: in the case of a boy, object cathexis is with the mother and identification with the father (pp. 105–6). This distinction becomes moot when read with Freud's (1923) complete Oedipus complex and the amalgamation of the biological sexes into a general parent undifferentiated by biological sex; however, the distinction of parental biological sex here indicates that the object cathexis and identification at stake relate to the rivalry thesis and the Oedipus complex, which is clearly based on the formula: object cathexis first and identification later. There is some confusion introduced about the sequence because of a crucial translation error in the English version of the *Standard edition*. The error is pointed out by Zepf and Hartmann (2005, p. 32, fn 2) and corrected in the *Revised standard edition*. Strachey's version (with italics added here to show the erroneous translation) reads: "At the same time as the identification with his father, *or a little later*, the boy has begun to develop a true object-cathexis towards his mother" (Freud, 1921, p. 105); the sentence must be corrected so that *or a little later* reads *or a little earlier* to match the German original, "*vielleicht sogar schon vorher*". This sequence has the effect of confirming the formula in 1923: the sequence in the Oedipus complex of object cathexis first and identification later. Read with Freud's 1923 amalgamation of the biological sexes into a general parent, this is now clearly an object cathexis and then identification sequence in the rivalry thesis of the Oedipus complex, and unrelated to primary identification.

A second clarification that helps to understand *primary* identification is the distinction Freud makes in 1921 to explain the difference between object cathexis and identification. Identification is a matter of *wanting to be*, while object cathexis is *wanting to have* (1921, p. 106) (in German: *sein* and *haben*). Freud shows a deep understanding of the implications of this: "The distinction ... depends upon whether the tie attaches to the subject or to the object of the ego" (p. 106), reflecting his later (1923, p. 34) four bisexual trends in the subject-object distinctions of the complete Oedipus complex already highlighted (in Chapter 2, pp. 75–6). The semantic distinction between *wanting to be* and *wanting to have* has profound philosophical and clinical implications that will be considered in Chapters 4 and 5, but for now the significance lies in how this distinction leads to primary identification. Freud carries on to state: "The former [wanting to be, i.e. identification] is therefore already possible before any sexual object-choice has been made" (p. 106); this resurfaces the problem of an early identification that predates sexual object choice, i.e. an immaculate identification that does not follow the predictable sequence of object cathexis first and then subsequent regressive identification. Here is the clue that opens the way to understanding primary identification as a *subject cathexis*, which is why primary identification resists "a clear metapsychological representation of the distinction" (p. 106) to later identification in consequence of object cathexis. "We can only see that [primary] identification endeavours to mould a person's own ego after the fashion of the one that has been taken as a 'model'" (p. 106). The concept of a model or surrogate thus unambiguously links primary identification to Freud's far more broadly outlined concept of *primary narcissism* (1905, 1914) and the related but somewhat gnomic form of *homosexual libido* and an initial *homosexual object choice*, linked to primary narcissism. Both primary narcissism and the homosexual object are placed in juxtaposition to a secondary object cathexis and secondary identification with the parent.

Primary and secondary narcissism feature frequently as terminology in texts written before 1921. Narcissism in this sense is an early shorthand formulation for the mechanism of cathexis and identification as it is developed later, and so the concept of (primary) identification has its roots in Freud's (primary) narcissism of the *Three essays* (1905). Primary narcissism is a central feature of the infantile stages that form the focus of the second of the *Three essays* ("Infantile sexuality" – 1905, pp. 173–206). Freud identifies the main patterns as follows: oral, anal, phallic and genital phases on the basis of the somatic zones that serve as the locus for libidinal pleasure. The predominant object in this infantile period is the subject itself, albeit in the specific somatic zones, and the libidinal aim of pleasure is achieved through activity, which is essentially self-stimulation (termed autoerotism, also masturbation, though this is not identical or synonymous with genital masturbation after puberty; 1905, pp. 185–93).

The libidinal instinct for pleasure is itself an offshoot of the first instinct – hunger – and its satisfaction, the instinct for self-preservation (1905, pp. 181–2; p. 198). The cycle of hunger and satisfaction is a rhythm of exchange: the child's economy of pleasure and its absence – "a search for some pleasure which has already been experienced and is now remembered" (1905, p. 181). This is where the three polarities of mental life emerge. Pleasure and unpleasure are joined by activity and passivity, and then the gradual division into subject and object emerges. The initial passivity of the infant is replaced by activity focused on feeding; for example, suckling instead of being suckled (1931, p. 236); then muscular control (1905, p. 186–7), for example, discharge of urine and excrement (1905, pp. 186–7) and expressions of sexual activity through autoerotism and masturbation (1905, pp. 185–91) coalescing finally in the child's will, termed the "instinct to mastery" by Freud (1905, pp. 193, 198; also sublimated in an instinct for knowledge p. 194; instinct to mastery further described in 1914, p. 85; 1915, p. 139; 1917, p. 327; 1920a, pp. 16, 35, 54; 1923, p. 29 fn 2; 1924a, p. 163).

In these early infantile stages, sexual activity is the infantile sexuality of autoerotism, but this does not mean it is independent of an object. The object is the self, and the libidinal pleasure is localised in the oral and anal and even genital zones. From the onset of nursing, and then extending to the care of the child, the oral and anal zones become sites for taking pleasure. Part of the pleasure is masturbatory (tactile and repetitive), but some degree of the pleasure is taken from the sharing of the zones with the alimentary functions, and indeed libidinal pleasure is initiated by the overlap of these alimentary and sexual functions in the common zones – "what is sexual includes what is excremental" (1905b, 98; see also 1912, p. 189; 1913, p. 336; 1926, p. 212; 1930, fn p. 100, and ed. fn p. 107).

The child in this period is its own first object. Secondary, external objects emerge but always in relation to the child; these are the breast/source of nourishment and then the mother/caregiver, in Freud's formulation (1905, p. 222). These intrusions are resolved into objects gradually by the repetition of absence and presence (*fort-da*, 1920a, pp. 14–17), a process in which the child seeks to master the absence by the change from passivity to activity. Object withdrawal is inevitable, however, and cannot be controlled by the child. The one object that does not withdraw is the child itself – its own body – and so this is elevated to the primary object and becomes the area where pleasure, now recognisably libidinal instead of focused on survival, can be mastered and maintained through autoerotism. This is a unity with the self. Freud calls this *primary narcissism* or *infantile narcissism* (1914) and goes on to show that the attitude of the parents to the child "is a revival and reproduction of their own narcissism" (1914, p. 91), creating a vast cycle of self-reproducing inter-generational narcissism. The culmination of this is the expectation that the child will exchange or substitute its self-love with the ego ideal (pp. 94–95), which is the parental narcissism. This is the process of identification with the parents. In Freud's later theory, parental narcissism and parental identification are clearly recognised as the foundation of the superego, with a concise description in Lecture 31:

> Thus a child's super-ego is in fact constructed on the model not of its parents but of its parents' super-ego; the contents which fill it are the same and it becomes the vehicle of tradition and of all the time-resisting judgements of value which have propagated themselves in this manner from generation to generation.
>
> (1933, p. 67)

As the world gradually resolves into objects for the child, facilitated in no small part by the advent of human language, the prototype self-as-object – the body of the self in all the permutations of autoerotism – is augmented by surrogate objects: the breast, the mother, the world. These are all pleasure objects in relation to the subject, and they are all narcissistic – a vigorous attempt to recover the state of early narcissism (1914, p. 100). This secondary narcissism may thus be termed the surrogate period of narcissism. The defining feature of pleasure is that it requires an object and only in this way can the subject experience pleasure. This is the foundation of economy. The advent of morality aims to make the self-as-object in the child unsuitable and forces the child to remain surrogate object to the narcissism of the parental subject. What unfolds for the child after the caesura of birth is a series of caesuras, where the narcissism of the child subject, vested in itself as the first object, is assailed by growing assault from forces outside as well as the demands of its own instincts for satisfaction. These assaults and caesuras are cumulatively comprehensible as the advent of morality – nothing more and nothing less than the restriction of the child's primary narcissism by the secondary narcissism of other subjects. This reinforces the parallel to the terms primary and secondary identification.

Between the *Three essays* in 1905 and the paper *On narcissism* in 1914, a direct parallel emerges in Freud's thinking between primary narcissism and something he calls homosexual libido with its own homosexual object. The earliest use of the phrase *homosexual libido* is in the Schreber case notes (1911). The concept then evolves from a discussion in relation to object love into the term *homosexual object* in the paper *On narcissism* (1914). The usage of homosexual object persists for about a decade (1917, pp. 426–7; 1919, pp. 199–200; 1921, p. 124; 1922, pp. 230–2), and the final mention is in the *Autobiographical study* (1925) in a summary of the *Three essays*, although in fact neither the term *homosexual libido* nor *homosexual object* was used in the 1905 edition. When homosexual libido is first deployed (1911, pp. 43, 45), it implies a sexual object of the same biological sex as the subject but not in the sense of a fixed or exclusive sexual orientation, rather as part of a fluid oscillation between heterosexual and homosexual feelings (p. 45). This fluidity is encountered repeatedly in a characteristic formulation: "Psycho-analysis enables us to point to some trace or other of a homosexual object-choice in everyone" (1925, p. 38).

There are three significant instances where this formulation is used by Freud that require special attention for the purposes of reconstructing the bisexuality thesis. First, there is the extensive comment about object love in *On narcissism*:

> We say that a human being has originally two sexual objects – himself and the woman who nurses him – and in doing so we are postulating a primary narcissism in everyone, which may in some cases manifest itself in a dominating fashion in his object-choice.
>
> (1914, p. 88)

The subsequent explanation (pp. 88–90) anticipates in detail the formula of object cathexis/identification in the 1921 and 1923 forms, and this serves as concrete evidence of a parallel between Freud's phrase primary narcissism with primary identification. It is interesting to note that even in 1914 the position of the mother is not exclusive and is extended to include both parents – the one who feeds the child and the one who protects the child (p. 90). This is echoed directly in Freud's footnote about "the parent" in *The ego and the id* (1923, p. 31).

The advent of the idea of two kinds of sexual object in *On narcissism*, one of which is the subject itself, is so important that it then finds its way into major revisions of two previous texts, notably the 1915 footnote to the *Three essays*: "all human beings are capable of making a homosexual object-choice and have in fact made one in their unconscious" (p. 145); and the 1919 footnote to the paper on Leonardo da Vinci (1910):

> everyone, even the most normal person, is capable of making a homosexual object-choice, and has done so at some time in his life, and either still adheres to it in his unconscious or else protects himself against it by vigorous counter-attitudes.
>
> (p. 99)

An almost identical formulation of the two kinds of sexual object in infantile development is introduced: a homosexual object, which is universal, and the parental object.

In *On narcissism* (1914), the expression *homosexual object* is used interchangeably with narcissistic object. This is important because it confirms that Freud's subsequent use of the term *primary narcissism* to describe this object attachment could then be considered his synonym for *primary identification*. However, the first time the expression primary identification is used in the context of psychoanalysis and Freud's theory of the infantile period happens to be in a text that is not by Freud. A paper by Trigant Burrow (1914) on "The genesis and meaning of 'homosexuality' and its relation to the problem of introverted mental states" focuses almost exclusively on developing the idea of primary identification. This paper was first presented by Burrow on 5 May 1914 at the fourth annual meeting of the American Psychoanalytic Association (APA), in Albany, New York State. This paper (although uneven in places) and other texts by Burrow are important but neglected contributions to the psychoanalytic theory of sexuality.

Burrow was an early supporter of Freud in the United States; they had met on Freud's visit to the USA in 1909, and Burrow was also present at the first meeting of the APA in Baltimore on 9 May 1911 (Jones, 1955, pp. 87–8). Between these two events, Burrow studied with Jung in Zurich. He firmly supported Freud after the schism with Jung, but then Burrow drifted away from the Freudian group in the late 1920s and was formally ejected from the main body of psychoanalysts in the early 1930s as his views became increasingly contentious. This is generally related to Burrow's theory around group analysis, which was incompatible with Freud's firm understanding of the singularity of the analyst-analysand relationship. Burrow's later group analysis theory receives far more attention today than his early psychoanalytic theory, where his committed support for Freud finds expression. There is no doubt that Burrow recognised the radical elements of Freud's sexual theory in this early period, although oddly these elements retained little significance in Burrow's later views, where he rejects the centrality of sexuality in human development and reverts to an idealised concept of love. Some of his later insights on the social dimension of neuroses are still innovative today (see, for example, Burrow, 1926 and especially 1927) and anticipate accounts such as those of Deleuze and Guattari, but in Burrow's work from the 1920s onwards his ideas become needlessly metaphysical, and his writing offers none of the rich metaphoric texture of the French tradition.

Lewes (1988) briefly mentions Burrow, although not by name – "an American psychiatrist" – and characterises him as "rather too general" (p. 57) without recognising the importance of Burrow's work; Lewes concludes mistakenly that Burrow's concept of primary identification is a "failure to have emerged from a symbiotic relation to the mother" (p. 57). Gay (1988) has only one comment – petty and unsubstantiated – to offer on Burrow: "a curious amalgam of physician and crank" (p. 476), and clearly Gay never bothered to read Burrow's actual psychoanalytical writings. The welcome republication of Burrow's main papers (2013) and recent studies by Schultz-Venrath (2015) and Drury and Tudor (2022) are evidence of a revived interest in Burrow's work. The collection of Burrow's papers edited by Pertegato and Pertegato (2013) stands out because it includes some previously unpublished material as well as certain early papers that have been hard to access. The selection and the introduction by Pertegato and Pertegato (2013) tend to emphasise Burrow's later work on group analysis, though they are clearly alert to the novel insights and contributions in Burrow's earlier psychoanalytic phase. Unfortunately, however, they ignore Burrow's focus on sexuality in this period and suggest instead that Burrow "reversed Freud's viewpoint" on sexuality in the genesis of pathology (p. liv). While this is a correct characterisation of Burrow's later work, it certainly is not accurate for his 1914 paper on the genesis of homosexuality. Schultz-Venrath (2015) focuses on the pivot in Burrow's relationship away from psychoanalytic circles, and Drury and Tudor (2022, pp. 189–98) concentrate purely on Burrow's work in the period after 1916 to demonstrate his theory of group analysis. Both essays are evidence of the ongoing trend to ignore Burrow's earlier psychoanalytic contributions in the area of sexuality.

In one of his earlier papers, Burrow (1913) suggests the infant in its initial period of life is in a primary and preconscious subjective phase; by subjective, Burrow means the child is focused on itself in a state that precedes relations with external objects. This lays the groundwork for the development of his concept of primary identification in the 1914 paper on the genesis of homosexuality, which is the focus of my interest. Primary identification in various formulations remains part of Burrow's thinking in the transition to his group analysis theory (1925a, 1925b and 1927) but then is abandoned in the group analysis paradigm.

In his 1914 paper, Burrow takes up Freud's position on the genesis of male homosexuality in the Leonardo da Vinci paper (Freud, 1910) and succinctly frames and addresses Freud's lack of attention to female homosexuality as well as the problem of the resolution of the female Oedipus complex that Freud struggles to formulate over decades and several papers (Freud, 1920b, 1924b, 1931). Most importantly, Burrow takes issue with the fact that the mother-identification genesis of homosexuality in the Leonardo da Vinci paper applies only to the male child, and Burrow proposes a new way of understanding identification that builds a universally applicable theory of the genesis of homosexuality, which correlates remarkably closely with Freud's universal homosexual object-choice (referenced above, 1914 and footnote addendums in 1905, 1910). Burrow's theory is based on identification of a special kind, which he unambiguously calls *primary identification*, using the idea that the child does not form a cathexis with the mother but with itself via the mother. This primary identification is directly relevant to Freud's radical bisexuality thesis. Although primary identification may seem to suggest a circularity in the primary narcissism of the infant co-extensive with the mother's narcissism reinvested in the child, Burrow actually argues that the child already has an object predating the mother in the form of the unity of the mother's body with its own body:

That is to say, the child's primary ego or consciousness being united to and one with the mother, regards along with the mother, its own body as the love-object. With the process of weaning, the infant is thrown more and more upon himself. Being left more and more to the contemplation of his own body, it becomes the constant and insistent object of interest – his hands and feet, his navel, his alimentary and genito-urinary organs and the functions pertaining thereto.

(pp. 278–9)

Burrow is merging Freud's concepts of physical autoerotism and the mental representation of this object as narcissism of the infantile phase to explain the subsequent identification as a self-identification that Burrow characterises as primary identification. This identification has a fundamental homosexual quality: "autoerotism or the love of one's own body is the love of that sex to which one's own body belongs and this, in the psychological interpretation, is precisely homosexuality" (p. 277). It is obvious that both subject and object homosexuality are implied here, by virtue of the subject and object being the same. Burrow takes this point to its logical conclusion, to provide a universal theory of homosexuality:

> Now it is clear that if the original, subjective relationship of the infant in respect to the mother leads to its first objectivating, so to speak, from the standpoint of the mother, i.e., as the mother with whom it is identified, and consequently leads to the infant's early regarding its own body as the mother regards it, i.e., as the chief love-object, then the result psychologically is in no respect different whether the child be male or female, for in either case since it loves itself, it loves the sex to which it belongs, and loving thus its own sex, it is homosexual.
>
> (1914, p. 280)

Burrow's concept of primary identification overcomes several problems with Freud's theory of homosexuality at that stage (Freud, 1910). The universal theory of homosexuality Burrow offers is applicable irrespective of biological sex. Furthermore, Burrow's theory also functions perfectly given the ignorance of the difference in biological sex at this early period of the infant's life. The infant's primary identification with its own sex is uncontaminated by knowledge of any difference in biological sex. Its own sex becomes the template by default. Primary identification also tallies well with Freud's later structural theory because primary identification has the necessary elements of the mechanism: object cathexis – the child's own body – and its loss, which produces the identification. The process of loss of the self as object is effected in particular via the complicated shame-injunction process, which I have explored already (Chapter 2, pp. 69–72), and this becomes the focus again in Chapter 4.

Primary identification in the way it is developed by Burrow links directly to Freud's idea of primary narcissism (1914) on a conceptual level, but the line of influence seems tricky to determine because Freud's text and Burrow's paper both emerge in 1914. It turns out that there is actually a third and earlier text that is the source of this key idea for Burrow and Freud. Burrow references and is building on a theory already put forward a few years before by Isidor Sadger, another of the enigmatic figures of this early period of psychoanalysis, whose contribution to the development of psychoanalysis has been overshadowed almost entirely by antipathy towards his ideas and his participation in the Vienna Psychoanalytic Society. Sadger has only recently been rescued from relative obscurity by the republication (Sadger, 1929) of his contentious biography of Freud. It is clear that Freud's idea of primary narcissism (1914) was influenced by two ideas from Sadger's work, namely Sadger's theory of narcissism and the closely related issue of the genesis of homosexuality and bisexuality. In the origins of an infant's attraction to objects, there are two kinds of objects. The term narcissism refers here to one kind, a form of self-identification which arises in distinction to love for an external object. The second kind is implicitly an external object-oriented attraction directed at the infant's caregiver. In turn, it is thus possible for the later external object choices to be influenced by both of these two kinds of initial object.

The lineage of these ideas can be traced as follows. Sadger presented a draft paper at the Vienna Psychoanalytic Society's meeting on 10 November 1909 (Nunberg & Federn, 1967, p. 307); in the discussion after Sadger's presentation, Freud then makes comments (pp. 312–3) on the paper; Freud's comments are incorporated verbatim by Sadger in the subsequent published version of his paper (Sadger, 1910, pp. 111–2); exactly the same phrases that Freud uses in his discussion of Sadger's presentation then also resurface in Freud's (1914, p. 88) work on narcissism a few years later. The relevant passages are as follows.

The text of Sadger's draft paper presented at the meeting on 10 November 1909 has not survived; it is only known from the summary of the presentation in the Society's minutes:

> A large role is played by autoerotism in the form of narcissism. In the types of people that the person loves one can recognize, in addition to the characteristics of the individuals who are loved homosexually and heterosexually, traits also of the person himself. Another of Sadger's patients still loves the type that evolved in him at the time when he came to do without the love for his mother.
>
> (Nunberg & Federn, 1967, p. 307)

Freud's observations during the discussion after Sadger's presentation are also summarised in the minutes of the meeting:

> Sadger's comment with regard to narcissism [above] seems new and valuable. This is not an isolated phenomenon but a necessary developmental stage in the transition from autoerotism to object love. Being enamored of oneself (of one's own genitals) is an indispensable stage of development. From there one passes over to similar objects. In general, man has two primary sexual objects and his future existence depends on the one upon which he remains fixated. These two sexual objects are for every man the woman (the mother, nurse, etc.) and his own person; and it follows from this that [the question] is to become free from both and not to linger on too long with either. Usually, one's own person is replaced by the father, who however soon enters the hostile position. It is at this point that homosexuality branches off. Man does not set himself free of himself so soon, as this case [of homosexuality presented by Sadger] very beautifully demonstrates.
>
> (Nunberg & Federn, 1967, pp. 312–3)

Freud recognises an original idea in Sadger's concept of narcissism and elegantly structures this idea into its component parts: the child and its body as one sexual object and the caregiver as another object available to the child. The extrapolation of these two early objects leads to a homosexual object, modelled on the child's own body, and a heterosexual one, modelled on the child's caregiver, which is assumed to be female. The second object offers an early and rudimentary formulation of the simple form of the Oedipus complex, although there is also the suggestion that a non-hostile relation to the father may develop if the father is seen as an object of attraction similar to the child's own body. The example discusses the situation for the male infant, in the general context of the case of male homosexuality that is the focus of Sadger's presentation; there is no reason to assume the theory is not also applicable to the female child.

For the subsequent published version of his paper, Sadger incorporates Freud's comments verbatim. The following passage is my English translation from the published paper in German (not previously translated):

> This is then an entirely new point that appears to me decisive regarding the genesis of homosexuality: the path to homosexuality always runs via narcissism, i.e. love for the self. I have shown this in all my case studies, and Freud confirmed this in response to my question about his homosexual patients. Narcissism is not an isolated phenomenon but rather a necessary development stage in the passage from autoerotism to later object love. Love for the self, behind which stands in a hidden form one's own genitals, is a development stage that is always present. From this stage, the individual proceeds to similar objects. Each person in principle has two primary and original sexual objects, and the future life of the individual is moulded by if and upon which of the two he/she finally remains fixed. For the male, these two objects are his mother (or the woman who nurses him) and his own person. To remain healthy he must rid himself of both, and not tarry too long with either of them. Shortly after this, the self is replaced by the father because the father, as the primary rival for the mother, steps in as adversary. Homosexuality bifurcates at this point, and the person selects the new sexual object according to the model of the self, the real self as much as the idealised self. The homosexual is unable to detach himself from himself, that is his destiny. He is more successful dissolving the cathexis with the mother. He does this by identifying himself with her.
>
> (Sadger, 1910, pp. 111–2, my translation)

To complete tracing the genealogy, Freud then reuses exactly the same phrases that he used in his comments on the discussion of Sadger's presentation in his long work on narcissism published in 1914:

> We say that a human being has originally two sexual objects – himself and the woman who nurses him – and in doing so we are postulating a primary narcissism in everyone, which may in some cases manifest itself in a dominating fashion in his object-choice.
>
> (Freud, 1914, p. 88, already quoted above)

The linkage in Burrow's paper to this idea comes via exactly the same passage from the published version of Sadger's paper (1910, pp. 111–2), which is referenced by Abraham Brill (1913, p. 338), who also quotes the main sentence, presumably in his own translation of it into English. Burrow's paper (1914) in turn references both Brill (1913) and Sadger (1910 via Brill, 1913), so the same influence from Sadger on Freud is therefore true for Burrow, whose argument for a universally applicable theory of the genesis of homosexuality correlates closely with Sadger's formulation.

There has been little recognition of the significance of this Sadger-Freud exchange until fairly recently. For example, Lewes (1988) has nothing substantial to say about Sadger nor does he recognise the influence of Sadger's work for Freud's theory of homosexuality and primary narcissism/identification. In a glancing reference to the November 1909 meeting, Gay (1988) assumes Freud was the sole progenitor of the concept of narcissism. The Sadger-Freud exchange is discussed by Dundes (2005) and at greater length by May (2015, pp. 3–39), although May's account fails somewhat to differentiate the two issues (narcissism and homosexuality). In this instance, May (pp. 33–4) concedes the line of transmission from Sadger to Freud but argues ungenerously that Sadger had no insight into his discovery and that Freud "revised Sadger's comments and transformed them into an insight of major significance" (p. 34). While there is no doubt that Freud's version has more nuance and also neutralises Sadger's crude clinical style and overbearing heteronormative perspective, demonstrated not least by the recurrent obsession in Sadger's work with curing homosexuals, May's argument that Sadger was a passive scientific utensil for Freud's discovery is not fair. It also relies considerably on the evidentiary weight of the Society minutes, which may or may not be an accurate, complete record of the discussion. The minutes would certainly not have been able to comprehend *in medias res* the complexity and implication of ideas being raised and worked out in collaborative discussion.

For the genealogy of the phrase primary identification, the point here is that the concept has its bedrock in this exchange between Sadger and Freud in 1909, which establishes the category of a primary self-object. While Freud and Burrow significantly extend Sadger's ideas about narcissism and the genesis of homosexuality, both Freud and Burrow rely on and adopt the concept of a primary and original narcissistic libidinal self-object that Sadger introduced. Attention is drawn to the chronology of Sadger's original paper about narcissism and the genesis of homosexuality because Sadger's paper is important to Burrow and Freud. Burrow refines Freud's (1910) genesis of homosexuality theory substantially by means of the universality of primary identification, which is not specific to biological sex. Primary identification is the actual term that Burrow introduces; the concept is extremely expedient, and Chapter 4 will return to it in a longer discussion. If Freud was aware of Burrow's 1914 text, he does not mention or reference it, but it is likely that Freud had seen the published version of Burrow's paper. More generally, it is possible to see elements in Freud's 1921 paper on group psychology as a response to Burrow's emerging idea of group analysis around that time. Freud certainly corresponded with Burrow, who frequently sent copies of his work to Freud. However, there does seem to have been a general antipathy in Freud's circle towards Burrow (Perte-gato & Pertegato, 2013, especially pp. lxxiv–xcv), and this would explain in part Freud's assiduous avoidance of the term primary identification, which so clearly has its origin in Burrow's 1914 text.

Whether via the influence of Sadger directly or Burrow's version, this universal theory of the genesis of homosexuality and primary narcissism (identification) in a self-object is added to the *Three essays* in the 1915 revision (1905, pp. 145–6) and repeated in the footnote added to the Leonardo piece in 1919 (1910, p. 99). Moreo-ver, the nascent bisexuality and Oedipus theses become central in *On narcissism* (1914), and they find their way into the two types of relationships described here: a narcissistic type focused on the child itself and an attachment type focused on the child's caregivers, with the notable inclusion of both biological sexes in this group-ing, and not just the mother.

A person may love:-

(1) According to the narcissistic type:

    (a) what he himself is (i.e. himself),
    (b) what he himself was,
    (c) what he himself would like to be,
    (d) someone who was once part of himself.

(2) According to the anaclitic (attachment) type:

    (a) the woman who feeds him,
    (b) the man who protects him,

and the succession of substitutes who take their place.

(1914, p. 90)

The first group – the narcissistic type – clearly corresponds to primary identifi-cation, and the second attachment type produces secondary identification. These two types of relationships and identifications are then revived in modified form in Freud's cathexis-and-identification formulations of 1921 and 1923. It is clear that Freud's early usage of the concept narcissism has significant overlap with the term identification in his later work.

In summary then, Freud implicitly, and even explicitly in places, presents a bi-sexuality thesis built on the basis of a special form of identification that can be characterised as primary. Via primary identification, the bisexuality thesis reveals an object cathexis of the self with the self. Sometimes this is termed primary narcis-sism or a homosexual object choice by Sadger, Burrow and Freud. There are two important issues to consider in this concept. Primary identification occurs at the early infant stage, so it takes place in the absence of knowledge of the difference in biological sex, with all the attendant implications. The use of the word homosexual in this context cannot therefore be equated with a literal homosexual identity or activity of the adult form. Rather the term represents an infant's self-cathexis and subsequent identification. Irrespective of how Sadger, Burrow and Freud use these variants, primary identification is not directly or mechanically the cause of manifest adult homosexuality, although there is conceivably a connection in the sense of a universal bisexual potential (latent and/or manifest) to take on this form later once the child has knowledge of the difference in biological sex.

However they are termed, these primary elements – primary narcissism, homosexual object choice – form the foundation for the primary identification of the infant child with itself on the basis of a prior object cathexis with itself. This meets the requirements of a proper alternate thesis for bisexuality, i.e. an identification in consequence of loss that predates the advent of rivalry and the Oedipus complex. The bisexuality thesis thus explains a non-oedipal period where the child's primary object cathexis and subsequent identification with itself produce an emergent id-ego structure of sufficient standing to serve as the nucleus for later ego and superego development. Initially in this development, the child also forms ties with the parents but as objects of its own bisexual libido – bisexual in the broad sense of a libidinal impulse as yet undifferentiated on the basis of biological sex. The parents (and later the broader social formation) in turn become caught up in the child's primary object cathexis and identification and play an active role by inhibiting the child's self-cathexis and self-identification and insisting on the *ascendancy* of parental identification, which is the genesis of the superego. In this confusion and battle of wills, the child is at a disadvantage and retreats into a desexualised or latency period, which is the culmination of the inhibition of its primary narcissism and the triumph of the parental will. Primary identification is thus more precisely the residue of the initial self-as-object cathexis. At puberty, by the latest, the child is then thrust from the ruins of primary identification into fixed reproductive relations to negotiate the rivalry of the Oedipus conflict, underpinned as it is by the archaeological foundation of bisexuality. At minimum, rivalry attempts to negate the preceding bisexuality. Even if the more complete Oedipus complex is taken as the outcome of the rivalry of the Oedipus complex, it negates bisexuality by fixing the biological sex of the subject as gender in place of the prevailing bisexual subject fluidity; and by fixing the sexual aim and object in a regime of reproduction, where non-reproductive aims and objects are at best sublimated, at worst repressed.

Summing up the reconstructed bisexuality thesis

A detailed technical reading and analysis of Freud's work shows the presence of a bisexuality thesis, built on the non-oedipal foundation of infantile sexuality and primary identification. This thesis stands in contrast to the better-known Oedipus complex with its focus on the reproductive regime and rivalry. There are many consequences to the bisexuality thesis, and more detailed consideration of the philosophical and clinical implications is given in the next two chapters. First though it is valuable to summarise the reconstruction process this far.

In *The ego and the id*, Freud explains the mechanism underlying the new structural model: object cathexis followed by loss and then by identification. This is the universal and unvarying mechanism for the formation of the ego and the superego. A lost libidinal object is reproduced in the mental apparatus as identification. The ego and the superego are formed out of the id on the basis of identification after the loss or prohibition of an object-cathexis. In elaborating these structures, Freud was troubled by discovering a form of early identification that seemed to deviate from this mechanism. However, my analysis and discussion so far shows that this primary identification follows the same structure. It is based on cathexis with the self (a subject cathexis) that by its internal unity of having and being the same object might appear from the outside to be objectless, but the infant has nevertheless found an object in the self. Primary identification predates cathexis with the parents. Subject cathexis also lays the foundation for a model of the ideal object, the perfect initial unity of the self, which is lost but then returns in the form of primary identification to serve as the model for all future objects. This self-identification has the appearance of primary narcissism and a pre-genital primary homosexuality, in which the child's own body is the model for the object. Later, once the genitals become the focus of the libidinal instinct via the reproductive regime, the homosexuality of primary identification may grow into the adult form or remain repressed by the general sexual inhibition that engulfs the child at this age; released in the form of adult heterosexuality, the libidinal drive still retains an unconscious universal homosexual residue. This explains the historical social fear of homosexuality, where the fear is not of the manifest homosexual person per se but a self-fear of awakening the repressed homosexual impulse entombed deep in the unconscious mental structure of the fixed heterosexual.

The range of surrogate objects at this early age of primary identification is gradually extended on the basis of the self-model to the parents in the form of external object cathexis. These objects are inherently bisexual (in the same pre-genital manner) from the initial perspective of the child subject. A more applicable term might be *ambisexual*, which Burrow (1914, p. 281) uses without reference. It appears that Ferenczi (1912) is the first to propose the term (as a way of distinguishing Freud's usage of the word bisexuality from Fliess's idea of the presence of both biological sexes in the same body). Ferenczi defines ambisexuality as "the child's psychical capacity for bestowing his erotism, originally objectless, on either the male or the female sex, or on both" (p. 156); in his later work, Ferenczi drops the term. While Freud makes reference to other terminological innovations by Ferenczi and his theories about homosexuality (1905, pp. 146–7), he never mentions or adopts ambisexual, even though this seems useful for addressing the subject aspect of bisexuality, which is doubly appropriate at the infantile stage.

The child is soon banished from this early paradise of self-centric polyvocal flux with the world when somatic reality increasingly asserts itself. The first loss is the self as object, out of which the first identification is born. Later losses are multiplied by the admixture of prohibition, especially in the shame-rivalry progression, where certain objects are prohibited and others permitted. The outcome of the process is always the same: object cathexis is lost or prohibited and is then transformed to produce identification with the object in the ego or superego. Prohibition can be interpreted as a special form of loss. The specific lever in the mechanism – loss or prohibition – determines whether a particular object cathexis produces identification in the ego or superego. Simple loss produces the ego while prohibition (in the shape of shame and rivalry) produces the superego.

In consequence of these observations, it is possible to say that the bisexuality and rivalry theses both have application. Bisexuality is the initial primal flux of the libido followed later by the introduction of rivalry. This also resolves what seemed so puzzling to Freud. Bisexuality and rivalry come to coexist in a dialectic relationship, with each seeking to negate the other. For a number of reasons, not least the self-replicating power of incumbent social forces, especially in the parental instance, rivalry holds sway and bisexuality is generally repressed.

In this universal dialectic, it is important to understand that bisexuality is not a state; rather, it is the outcome of an interplay between homosexual and heterosexual impulses, further coloured by tensions introduced by socially constructed values (injunctions) that shape sexual aims and objects, in which the reproductive always trumps the non-reproductive regime. Socially constructed inhibition and rivalry commence in the infantile period but always subsequent to the self-cathexis and loss that produces primary identification. Inhibition and rivalry in the multitudinous forms of social values are targeted against subject cathexis and primary identification; thereafter a dialectic tug-of-war in the development of the individual is established, with the hand of society pressed firmly on the scales in favour of parental identification, in the form of heterosexuality and gender as fixed states that arrest the dialectic. In recent decades, manifest homosexuality has been somewhat released from inhibition, indexed by full legal equality with heterosexuality in a few dozen jurisdictions around the world, but even here homosexuality is only recognised and tolerated as a fixed and exclusive form of orientation that cohabits unthreateningly within the rivalry paradigm of reproduction. In these jurisdictions, other variations of sexual relations and gender identities are also now asserting a claim for recognition and tolerance. In reality, however, sexuality in its orientation and gender are not fixed endogenously but by this exogenous action of social formation.

The dialectic process is illuminated by recognising the bisexuality thesis. In this thesis, there is the innate universal potential for an ambisexual polyvocality of desire within each person: an unfixed, free-ranging bisexuality of subject-object, active-passive and male-female libidinal flux, which rivalry and the Oedipus complex seek to arrest.

Reference list

Please note: References follow the system of historical layering, with a distinction between source texts and access texts. If the source date is different to the access date, page references are always for the access text, but the reference year is that of the source text. For more in this regard, please see the comment on historical layering in the Introduction, p. 5.

Bondi, S.A. (1994). El sexo de los ángeles. In M. Lemlij, ed., *Mujeres Por Mujeres*. Lima: Biblioteca Peruana de Psicoanálisis. Trans as "The ambiguity of bisexuality in psychoanalysis". In *Studies on femininity*, M. Alizade, ed. London: Routledge.

Brill, A.A. (1913). The conception of homosexuality. *Journal of the American Medical Association*, 61(5), 335–40.

Burrow, T. (1913). Psychoanalysis and life. First presented on 14 October to the New York Academy of Medicine. In E.G. Pertegato and G.O. Pertegato, eds., *From psychoanalysis to group analysis: The pioneering work of Trigant Burrow*. London: Karnac Books.

Burrow, T. (1914). The genesis and meaning of "homosexuality" and its relation to the problem of introverted mental states. First presented on 5 May at the fourth annual meeting of the American Psychoanalytic Association. Published in 1917 in *The Psychoanalytic Review*, 4(3), 272–84. In E.G. Pertegato and G.O. Pertegato, eds., 2013. References are to the 1917 publication.

Burrow, T. (1925a). The laboratory method in psychoanalysis: Its inception and development. First presented in September at the Ninth Congress of the International Psycho-Analytical Association. Published in 1926 in the *American Journal of Psychiatry*, 5(3), 345–55. In E.G. Pertegato and G.O. Pertegato, eds., 2013.

Burrow, T. (1925b). The group method of analysis. First presented on 14 November to the Washington Psychoanalytic Society. Published in *The Psychoanalytic Review*, 14(3), 268–80. In E.G. Pertegato and G.O. Pertegato, eds., 2013.

Burrow, T. (1926). Psychoanalysis in theory and in life. *The Journal of Nervous and Mental Disease*, 64, 209–24. In E.G. Pertegato and G.O. Pertegato, eds., 2013.

Burrow, T. (1927). *The social basis of consciousness: A study in organic psychology based upon a synthetic and societal concept of the neuroses*. London: K. Paul, Trench, Trubner & Co.

Compton, A. (1985). The concept of identification in the work of Freud, Ferenczi, and Abraham: A review and commentary. *The Psychoanalytic Quarterly*, 54(2), 200–33.

Drury, N. and Tudor, K. (2022). Trigant Burrow and the social world. *International Journal of Applied Psychoanalytic Studies*, 19(2), 187–201.

Dundes, A. (2005). Introduction. In I. Sadger, *Recollecting Freud*. Madison: University of Wisconsin Press.

Ferenczi, S. (1912). Über die Rolle der Homosexualität in der Pathogenese der Paranoia. *Jahrbuch der Psychoanalyse*, Band III, 101–19. Trans. by E. Jones as "On the part played by homosexuality in the pathogenesis of paranoia". In *First contributions to psychoanalysis. The International Psycho-Analytical Library*, 45, 131–56. Boston: Richard G. Badger, 1916.

Freud, S. (1905). Three essays on the theory of sexuality. In J. Strachey, ed. and trans., *The standard edition of the complete psychological works of Sigmund Freud, 24 vols*. London: Hogarth Press, 1953–1974. 7:125–245.

Freud, S. (1905b). Jokes and their relation to the unconscious. *Standard ed.*, 8:1–274.

Freud, S. (1910). Leonardo da Vinci and a memory of his childhood. *Standard ed.*, 11:59–137.

Freud, S. (1911). Psycho-analytic notes on an autobiographical account of a case of paranoia (dementia paranoides). *Standard ed.*, 12:1–82.

Freud, S. (1912). On the universal tendency to debasement in the sphere of love (Contributions to the psychology of love II). *Standard ed.*, 11:177–90.

Freud, S. (1913). Preface to Bourke's *Scatalogic rites of all nations. Standard ed.*, 12:333–7.
Freud, S. (1914). On narcissism. *Standard ed.*, 14:67–104.
Freud, S. (1915). Instincts and their vicissitudes. *Standard ed.*, 14:109–40.
Freud, S. (1917). Introductory lectures on psycho-analysis (Part III). *Standard ed.*, 16: 241–463.
Freud, S. (1919). 'A child is being beaten': A contribution to the study of the origin of sexual perversions. *Standard ed.*, 17:175–204.
Freud, S. (1920a). Beyond the pleasure principle. *Standard ed.*, 18:1–63.
Freud, S. (1920b). The psychogenesis of a case of homosexuality in a woman. *Standard ed.*, 18:147–72.
Freud, S. (1921). Group psychology and the analysis of the ego. *Standard ed.*, 18:65–143.
Freud, S. (1922). Some neurotic mechanisms in jealousy, paranoia and homosexuality. *Standard ed.*, 18:221–32.
Freud, S. (1923). The ego and the id. *Standard ed.*, 19:1–66.
Freud, S. (1924a). The economic problem of masochism. *Standard ed.*, 19:155–70.
Freud, S. (1924b). The dissolution of the Oedipus complex. *Standard ed.*, 19:173–79.
Freud, S. (1925). An autobiographical study. *Standard ed.*, 20:1–74.
Freud, S. (1926). The question of lay analysis. *Standard ed.*, 20:177–258.
Freud, S. (1930). Civilization and its discontents. *Standard ed.*, 21:57–145.
Freud, S. (1931). Female sexuality. *Standard ed.*, 21:223–43.
Freud, S. (1933). New introductory lectures on psycho-analysis. *Standard ed.*, 22:1–182.
Gay, P. (1988). *Freud: A life for our time.* New York: Norton, 2006.
Jones, E. (1955). *The life and work of Sigmund Freud. Vol 2: The years of maturity 1901–1919.* New York: Basic Books.
Laplanche, J. (1970). *Vie et mort en psychanalyse.* Paris: Flamarrion. Trans. by J. Mehlman as *Life and death in psychoanalysis.* Baltimore: Johns Hopkins University Press, 1990.
Lewes, K. (1988). *The psychoanalytic theory of male homosexuality.* New York: Simon & Schuster.
May, U. (2015). *Freud at work: On the history of psychoanalytic theory and Practice, with an analysis of Freud's patient record books.* Trans. D. Haller, B. Mathes, M. Molnar, P. Slotkin, & D. Winter. London: Routledge, 2018.
Nunberg, H. and Federn, E. (1967). *Minutes of the Vienna Psychoanalytic Society, Volume 2: 1908–1910.* Trans. M. Nunberg. New York: International University Press.
Pertegato, E.G. and Pertegato, G.O. (2013). Introduction. In *From psychoanalysis to group analysis: The pioneering work of Trigant Burrow.* London: Karnac Books.
Sadger, I. (1910). Ein Fall von multipler Perversion mit hysterischen Absenzen. *Jahrbuch für psychoanalytische und psychopathologische Forschungen*, 2, 59–133.
Sadger, I. (1929). *Sigmund Freud: Persönliche Erinnerungen.* Tübingen and Berlin: Diskord, 2006. Trans by J.M. Jacobsen and A. Dundes as *Recollecting Freud.* Madison: University of Wisconsin Press, 2005.
Schultz-Venrath, U. (2015). Die Entdeckung der 'Gruppenmethode in der Psychoanalyse' (1926) von Trigant Burrow – ein verhinderter Paradigmawechsel? *Gruppenpsychotherapie und Gruppendynamik*, 51(1), 7–17.
Zepf, S. and Hartmann, S. (2005). Konzepte der Identifizierung: Versuch ihrer theoretischen und klinischen Differenzierung. *Forum der Psychoanalyse*, 21, 30–42.

Chapter 4

The bisexual dialectic

A close textual reading in the previous two chapters has revealed the presence in Freud's work of an alternate thesis to the well-known Oedipus complex and rivalry thesis. The bisexuality thesis that has been reconstructed presents a subject-centred universal homosexuality, which precedes and then is concurrent with the development of object heterosexuality and socially constructed gender. This is in concord with the dual regimes of non-reproductive and reproductive sexuality at the heart of Freud's sexual theory. The bisexuality thesis was reconstructed from a number of textual sources, especially Freud (1923), Burrow (1914) and Sadger (1910), and described in detail. The bisexuality thesis is premised on a primary form of identification with the self after primary object cathexis, termed homosexual object choice and primary narcissism by Freud, to serve as the nucleus of an id-ego constellation that chronologically predates the advent of the superego. In turn, the superego is produced in response to injunctions ensuing from shame and rivalry, initially focused in a parental cathexis and identification sequence but then extended to broader social relations on the same parental model. This is termed secondary identification. Rivalry in consequence of the Oedipus complex functions to negate or (at minimum) repress much of the primary bisexual character and aims to produce in place of bisexuality a relatively fixed structure of social gender and sexual orientation aligned to biological sex and the reproductive regime. Shame is an additional component of repression and is a precursor to rivalry.

The material in this chapter and in Chapter 5 is a direct development of the reconstructed bisexuality thesis. These two chapters are a free-ranging discussion with a less conventional style of writing, and the novelty of the insights may surprise some readers. The objective in the presentation is ideological neutrality that is free of bias, although such a scientific goal is acknowledged to be inherently qualified and conditional. The starting point and tether for this discussion is the dialectic subject, which is the point where the previous chapter halted. The consequences of Freud's bisexuality thesis together encapsulate and describe the dialectic of the subject and illustrate the potential for an ambisexual polyvocality of desire within each person.

The paradigm of a dialectic subject presented here stands in contrast to theories of the subject predicated on what is commonly described as a split in subjectivity.

DOI: 10.4324/9781003498919-5

The idea of split subjectivity is now widely accepted and dominant; it is attributed in no small degree to Freud's tripartite model of the mental apparatus premised on the unconscious but in recent decades has been especially associated with the work of Lacan and his followers. However, the dialectic of the subject shows it is erroneous to posit a split, either as the normal or the pathological condition of the subject, because the idea of a split assumes that the subject was once something whole and might aspire to or recuperate wholeness again. The word *split* has semantic meaning only in relation to the word or concept of *wholeness*. By contrast, the paradigm of dialectic subjectivity – drawn from the reconstruction of Freud's bisexuality thesis – shows there is no split subject, only a developing subject always emerging from the dialectic. By arresting the dialectic, social and economic forces can produce the impression of a split by restraining and inhibiting the emergent process. The dialectic in the subject is neither avoidable nor pathogenic in itself; rather, the dialectic is the very nature of the primal libidinal force upon which the entire mental apparatus is constructed. The dialectic constitutes the subject in the diachronic and synchronic view. There is no solid subject to start with or at any stage of the dialectic, but the illusion of solidity is created by arresting the dialectic. Pathogenesis in the broadest sense of the word can then be defined as the result of arresting the dialectic, against which the dialectic subject strains, producing symptoms.

The only material form of division that is known by the subject – by virtue of being a physical entity – is the general split of matter into subject and object as (more or less) distinct entities. This is as much a linguistic as a biological reality. The bisexuality thesis with its focus on the early infantile period shows an interesting and important consequence of the subject-object dichotomy. At the start in infancy, the subject and object are separate, but they are identical with each other; this creates a primal unified subject-object that serves as a model or master value to the infant, and which in turn is overwritten and replaced by other master values. The master value is understood as having the features shown in the concept of narcissism (Freud, 1914) and identification (1921, 1923). In this view, it must be clarified that there is only a relational value to the subject: there is no *a priori* standard by which either a unified or split subject can be theorised. Like all value, the subject is always a relational value because there is no solid or concrete starting point. The value of the subject is dynamic and is produced continuously in a process of relations, the perspective termed *relativism*. This has already been explored in Freud's methodology (Introduction, pp. 13–21) and will return to the focus in the next chapter (pp. 134–44). Where the subject is portrayed as fixed (in either a unified or a split state), this is always by virtue of a temporary stasis that is the nomination of one particular value, and nomination is achieved by arresting the dialectic. This is a restatement of Nietzsche's concept of *becoming*, which in turn is a development of the original formulation by Heraclitus (c. 500BCE, p. 53) of flux and change: "One cannot step twice into the same river, nor can one grasp any mortal substance in a stable condition, but it scatters and again gathers; it forms and dissolves, and approaches and departs".

The reconstruction of the bisexuality thesis shows that this thesis and Freud's structural model go hand in hand. A consolidated view of the structural model will make clear that this model is a consequence of the bisexuality thesis. The formation of the ego and superego takes place as identification in consequence of loss and prohibition, respectively. The basic mechanism is clear – object attachment, followed by loss, followed by identification with the lost object. This is how both the ego and superego are produced, and only the differentiated process that produces an ego and a superego requires some discussion. There is no reason to believe the differentiated process does not operate universally (*system*), although there is scope for significant individual variation that in turn produces individualisation (*instances*) within the species. The larger the sample group, the less apparent will be the individual effects as social formations increasingly level differences when they grow in size.

Identification is of two kinds, primary and secondary. Primary identification takes place in the early infantile (*preoedipal*) period, where the infant initially takes itself as object (autoerotism) to produce what can be described as a primal unity. However, this unity is unsustainable under the impinging force of the reality principle, and the inevitable loss of the self as object generates an identification that produces the initial ego kernel. In addition, there is also a mechanism of injunction that is brought to bear on the primal unity, and this then gives rise to the process of secondary identification, which produces the superego. The differentiated sequence of identification and its relation to the structural model are discussed in detail in the following sections. First there is a detailed review of ego formation via primary identification; this is followed by the superego in its secondary identifications.

Primal unity and primary identification

For a full understanding of the structural model, it is essential to remember that the ego and superego are not splits but growths out of the id. They are regions of the id, still connected to and drawing their energy from the id:

> the ego is identical with the id, and is merely a specially differentiated part of it. If we think of this part by itself in contradistinction to the whole, or if a real split has occurred between the two, the weakness of the ego becomes apparent. But if the ego remains bound up with the id and indistinguishable from it, then it displays its strength. The same is true of the relation between the ego and the super-ego. In many situations the two are merged; and as a rule we can only distinguish one from the other when there is a tension or conflict between them.
>
> (Freud, 1926, p. 97)

The original and primal unity of the id suffers injury on two fronts; each injury becomes the site for the subsequent outgrowths, one the ego and one the superego. First there is the component of loss of unity, and then later the aspect of prohibition. These take the form of two dialectic conflicts. The bisexuality thesis draws attention to the temporal sequence of the two injuries, where loss precedes prohibition. The dialectic commences with the first injury: the loss and search for primal unity. Each cycle of loss and rediscovery of the initial self-unity reinforces the nascent ego, fed by the id. This is the libidinal engine of desire. At its simplest, the dialectic is initiated by physical birth and is the expression of a biological desire (or primal *will*) to continue living despite the harsh new extra-uterine reality. Freud refers to the physical break initiated by the child's birth as the caesura (*die Caesur, die Zäsur*) of the act of birth (1926, p. 138), and the word is useful to describe a series of later and similarly momentous interruptions and challenges to the initial self-contained unity. Here the id is clearly seen to underpin primal unity. The earliest stirring into life of the ego is an initial trace – or consciousness – of the lost self-object and diminishing self-unity, culminating in primary identification. This is a momentous breakthrough for the infant. At the same time, the infant has to contend with the parents, who have other designs: imprinting their own desires upon the infant object. It is here that prohibition – in the form of shame and rivalry – enters the field to redirect the child's desire away from itself and towards the parents in the recurring formula that produces secondary identification and the superego.

Primal unity is characterised by the union of object cathexis and identification: to have and to be the same object. The apparent contradiction (Freud, 1921, p. 106) of having and being the same object is resolved in the initial unity of having and being the self. There is only a contradiction later, from the perspective after unity has been lost. At that prelapsarian time, in that unity with the self, the subject and object are identical with each other. The primal loss enters when the unity cannot be maintained. Even before the advent of parental intervention through shame and rivalry, the primal unity is impossible to maintain after birth because there are stoppages in the flows of nutrition and care. These stoppages have the effect of interrupting the pleasure that is the aim and expression of primal unity. Each interruption impinges on the unity and pleasure, breaking down the harmony of being and having the same object. *To be* and *to have* become discrete verbs. Being comes to stand for a state of not having. We are because we do not have. To have, or more precisely *not to have*, then precedes being. *Non habeo ergo sum*. I do not have, therefore I am.

This first conflict has philosophical, psychological and economic dimensions. The conflict arises from desiring to be and to have the same object, the self. Need interrupts the primal unity of self because it introduces the sequence of loss, exteriority and the exterior object. The conflict between being and having is produced by the real exteriority of objects of nutrition and care. This exteriority is effectively the first economy and underlines the essential continuity in the duality of production and consumption that Marx (1857) eloquently points out, starting with the example of humans producing their bodies by the consumption of nutrition:

> Consumption is directly also production, just as in nature consumption of elements and chemical substances is production of a plant. It is obvious that man produces his own body, e.g., through nutrition, a form of consumption. But the same applies to any other kind of consumption which in one way or another produces man in some aspect.
>
> (p. 28)

This dualistic continuity is a concept that inescapably underlies all economic theory, but it is useful here to illustrate the rupture of the initial economy of the infant after birth in the primal state. The object of food must be destroyed if it is to become nutrition. Having becomes being. In this practical sense, the subject is objectless because the subject must necessarily destroy the object of food. Having the object can only be of temporary duration if being is to be sustained. The infant subject must destroy the external object by ingestion in order to sustain the self-object, but the sustenance is always only of temporary duration. The presence and absence of the object – food, the breast, care – is the earliest form of the experience that is later articulated in the fort-da game (Freud, 1920), which rehearses and works through the loss of unity. This cycle lays down the structure and pattern of both the survival and sexual drives. The object is thus present until it is destroyed or lost. Having also destroys being – because simply having the object without the becoming that the consumption of the object allows will gradually destroy being. This highlights again the circularity of economy. The cycle of presence and absence is predicated on primal unity, remembered and sought again each time the memory of unity prompts the awareness of loss. External objects can never restore the primal unity in a practical sense because there is no material way for the unity to be restored permanently. Food runs out and has to be replenished; care comes and goes, is present and then lost.

These early years of the infant's life replicate the initial caesura of birth, where the intrauterine state – a proper unity of production and consumption – is replaced with the reality of discrete sites of production and consumption. The disconnected sites (e.g. the child and its nourishment) are initially bridged by the caregiver, but increasingly the subject will be called upon to reproduce the unity of production and consumption by its own labour if it is to survive. All subsequent objects are therefore surrogates for the first object of unity, but it is important to remember that the object in a psychological and a philosophical sense is always an illusion. In both these senses, the subject is always objectless, throughout its life and not only as an infant, because the object is as elusive as it is an illusion. However, for practical reasons of self-preservation, being demands a material object. The external object is always a surrogate for the original unity: "a search for some pleasure which has already been experienced and is now remembered" (Freud, 1905, p. 181). Analogous to physical nutrition, which creates and sustains the body, identification is the mechanism on the level of the mental system to replace having with being in the subsequent development, first of the ego and then later of the superego.

Secondary identification: shame and rivalry

The initial kernel ego is thus produced by the impinging reality of the postnatal externality of objects of care. While the infant cannot control the objects of care, to a large degree this early ego retains a significant physical object in the infant's own body. This is one object that does not withdraw, and it becomes a primary object and the area of pleasure, both libidinal pleasure and the pleasure associated with satisfaction of survival needs. Here pleasure can be mastered and maintained through autoerotism. This is a unity with the self that corresponds to Freud's concept of the polymorphous (1905), later called primary narcissism and infantile narcissism (1914), which corresponds to primary identification as traced so far in the discussion. Freud recognises that there is a circularity to this identification, as the attitude of the parents to the child "is a revival and reproduction of their own narcissism" (1914, p. 91), creating an inter-generational cycle of parental identification in which the child is expected to exchange or substitute its primary identification with the secondary identification that is the superego (pp. 94–5). In the internalisation of parental identification, "a child's super-ego is in fact constructed on the model ... of its parents' super-ego" so that the contents of the super-ego are the same across generations, and the superego as a master value "becomes the vehicle of tradition and of all the time-resisting judgements of value which have propagated themselves in this manner from generation to generation" (1933, p. 67).

There is a circularity here that unsettles many commentators, and perhaps understandably so because it presents a chicken-and-egg quandary: which comes first, the child or the parent. A good example of this disquiet is the disorientation of infinite regression expressed by Deleuze and Guattari (1972): "the father must have been a child, but was able to be a child only in relation to a father, who was himself a child, in relation to another father" (p. 273). Apart from the limitations to their analysis of considering only the simple form of the Oedipus complex and from the perspective of the male, their regression delirium traps their view in a system with no apparent exteriority, which they describe in their extravagant metaphors as follows: "There are no desiring-machines that exist outside the social machines that they form on a large scale; and no social machines without the desiring-machines that inhabit them on a small scale" (p. 340). The quandary becomes less threatening, however, when viewed from the perspective of relativism opened up by the bisexuality thesis. No doubt a circular element is unavoidable later on, especially given the inescapable biological circularity of sexual reproduction, but the solution I am proposing is the element of primal unity and primary identification vested in the infant-child that provides a starting point of sorts in the subject's mental formation, and entirely precedes secondary identification with the parents. Primary identification is a brief tabula rasa out of which the child's ego emerges to write the opening lines of the narrative. Despite the later trials the ego must face, of which to be sure there are many, primary identification endows the ego with some degree of agency that allows a running start. Not least of these later trials is the secondary identification forced on the infant by shame and rivalry. Nevertheless, the bisexuality thesis holds out the possibility of an alternative to rivalry.

For the child, its prototype self-as-object – the body of the self in all its permutations of autoerotism – is transformed into primary identification, which in turn is augmented by surrogate objects: the breast, the mother, the world. These objects represent a vigorous attempt to recover the state of early primal unity. This is the start of the period of secondary identification, or secondary narcissism as Freud terms it (1914). Secondary identification persists for the remainder of the individual human life and is characterised by surrogate objects. Shame and rivalry aim to make the self-as-object in the child unsuitable and embargoed for the child, and to force the child to become and remain the surrogate object available to the parental subject. The primary identification of the child subject, vested in itself as the first object, is assailed increasingly by forces from outside as well as the demands of its own instincts and will for satisfaction. These external assaults are cumulatively comprehensible as the advent of morality in the popular sense, but this is nothing more and nothing less than the restriction of the child's identification by other subjects. Following the injurious primary caesura introduced by physical reality, there is a second injury to the infant's self-unity. This injury is the consequence of the psychological reality of the parents in the form of shame and rivalry as the specific modalities of injunction. The discussion of the introduction of injunction examines the two steps that injunction follows: first shame then rivalry. This heralds the formation of the superego.

The reconstruction of the bisexuality thesis shows that the ego's formation in primary identification gives it a homosexual quality, especially observable in the early primal period. This homosexual side of bisexuality is universally repressed into the unconscious, first by shame and then later by the rivalry of the Oedipus complex (especially under the influence of puberty) to enhance only the heterosexual side of the bisexual potentiality. The shame and rivalry modification is the formation of the superego, which is based on the secondary identification that is championed by the parental instance. However, the bisexuality thesis suggests there are also potentially some aspects of secondary identification that are informed directly by primary identification, independently of the parental instance. These would be aspects of primary identification that escape shame and rivalry, and presumably allow for the development of manifest rather than repressed homosexuality. To say the ego – or subject – has a primary homosexual quality would imply that all subjects are initially valued by the ego – as subjects and objects – via the measure of equivalence or non-equivalence on the basis of the ego's psychological reality founded on an internal unity. Conflict (intra and inter ego) thus enters the picture forced by the imperative that some external and secondary value (parental, superego) should be the basis for reality. The extent to which each individual negotiates this conflict (i.e. accedes to the external demands or diverges from them) is the degree of individuation, and potentially individual freedom. For most people, there is a stasis with repression of the homosexual quality; this stasis precludes the fullness of the bisexual potential. This perspective opens the door to looking at repression as a force that must be undone in the clinical situation, which will be the focus of the next chapter.

Shame

The true initiation of secondary identification thus takes place when the child's pleasurable primal connection with its own body is inhibited and prohibited. The early confusion of the common zones is set straight by the fixed separation of the functions, which is harshly trained by the caregiver and internalised by the child. This is no small accomplishment. Firstly, the caregiver plays an ambivalent role, now initiating, then disapproving of the pleasure. Secondly, a distinction must be established for the child between the ingestion-excretion functions of the mouth-anus-penis/clitoris-vagina series and the general and undifferentiated pleasure function these zones incite and provide. The result is an ambivalent gradation of pleasure, with some alimentary pleasure permitted (feeding) and some prohibited (pleasure from excretion and controlling these flows, masturbation), and a further line is drawn at tactile self-stimulation, even in otherwise permissible zones. In addition to arresting the pleasures of autoerotism, the prohibition also differentiates and segregates feeding from excretion and excretion from sexual activity. All this further confounds the initial, pleasurable intermingling of the zones and the experience of the body as object. The result is a blanket association of shame and disgust extending to all the common zones of feeding/excretion/sexual pleasure, and hence to all infantile sexual activity: "through a long series of generations the genitals have become for us the *pudenda*, objects of shame, and even (as a result of further successful sexual repressions) of disgust" (Freud, 1910, p. 96). An older German expression for the genitals is exactly *die Schamteile* or *der Schambereich* – literally the shame parts or zone. This Germanic form still circulates in the *schaamdelen/ skaamdele* of Dutch/Afrikaans with the equivalent *les parties honteuses* in French. Shame (*die Scham*) is derived from Proto-Germanic *skamo* (Kroonen, 2013, pp. 440–1), in turn possibly derived from the Proto-Indo-European *kau* = shame or *k̂em* = to cover (Pokorny, 1959, pp. 535, 555). A major mythological manifestation of this morality in Western discourse is the covering of their genitals out of shame by Adam and Eve in the Book of Genesis and their subsequent expulsion from Paradise, where "Paradise itself is no more than the group phantasy of the childhood of the individual" before shame (Freud, 1900, p. 245). Based on Freud's work, a provisional definition of shame was suggested in Chapter 2 as follows: the devaluation and inhibition of infantile narcissism and pleasure (p. 71), but further precision about shame is called for because the nature of shame has caused much debate and confusion.

In the very substantial literature on the topic (Scheler, 1913; Sartre, 1943; Hazard, 1969; Lewis, H.B., 1971; Wurmser, 1981; Nathanson, 1987, 1992; Morrison 1989, 1996; Lewis, M., 1992; Tangney & Fischer, 1995; Lansky & Morrison, 1997; Kühn et al., 1997; Gilbert & Andrews, 1998; Metcalf, 2000; Westerink, 2005; Maibom, 2010; Dearing & Tangney, 2011; Hilgers, 2013; Werden, 2015; Zahavi, 2015), shame is generally characterised as an affect or emotion, but this says very little and describes rather than analyses the phenomenon of shame. More recently, shame linked to the enforcement of morality has also increasingly come to be regarded in an affirmative light (Tangney & Dearing, 2002; Calhoun, 2004; Nussbaum, 2004; Vanderheiden & Mayer, 2017; Thomason, 2018; Samnotra, 2020; Flanagan, 2021). Barnard-Naude (2021) is a leading example of the rehabilitation of shame as the foundation for morality, based on an intractable and incoherent misreading of Freud adopted via Lacan's hazy and erroneous subdivision of the superego into ever more parts. This moralistic view recycles the revisionist de-radicalised psychoanalysis and uses it to valorise and endorse the agency of the superego at the expense of the ego, thereby refurbishing Lacan's intrinsic conservatism with a fresh coat of magisterium authority and virtue signalling. The pathologising of the ego via shame that is unconsciously demonstrated by such work (e.g. Barnard-Naude, 2021, pp. 16, 20) is exactly the power of injunction in the formation and ascendancy of the superego.

While such moralising serves to confirm my view that shame is the devaluation of the ego, it is now possible in the light of the bisexuality thesis to define shame more accurately as the *symptom* of injunction. The mechanism of injunction works to prohibit self-identification, and then forces identification with the parents instead, in an internalising by the infant of the parental instance. This is tightly connected to shame, which injunction produces as a symptom. The question of pathologising the ego deserves much more detailed consideration. It is obvious that shame is a form of injunction, but the nature of the injunction is interesting. Shame is produced by a type of injunction relating specifically to self-desire. That this self-desire is so worthy of injunction in turn shows it to be a special form of desire. Self-desire is nothing less than *the primal and original expression of incest*. This makes the inhibition and repression of primal unity the initial instance of the incest taboo and relocates the agency of the incest taboo all the way back to the earliest shame mechanism in infancy. It both simplifies and complicates the picture. Put simply, shame in the infantile period operates as an incest taboo in the simplest definition as the prohibition of a primary cathexis with the self as object (self-kinship). There is an obvious and self-evident structural parallel with the more easily recognisable later instances of the incest taboo: a prohibition directed towards expressions of cathexis with the parents (in secondary identification). The parallel confirms the point made in Chapter 2 (p. 81) that the institution of the incest taboo must extend also to incestuous homosexual relations for the taboo to be universal. Now it is important to extend this insight far enough back to the very genesis of the primary, homosexual side of desire in the preoedipal phase. The implications for this early period are as follows. The insight that the prohibition of self-desire is structurally a form of incest taboo – a self-incest taboo, or *subject as object taboo* – clears up the picture of this early period of prohibition by linking shame not only to the shameful body parts but also to the infant's body as a whole, and consequently to the infant's emerging ego, which is formed as the residue of the attachment to the self as object. In addition, this new insight has the potential to explain the specific role of shame in the broader incest taboo that seems to prohibit more strongly the homosexual side of bisexual desire, i.e. the desire of the self, or what Freud calls narcissistic desire. Whereas social convention later partially releases the reproductive sexual function from shame to produce heterosexuality, the same courtesy is not extended to homosexual desire. Judith Butler mistakenly calls this ongoing restraint of homosexuality a homosexual taboo (1990, p. 86), but the taboo against homosexuality is not separate from the broader incest taboo; it simply operates in this specific way by applying first to the self as its own object and from there to other similar bodies as sexual objects. An association is created of the initial incest taboo of the self as object to all homosexual (i.e. similar or same-sex) objects. This early form of the incest taboo also explains the strength of the repression of the adult homosexual (and hence bisexual) component of desire. The early time of its introduction plus the intensity and physical proximity of the taboo applied against the infant's body itself will combine with the shame of the taboo mechanism to form an impenetrable barrier that persists for life. Homosexuality is repressed into the unconscious, below this barrier, and for most people this is where it will remain. Although it still plays an important individual and social role unconsciously, it can now be described as *unconscious homosexuality*. More will be said about repressed and unconscious homosexuality in the next chapter.

The complexity of the view now is the way in which this early form of the incest taboo as a subject taboo is extended to the object in the later phases, especially the heterosexual object. In effect, the later general incest taboo is building on the already strong basis of this subject taboo. The subject taboo illustrates the double function of any taboo – not only the negation of one set of actions (homosexuality, incest) but also the affirmation of other actions (exogamous and exclusive heterosexuality, procreation). There is thus the *double nature of prohibition* at work in the formation of the superego. This early self-incest taboo or subject-incest taboo is a significant breakthrough in understanding how shame functions. It lends support to and expands the model of injunction. The historical discourse around the prohibition and punishment of masturbation is a powerful example of the subject-incest taboo at work, and masturbation in both its infantile and adult forms offers an interesting line of prospective enquiry in light of the bisexuality thesis.

In considering shame as the symptom of prohibition, a group of related symptoms emerges that includes disgust, guilt, fear and anxiety. Attempts have been made in the literature to distinguish between these elements along the developmental and chronological lines of an individual subject or an entire culture. If development is indeed the focus, then this can only proceed from fear to guilt and shame. Fear is the most primitive tool aroused by the deployment of unmasked violence to enforce injunctions. Guilt and shame are a response to more strategic and less violent means, if teleology or development is to be invoked. An alternate view, commencing with Thomas Hobbes (1651) and reiterated most recently by Foucault (1975–76), holds that violence is inherent in and underlies all social formations.

The literature also frequently suggests that distinctions between these symptoms – shame, disgust, guilt, fear, anxiety – follow the dichotomy of internal and external, but this is false, as is the idea of an internalised versus an external agency that the developmental argument suggests. All of these symptomatic responses to injunction are produced internally in proportion to the external force applied. This external force can range from brute physical harm to more coercive forms of violence, such as threats, the withholding of resources and affection, and even expulsion from the social body, which is a permanent stoppage of resources. On this point there can be no doubt: the initial injunction always comes from outside, although this force may co-opt or exploit internal needs such as hunger, vulnerability and desire. Through repetition, these external forces and agents become internalised in the superego; they leave a memory trace along a very basic axis of cause and effect. Such internalisation applies to all these symptomatic responses. Fear is no less internalised than guilt and shame. Fear produced as a mechanism of prohibition may need more frequent reinforcement, but this is not very different to guilt and shame, which also require life-long reminders. Only the smallest use of intoxicating substances (e.g. alcohol) will quickly stifle inhibition and propel the uninhibited search for pleasure to the surface in its stead. Injunction is not set in place once and permanently in the developing infant and then left to operate smoothly for life – it requires mechanisms of reward and punishment to be perpetuated in renewal, and even so injunction will break down and fade as dementia sets in at old age or when other forms of mental erosion occur, such as trauma, which is the result of extreme force on the mind and the body, and anxiety, an overwhelming and debilitating state of chronic fear, guilt and shame. This is to understand the symptoms of trauma and anxiety as a barometer for *too much force*, but it should be evident that all force is too much force, whether physical or mental, especially in the case of the child, who is essentially still defenceless and inexperienced in wielding force itself, which is why the subjugation occurs early on in the life of the child.

No obvious alternatives to shame present themselves, though surely there must be a better way of making and transmitting culture and society than through physical and mental violence. So-called progressive consensus does not offer a ready alternative; it merely advocates for the replacement of physical violence with the mental form, which is no less effective at producing fear, guilt and shame, and no less traumatic or anxiety inducing. An alternative is therefore a crucial question, not only for the individual developmental path but also for the species. What is the optimal mechanism for obtaining consent and cooperation, to the extent that these are necessary for the welfare of the child and, by extension, the social group (in the form, for example, of government)? In my own view, the social group should be resisted and accorded a far more limited and mutually cooperative role, although of course social formations are tightly linked to the material economic forms of society, by design. In practice, there are only a few examples of a cooperative form of social group that come to mind, such as the peer-based non-competitive collaboration of the Scout Movement and supported self-construction of children in the Montessori Method. Both practices emphasise the centrality of the individual in determining his or her own development, with support rather than injunction from outside. This correlates with the absence of rivalry in bisexuality and shows non-rivalry as a potential revolutionary act, echoing the aspirations of liberty, equality and fraternity crystallised by the French Revolution. There is also the more recent example of *Pride*: a concept and form of action pioneered by the gay and lesbian movement of the late 20th century as a mechanism to offset and diminish shame. Even as Pride and Christopher Street Day events have grown in profile and scale and have morphed into an overwhelmingly commercial festivity, the historical consequences of this intervention for the emancipation of desire cannot be underestimated today, although it is also important to remember that Pride has at its foundation an action (or at least the threat) of violent resistance to injunction. This is also in keeping with the structure of any revolution: the triad of liberty, equality and fraternity are seldom handed out willingly by tyrants.

There is one further component to the shame-guilt-fear-anxiety composite that has not yet been considered; it came to the fore in the last decades of the 20th century and is now almost predominant in many societies and cultures, especially in rich countries: *emotional neglect*. A useful synonym for this neglect is *alienation*. More and more children are raised by the induction of a generalised and impersonal injunction (via schools, media, peers) premised on parental neglect, rather than fear, shame and guilt. Neglect of course also results in anxiety. In addition, neglect produces a vacuum where previously secondary identification with the immediate biological parents and family held direct sway, and this vacuum is quickly filled by a wide range of political and economic agents in the broader social forms of parental identification that exist beyond the traditional parental and family paradigm. The close family and clan context previously characterised human evolution, so the implications of its dissolution for the future of the species are of great interest.

Emotional neglect and alienation as features of late modernity are clearly linked to and accelerated by the advent of electronic media. Widespread social and economic penetration by radio and television in the second half of the 20th century was merely the advance guard for the internet today. This is an interesting thought, one that has much potential for explaining the current form of secondary identification which is so heavily inflected by alienation. To state the obvious: neglect (i.e. abdication by the immediate parental instance) in combination with the disembodied and distanced agency of electronic media produces a stunted individual who is deprived of the fuller range of human expression, relations and development that comes from being raised in close nurturing groups. This is comparable to the way a shallow learning of language produces a stunted or deprived form of expression lacking in range and confidence.

It seems contradictory here to privilege family and parental care even though they are the direct channel for the transmission of parental identification. In principle, however, parental identification is not altered by these impersonal electronic and non-familial means of transmission, merely displaced to profit-making corporations or populist leaders and reduced in individual nuance and complexity. The child in such an environment of emotional neglect misses out on the physical proximity and intimacy inherent to nurturing, which is a necessary human phenomenon seen from the perspective of evolution. Physical proximity and care are also essential ingredients in the development of primal unity and the formation of non-rival relationships predicted by the bisexuality thesis, as much with parents as with other adults and with peers. This situation in late modernity is not very different, however, to the vast majority of people living in pre-modern and early modern social formations, where deprivation of physical and emotional care is characteristic outside of small aristocratic elites and the middle classes, for a number of socio-economic reasons and producing a range of differentiated outcomes. It is tempting then to investigate the degree to which the ego and superego are formations that emerge in and are characterised by class and culture.

Such speculation moves into the territory of making value judgements, and about something that is ultimately impossible to value objectively, which prompts only questions: Is this or that individual expression richer or poorer? Is Leonardo da Vinci's creative expression, to take a random example, better than video games or social media? Did Da Vinci's creativity give him any more pleasure than video and social role-playing games stimulate now for their consumers? Freud's focus in general on pleasure is drawn from observations of empirical reality, in which pleasure and unpleasure have a fundamental and dialectical role in the organisation of behaviour. Is pleasure in its quantitative consumption even a compelling measure of value compared to the qualitative matter of productive expression (creativity, originality, complexity).

It is worth noting that the act of selecting one value above others in human society is the act of nomination. Each measure of value is a form of nomination. In line with the dialectic principle outlined so far, all social and economic nomination is therefore reducible or traceable to two master values: the self-signifier of primary identification and the injunction performed by parental identification, which in turn is simply an aggregated system of social values. In liberal democracies, discussion of social value is often reduced to arguments for or against diversity based on the nominations of personal taste, especially since the discussion takes place in the omelette of mass socialisation, where there is no objective way to identify a true and unique individual subject, or to distinguish such a subject from the uniform scar tissue of shame and mass-induced learned responses to injunction. Nevertheless, the idea of diversity is a serviceable index at present for dialectic movement and resistance to static nomination in tolerant societies. In most other jurisdictions around the world, there is little or no room at all for accommodating individual diversity as a qualitative measure of value in even this very modest manner.

From an ideal perspective, value judgements made in a system of values should ultimately reflect an emancipatory aesthetic: the creative aesthetic of the dialectic. This is an aesthetic based on the ongoing synthesis of becoming and resistance to the restraint of stasis. While this would be an interesting point to develop, it is ultimately circular, leading as much to individual pleasure as to the conventions (e.g. tolerance) necessary for any form of fluid social or species being. Ultimately, creativity and the dialectic stand in conflict with the stasis of injunction, which is an act of nomination that suspends the dialectic. The injunction says that the subject must be or must have only certain objects, and so the conflicts of secondary identification arise in response to the shame-rivalry nexus. Injunction and the conflict it produces are thus always relative, reactionary and productive of the injunction itself. Primary identification, as impossible and hallucinatory as it is, precedes injunction, and the injunction sets out to break the primary identification residue of being and having the same object. The dialectic is thus set in motion. Whereas injunction should ideally be nothing more than the bearer of a basic and honest reality principle, injunction in the parental system of shame and rivalry forces its own impossible and hallucinatory identification with the parent onto the child. This restricts the dialectic to a much more limited (and unequal) battle between ego and superego.

Rivalry

In the Oedipus complex, the mechanism of rivalry is used to solidify socially constructed gender as a psychological reality. Furthermore, this new social representation of biological sex is fixed on the genitals through their partial release from shame, and this release is accomplished via the concomitant introduction of rivalry. Castration in its double armature of genital anxiety and envy is often presented as the crux of the Oedipus complex, but this is wrong. Castration anxiety and penis envy are just symptoms of the component of rivalry taking over from shame. The symptoms of genital anxiety and envy occur after the child becomes aware of the difference of biological sex. Where shame was generalised before this awareness, the concerns around castration are a new sub-division of shame into specific components and anatomical areas on the basis of biological sex. When considering castration, it is important to emphasise the following points. Anxiety and envy around castration are a specific manifestation of rivalry linked to biological sex. Although it comes later, and follows on from the generalised shame of the infantile period that is not implicitly linked to biological sex, castration builds on this already existing foundation of shame to stimulate the rivalry of the Oedipus complex. In a concrete manner, castration anxiety and penis envy are the ways the empirical reality of biological sex is constructed and fixed as gender in psychological reality; biological sex is re-created and represented in a psychological and social construct. In contrast to biological sex, the definition of social sex is thus the socially constructed nodal point in an individual that lies somewhere on an axis of resolution between subject and object identification. This definition shifts the focus to where it should be: the construction process itself and the compromise produced between identifications of subject and object; the preoedipal and oedipal; the individual and society. The outcome will be the degree to which an individual accepts the stereotypical identifications thrust on it by society.

In a broader perspective, rivalry ensures a divide and conquer approach where boys are differentiated and split off from girls. Girls are prepared for a lifetime of object status, with the promise of a baby to serve as the focus for their depreciated identification. Boys can be more problematic. Not only are they often physically stronger and more recalcitrant to shame; they are also typically brought up with more indulgence by their parents in anticipation of their future preferential status. However, the net result of rivalry with the parent is that the wills of both boys and girls are broken. Firstly, there is the manifest rivalry of parental identification which asserts itself over all objects. For the child, the rivalry of the Oedipus complex is the rivalry of seeking its own subjectivity beyond primary identification by seeking an external object. While rivalry is instrumentalised by the parent, the child's engagement on such unequal terms produces the inevitable and preordained loss of this battle to the parental will – the parent always wins simply because the child does not have the physical and mental resources for anything approaching an even competition. From the perspective of the complete Oedipus complex, it is immaterial that a male child should desire the mother (positive) or the father (negative), and equally immaterial that a female child should struggle to negotiate her desire for the competing wills of the mother or the father. The essential outcome of the rivalry of the Oedipus complex is that the child of either sex is forced to concede the subject position to the parent. This outcome produces the child as an object that confirms and affirms the identification and subjectivity of the parents. In consequence, the child adopts the fixed roles accorded to it in the form of gender and sexual orientation. Some children may experience greater difficulty in this process, due to the relative strength of their primary identification. Furthermore, there is some potential for the child to find a non-rival bond with the parent, as Freud's bisexuality thesis suggests.

A second aspect of rivalry is that competition and rivalry are introduced between children to break the potential for rebellion. Rivalry finds its expression in the competition for parental favour, but also in the ritualised rivalry and concomitant libidinal sublimation in education, sport and other structures of economic status, and finally the solidification of all these social dimensions into nation, class and race. The symptomatic aggressiveness of the child whose will is being restrained and broken cannot be underestimated, and this active expression of its expansive will is the focus of the parental breaking of the will by yoking and channelling it into forms that minimise the threat to the parent and maximise productivity in the political economy later as adults. This continues for life in the extraction of labour, which is nothing but directed activity – a form of active passivity standing in contrast to direct action. The reward over time: a gradual promotion from object to subject, a drip feed of pleasure, in exchange for loyalty and labour rendered.

The Oedipus complex consolidates not only activity and passivity but all three polarities in a manner that solidifies them and thereby restricts their inherent dialectic potential as continuums. The most egregious consolidations take place as the continuum of active and passive is frozen into the social stereotypes that are gender. In the process, subject and object are also consolidated, with the parental position privileged as the central subject. This commonly takes the form of the father, with the mother and children as objects of his little empire, although even here, the mother has an intermediary status as primary caregiver and representative of the parental will. In addition, promises are made (of future ascendancy for boys and future babies for girls) in exchange for present obedience and objectification. This underpins the aggregation and formation into a hierarchy of competing wills – which can be understood as the definition for society. A pool of terms is created by a process of aggregation, where degrees of subjectivity are incrementally accessed, like progressive levels in a video game, in exchange for cementation in the hierarchies of the controlling parental will. Not only does this lay down the pattern for the diachronic reproduction of the familial empire into the future; it also embodies on a micro scale the macro pattern of the synchronic heterosexual empires of men and their forces of social reproduction. This structure is described as a hierarchy, and this may be the manifest form in many instances, starting with the nuclear family, but in effect it is a grand alliance of ever-greater agglomerations of rival wills. Each parental will is a subject with its circle of objects, and in turn this subject owes allegiance as object to a greater subject's will: circles or spheres of power by secondary identification overlap into fabrics of ever-greater empires, all standing in relation to the overriding parental identification.

Over the millennia of human history, the biggest loser in this struggle of wills has been the female – she is stripped of almost all subjectivity, pleasure and activity. In exchange, she is given initial mastery over any child she produces, her own small but domestic empire of identification as compensation, though this unequal exchange entails a vast sacrifice of her labour not only in service of the child's needs but more importantly those of the child's father. That she should accept this obviously poor exchange for the far greater value of her own subjectivity is testimony to the power of the shame and rivalry mechanisms at work in the social construction of gender. The male emerges better off, with a promissory note for a portion of his own future subjectivity in exchange for present submission as object to the parental will. This bond is not worth the paper it is written on, for he has acceded to a lifetime of submission in exchange for the scraps of pleasure the superego will brush in his direction. It is a mystery that anyone would agree to this obviously rotten deal, which of course is why it must be fixed in place while the child is still young and defenceless. In practice there is slippage in the process of solidification. Some women demand equality with men, and over the last hundred years they have been given the same empty promissory note for future subjectivity as their brothers receive. In practice this is a shift in weave of the empire fabric, with others – domestic workers, nannies, cleaners, teachers, carers for the aged – forced to shoulder the burden relinquished by the emancipated woman. The circles remain the same. Women and men never demand an end to this system of differentiation between women and men, simply a reapportionment of the scraps. The same applies *mutatis mutandis* for the working class and the colonised, and for all the other object classes within ideologies (nation, race, class, creed) that are visible manifestations of the graded rivalry of the Oedipus complex. Every person is located in a force field of relations to all others, and the field is structured in gradations along the three axes of subject and object, activity and passivity, pleasure and unpleasure. The question then is the degree to which these relations are pre-determined and static or negotiated and dynamic.

From individual to society and economy

To summarise the discussion so far: the formation of the individual's ego and superego takes place as identification in consequence of loss and prohibition, respectively. The differentiated mechanism is clear. If there were only loss or only prohibition, the outcome would be only an ego or a superego, respectively. Hence it is possible to describe a ratio of loss to prohibition, since the situation is never pure loss or pure injunction. This line of thought throws light on the development of each individual and also the development of social groups. The idea of a ratio allows for understanding the wide spectrum of different outcomes that is encountered in the human species. The identifications in consequence of loss and prohibition have certain common elements. The most universal of these is the relation to the preceding state of primal unity. The destruction of this unity – first by primal loss of the self as object and later by the prohibition that seeks to determine the typology of surrogate objects permitted in place of the original unity – produces a universal scenario. This scenario has been characterised as the incest taboo, although even this universal scenario will be embossed by local cultural and personal factors.

The ratio of loss to prohibition is not static. In a broad development, loss of the initial unity will predominate at the start but then will be outweighed over time by the growing number of injunctions. The mechanisms of loss and injunction are the engine of both desire and the dialectic. Desire, first and foremost, is a relationship to an object, if for no other reason than the semiotic argument that the subject and object exist in a mutual relationship of signification. There can be no desire – and hence no subject – without an object. The object need not be real in an empirical sense, and most often it is not; it is an illusion projected by the desiring subject, but even as an illusion the object exists and must exist to produce desire.

The basic structure of desire is outlined in Plato's *Symposium* and serves as the implicit foundation for the reworking of the concept in Freud's understanding of libido. This deflates the ambition of Deleuze and Guattari (1972, p. 25) to put forward a different model to the Platonic logic of desire, because they still fundamentally rely on Freud's Oedipus theory. Similarly, Lacan's conception of desire revolves around the phallic object and does not go outside the Oedipal period and rivalry. Both projects are limited by their focus on the Oedipus complex and neither considers the possibility of the alternatives opened up by Freud's bisexuality thesis. The question of why one object is desired and not another also implodes the reckless contemporary view (e.g. Garcia, 2010) that there is no difference between objects. Such provocation is a tedious reaction to convention and is just another *jeu* (game, jest) in the French philosophical and psychoanalytic tradition.

There is a single law of desire: we only desire that which we do not have. All desire comes down to this simple statement. Famously, it originates in the *Symposium* in the following formulation:

> Then this man and everyone who feels desire, desires what is not in his possession or presence, so that what he does not have, or what he is not, or what he lacks, these are the sorts of things that are the objects of desire and love.
>
> (pp. 35–6)

There are two parts to this law: desire is of some thing – some object – and the object is some thing that is lacked. Desire by definition must have its object. This leads directly to the question: Why one object and not another? Why this object and not that? This in turn indicates two types of desire, along the same lines as Freud's bifurcation – need and pleasure. Need is defined more precisely as the survival needs, which is not to suggest that pleasure is gratuitous. The role of pleasure shows clearly that it is just as much a need as food and water. The distinction becomes one of degrees. For real hunger, any form of food will suffice, whereas pleasure is far harder to pin down, beyond a broad characterisation of the libido. This bifurcation of desire does not say anything about the object though, only about the subject. Leave aside the survival needs for the moment, which are universal and serve only as an analogy for the pleasure needs, and the following reformulation of the law in line with the bisexuality thesis functions as a proposition: we only desire that which we do not have, and we do not have it because it is lost or prohibited.

In the simplest form, desire is for some object (real or imagined) that the subject does not currently have. This object is a lack in the sense of an absence. The analogy to nourishment: hunger and thirst are instinctual symptoms of the absence of food and water. For reasons that fascinate, these symptoms of absence may be transferred and attached to other situations where the subject experiences the absence of an object, and so one object – more easily obtainable – may be substituted for another that is desired but less available. This is reflected in Freud's idea of displacement, and also in transference, in the psychoanalytic model of clinical treatment. These manifest variations may disguise but do not alter the underlying mechanism. In contrast to the self-preservation instinct, the manifest and latent forms of desire in the sexual drive (to use Freud's libido as the trope for pleasure) become even more complex, given the intricate and bifurcated character generally of human sexuality and its position in human culture.

What then is the source of sexual desire? It cannot flow from the object, for otherwise there would be only the simplest sexual reproductive contact, merely functioning to produce the next generation. Despite all efforts by ideological formations to reduce sexuality to biological reproduction, this has never been entirely successful or permanent. These self-appointed guardians of the reproductive regime – religions, political interests, social structures, economic forces – are deeply invested in sublimating or repressing the libido, and they play a major role in redirecting and channelling human desire. Such obviously ideological endeavours to channel sexual desire point to one of the two mechanisms driving the selection of one object over another. Some object (or sometimes a sexual aim attached to an object) is prohibited and therefore the object is desired. In turn, this desire is redirected to permitted objects. However, even as the productive force of prohibition is acknowledged to play a mechanical role in this manner, prohibition must come *after* desire and not before. There is no reason to prohibit something that does not already exist. So while prohibition plays a role in the selection of one object over another, it does not account for the original nature of desire itself.

The chronologically earlier mechanism driving the selection of the object gives a clearer understanding of desire. Preceding the injunction, desire is a symptom of *loss*. It is important to emphasise here that loss is different to the Lacanian concept of lack. Without diminishing hunger's physiological triggers, the hunger for food is based on a previous state of satiation, and in this way desire is a response to the loss of an object that previously was possessed so that there was no desire – only pleasure. We need to have lost something to desire it, or it needs to be prohibited, which is a specific kind of loss.

This arranges desire and pleasure in a dialectic relation, so much so that the one can be defined as the absence of the other: desire is the absence of pleasure, pleasure is the absence of desire. If desire itself is experienced as pleasure, this is because of the anticipation of pleasure that pervades desire, bringing to mind the German expression: *Vorfreude ist die schönste Freude* (there's no pleasure like anticipation). Similarly, if pleasure retains an element of desire, this is due exactly to the temporal dimension of desire that Plato identifies: the desire to remain in possession of the object in the future (p. 35). There is a further question, about the attainability of the object: Can desire find satisfaction? This, however, reflects a static understanding of desire, which the dialectic view seeks to undo; it is not so much the attainment of the object but the desire itself which is the focus of the dialectic, and attainment can be best described as a momentary and always fleeting stasis in the dialectic.

It is not sufficient to say that we desire something that we do not have. We need to have knowledge of the object to desire it, in order to distinguish it from the cosmos of objects that assails us. We need to have lost this thing in order to desire it, or it needs to be prohibited, which is a different kind of loss, but a loss nonetheless. There is also the possibility of a confusion or substitution of one lost object for another, which functions as a surrogate. Desire precedes prohibition; prohibition reprogrammes desire.

The universality of the primal loss that produces primary identification serves as a common or defining feature of the species. More than that, however, it gives rise to the second mechanism (prohibition) in the following formula: because there is loss, there will also be injunction. Injunction is the diachronic drama of loss playing out over time. It comes as no surprise that the reproduction of the species should be the terrain for the transformation of the universal loss into specific injunctions, which are advantageous to some at the cost of intensified loss to others. This produces an asymmetrical exchange in the economy. The vulnerability of the child places it at a distinct disadvantage and makes possible the transformation of a common but nebulous initial loss (reflected in primary identification) into a set of specific codified prohibitions and secondary identifications. It is as if the libidinal desire of the infant must be used to augment the force required to sustain the ego and (especially) superego formations of the parents, and in turn the broader formations of society and the economy. This concept can be extended *mutatis mutandis* from the child to groups such as slaves, workers, colonised subjects and women, who are forcibly kept in a state equivalent to that of minor children, and in that state exploited.

There is a social contract, but not in the synchronic sense used by Jean-Jacques Rousseau. The social contract is a one-sided treaty (as all treaties turn out to be) dictated by the existing parental generation, to which the new generation must agree *in toto* and privately hope to contest certain clauses later so as to adjust the ratio more equitably. In the process, however, the new generation becomes integrated into the existing parental order and any modified terms come not only at the cost of the next generation but are once more transferred as a contractual burden to each subsequent generation. In a graphic way, this is illustrated by the straightforward hierarchy and progression system found, for example, between seniors and juniors in a school or work environment or between new and old immigrants, as is seen in the USA and Europe today. The transfer of the present burden to future generations is also illustrated – most urgently – by the unfolding global environmental crisis and the bankruptcy of social welfare and pension systems, even those that do not yet operate on the principle of pay-as-you-go, where the current generation of beneficiaries are drawing down far more benefit than is sustainable.

In practical terms, the social contract installs the injunctions, and these take on the force of a constitution, a Basic Law or *Grundgesetz*. All the codified laws, from before the Roman era up to and including the contemporary legislation and decrees enacted by elected representatives and self-appointed dictators, are simply the present manifestation of loss transfigured into injunctions. The laws say: you have lost yourself, and you must restrict your search – your desire – for yourself to the aims and objects permitted by the law. These aims and objects always support the existing generation of incumbency – where the apex of incumbency is certainly property ownership defended by the law – and guard it from usurpation. This is the manner by which parental identification protects itself. The law is set in place to protect the incumbents, but more than that it seeks to enlist the libido of the new generation in service of the old. This requires the repression and sublimation of the libido, so that desexualisation – forcing the libido underground and pressing it into service, in the good old sense of the word: employment; making it serviceable – is the start of the social formation. This social contract has the character of the enthralling force of Hobbes's Leviathan: the new generation stands in thrall to the incumbents. While it is a contract between the generations not to make war against each other, the peace treaty serves to protect the vested interests of the current generation and the asymmetry of its power.

The intergenerational contract is inherently flawed and unstable from the start, which is why it has to be inscribed at an early age in the form of the superego with the injunctions of shame and rivalry. The contract is flawed in a general way because one party is in a disadvantageous position by design, but the fundamental flaw is that the present generation is always acting *in male fides*: it seeks to perpetuate and reproduce itself in the new generation. This is done in the overall sense of privileging parental identification but also by the parent striking each new coin in its own vain image. There is a genetic similarity or affinity between the generations that allows the contract to hold, despite the bad faith. The factor of genetic similarity has a core evolutionary function but, in addition, the similitude is based on minting the child in the image of the parents. There is a degree of shared or common identification, if only because of the action of parental identification on the tabula rasa of the child. The outcome is assured by the action of the child's identification with the parent on the basis of injunction.

The similitude between generations allows the contract to hold to a sufficient degree for the formation of social units. Modernity is characterised by the proliferation and ever-grander scale of these units, which in turn is predicated upon the growing uniformity of identification on the basis of injunction that can be facilitated by modern technology and media. This produces a servile human species living in a vast open-air prison-factory that encompasses the entire planet (Adorno, 1951, p. 33; Gadamer, 1973, p. 491).

The thraldom (exactly in the sense of awe in consequence of force) by which the contract is secured and held in place is also clustered around an unconscious homosexual impulse on the basis of non-familial similitude and non-rivalry that has its roots in primary identification. This unconscious impulse to form alliances between men, between women, and also between men and women (in an expression of their subject homosexuality and in a sublimated form of the heterosexual impulse that is non-reproductive) is able to override or at least partly ameliorate the rivalry of the Oedipus complex. The homosexual impulse must therefore also be a direct component of evolution for it to persist. This means that both rivalry and bisexuality have an evolutionary reason for their continued presence, and they are both of value to the survival of the species for the latent and manifest forms of homosexuality to persist.

The universal but latent homosexual form becomes manifest in some cases. In the manifest form, the libido takes a specific object, whereas in the latent form there is a sublimation of the libido into wider social feelings, ties and identification, exactly along the lines Freud (1921) sketches in general for the sublimated sexuality that is identification at work in the formation of groups. Seen from the perspective of the bisexuality thesis, group formation on the basis of identification could also function by the sublimation of the heterosexual impulse, e.g. taking on the form of female leadership, although this is less commonly encountered. This requires the heterosexual male to sublimate his view of women as reproductive objects in order to see them in a non-reproductive light. Unconscious homosexuality facilitates this process. Given the traditionally dominant position of men in general, latent male homosexuality is probably more important by virtue of the role it plays in managing the aggressive-possessive and ultimately destructive forces that dominate relationships between men historically and in evolutionary circumstances as a consequence of rivalry. Without latent homosexuality, men would destroy each other in an orgy of war. The manifest form is simply an overflowing of this latency.

The group sublimation mechanism rests on the success of the repression of the libido into the social, via injunction. The bisexuality thesis shows that both homosexual and heterosexual impulses are repressed. In addition, the libido can equally be sublimated into human labour, so that the genesis of the economy is seen to match the genesis of social formations in the superego. It is inevitable that humans must alienate a portion of their time in the form of labour to produce objects (food, shelter, etc.) necessary to meet their needs. However, this inevitability is transformed from a simple barter economy of exchange into an extractive mechanism of such diabolical proportions that it is able to transcend place and time and liberate a small minority of people from the onerous labour and grim subsistence to which the majority are consigned in perpetuity. The structure of the human economy reproduces the asymmetrical relation between parent and child. While all economy depends on the exchange of products between producers and consumers, it is abundantly apparent that human exchange is always asymmetrical, benefiting one party at the cost of the other. Beyond the specific forms of this or that national economy, there is a universal human urge produced by rivalry to strike an unequal bargain. This invariable factor is benignly termed *profit*. Profit is extracted not only by manipulating the inherent complexity of exchanging unlike objects (i.e. values) but also by defining the structural framework of all economies in human history, from slavery to capitalism, so as to ensure that one party to the exchange is worse off than the other, in perpetuity. It is worth remembering that even the performance of social conduct (morality, altruism) is a form of labour and exchange – people conform to codes of socially condoned and prohibited behaviour, engrained by shame and injunction, in the expectation of reciprocation. Even here, the exchange is fundamentally unstable and asymmetrical, and this can be traced back to the formation of the superego in the mental apparatus. The global scale of society and the economy in modernity only exacerbates the asymmetry.

In a society that sends (some of) its sons to work in factories and die in wars, the homosexuality of primary identification must be repressed into the unconscious and sublimated into groups. There is a double and contrary action in the repression: homosexuality must be repressed in order to override the non-reproductive mutual affinity it produces. At the same time, there is a residue of this affinity that allows the sons (and the daughters too, in places where they are also sent to work or to make war) to cooperate together in the desexualised manner necessary for the teamwork (as it is so quaintly called) of labour and war. This is the limited group cooperation against mutual rivals produced by repressed homosexuality. The broad society seen in the modern world is the product of this repression of homosexuality. Repression of the homosexual component of bisexuality manufactures rivalry. The more repressive a society is of homosexuality (and by implication, of bisexuality), the more warlike and aggressive the society will become. If homosexuality were not repressed and sublimated into work and war, then there would be a totally different kind of society, one in which unrepressed homosexual feelings would be fully integrated and interwoven into the fabric of society that by definition would then be fully bisexual. These horizontal homosexual bonds between members would prevent, or at the very least inhibit and countermand, the vertical bonds of a society build only on rivalry. Instead of being kept below the surface, yet active, homosexuality would be integrated openly, and it would counterbalance aggression, exploitation and profit. This is the invincible army of lovers that Plato suggests in the *Symposium* (p. 9). Instead, today there is only the army of repression.

By definition, war is the failure to see all other men and women as the equivalent of the self. This is the point of the bisexual impulse, and specifically the homosexual component: to recognise the equivalence and the similarities between people. This recognition stands in contrast to a focus purely on the competitive aspect that in its undiluted form is war, which is the result of the survival and reproductive drive. Fraternity is a good term for this equality-similarity theme, and it stands in contrast to the paternity-patriarchy structure of the reproductive impulse.

It seems futile to speculate about the possibility of an economy or society structured on principles of non-rivalry. If there were to be a form of economy and society wholly consistent with the unrepressed non-rivalry of the bisexuality thesis, it would be so radical, so wholly incompatible with parental identification, that it would necessitate a complete negation of the nominative principles of asymmetry in the parental economy of war, profit, property, ownership and reproduction. A society and economy of non-rivalry would be built upon a far smaller human component in a collaborative relationship with the natural environment rather than one premised on unconstrained environmental extraction and plunder to feed the immeasurable growth and hunger of the human population. Without rivalry, the ontology of being and having – of me and mine – would fall away into a world of becoming in which the dialectic subject was resolved once and for all by affirmation of primal unity and the interconnectedness of all life. Such speculation though is an entirely different subject.

Dialectic of the bisexual subject

In a conversation with Annamaria Carusi in 1997, she made an observation that has stayed with me in crystal clarity ever since: all we can hope to do is *keep the dialectic open*. The phrase strikes me again now in the context of the dialectic of the subject, and it is on this note that the chapter ends with some final observations.

It is possible to view this or that subject position as conservative or radical, and then to promote, adopt or contest such a position on the basis of taste and conviction. For example, I suggested in Chapter 1 that certain psychoanalytic theories are inherently conservative. In my view, they are deeply committed to conserving parental power and enhancing the rivalry of the Oedipus complex, so much so that it blinds these theories to any alternative position. By contrast, an evaluation of Freud's work from a radical perspective opens up the possibility of reinterpreting this material with a revolutionary focus. Beyond taste and conviction, which are fickle masters, the model of the dialectic subject offers a solid and neutral foundation to advance a theory that integrates the analysis of Freud's texts and challenges readers of this theory in a revolutionary manner.

The discussion in this chapter of several consequences of Freud's radical thesis of bisexuality has explored aspects of desire linked to primary non-oedipal unity and shown how shame and injunction function to redirect this unity away from the subject. Realignment is also carried through in the emergence of law, society and the economy. In all of these areas, a contrast emerges between rivalry and non-rivalry. By focusing on non-rivalry, some radical conclusions arise from these consequences.

The dialectic subject is a central consequence of the bisexuality thesis. An important distinction arises between the nomination impulse of rivalry and the dialectic bisexual subject who resists nomination. Ultimately, all value is a nomination, including cathexis and identification, but the contrast between the movement of the dialectic and the stasis of nomination foregrounds and highlights *the relative nature of value*, which is otherwise hidden by the nominative force of rivalry. This shows nomination to be the act that arrests the dialectic.

Keeping the dialectic open means reducing nominations. In a general way, this implies reducing the nominative power of the impersonal agencies (the law, society, the economy, etc.) and challenging the power of the minority of humans who are the makers of these agencies, with all the implications this has for upending social and economic formations. At the individual level, keeping the dialectic open entails a subject who makes conscious the mechanisms of cathexis and identification and thereafter engages actively with them in order to utilise the dialectic as a force for freedom.

Humans are derivatives, constituted by universal loss and injunction. If there is something that might be said to be essentially the self, it is not this universal derivative content but rather the manner – the active agency – by which the content is navigated. This navigation is the individual *will* in all its expressions: the will to power, the will to freedom, the will to navigate desire. The will, however, is also constituted by desire, producing circularity in the subject. This fundamental circularity in its open form is the dialectic, but it also makes the individual will vulnerable to being harnessed back into the service of the will of others, of being led back into the traces of loss and injunction. This is the work of nomination.

Reaction against injunction to produce a form of counter-definition may appear to be a first step on the path back to the open dialectic, but it is in fact a *cul de sac*, always returning the subject to the injunction from which the counter-definition springs. This is strongly reminiscent of Freud's concept of anticathexis in the formation of repression (1915, p. 181; 1917, p. 360), which is the focus in the next chapter. Carusi (1991) keenly describes the problem of counter-definition in the post-colonial context. Counter-definitions may re-constitute the self but only as another negative value, another negation that is the outcome of rivalry. If some object is to be accorded value, this must be because we value it for itself, and yet it is unavoidable that my-self is one and the same as it-self in the dialectic of subject and object.

Nomination is inevitable. The importance of the dialectic is the ability it endows to resist the permanent stasis that comes from the nomination of one value (idea, term, function, instance, object) as a master value. Where a master value is absolutely unavoidable for survival, it should be nominated by democratic consensus and scientific integrity. Furthermore, the dialectic reminds us to recognise that values are materially and historically determined but in the provisionality and randomness of conventionalised meanings. The open dialectic opens up a path back to our inherent bisexuality and reminds us that a stranger may just as easily become a brother, a sister, a lover. In its simplest form, this is the dialectic of making our own non-biological family by seeking out and cultivating bonds of non-rivalry that incorporate a range of mutually affirming and nurturing relationships and that challenge the narrow confines of parental injunction and biological reproduction.

The possibility of non-reproductive relations encapsulated in the bisexuality thesis returns the discussion full circle to Plato's *Symposium*. Although the term is hardly up to the task, such non-rival relations are commonly given the name *platonic love* because the original description comes from Plato. In contrast to the form of desire that is procreation, the speech by Socrates at the end of the *Symposium* explores aesthetic nomination in the form of intellectual and artistic collaboration to produce a mutual pregnancy of the mind (pp. 46–7). This act of creative collaboration is an ancient description of what I here call a non-rival relation. In this perspective, procreation has a radical and liberating bisexual alternative: *co-creation*. The act of co-creation is intrinsic to the openness of the dialectic. The bisexuality thesis repeats the final lesson of Socrates in the *Symposium*: it is not only the object we desire but also how we desire the object that is of value.

Reference list

Please note: References follow the system of historical layering, with a distinction between source texts and access texts. If the source date is different to the access date, page references are always for the access text, but the reference year is that of the source text. For more in this regard, please see the comment on historical layering in the Introduction, p. 5.

Adorno, T. (1951). Cultural criticism and society. In *Prisms*. Trans. S. and S. Weber. London: Neville Spearman, 1967.

Barnard-Naude, J. (2021). An ordeal of the real: Shame and the superego. *Acta Academica*, 53(1), 1–22.

Burrow, T. (1914). The genesis and meaning of "homosexuality" and its relation to the problem of introverted mental states. First presented on 5 May at the fourth annual meeting of the American Psychoanalytic Association. Published in 1917 in *The Psychoanalytic Review*, 4(3), 272–84.

Butler, J. (1990). *Gender Trouble: Feminism and the subversion of identity*. New York: Routledge, 2006.

Calhoun, C. (2004). An apology for moral shame. *The Journal of Political Philosophy*, 12, 127–46.

Carusi, A. (1991). The postcolonial other as a problem for political action. *Journal of Literary Studies/Tydskrif vir Literatuurwetenskap*, 7(3–4), 228–38.

Dearing, R.L. and Tangney, J.P. (2011). *Shame in the therapy hour*. Washington DC: American Psychological Association.

Deleuze, G. and Guattari, F. (1972). *Capitalisme et schizophrénie: L'anti-Œdipe*. Paris: Éditions de Minuit. Trans. by R. Hurley, M. Seem and H. Lane as *Anti-Oedipus: Capitalism and schizophrenia*. Minneapolis: University of Minnesota Press, 1983.

Flanagan, O. (2021). *How to do things with emotions: The morality of anger and shame across cultures*. Princeton: Princeton University Press.

Foucault, M. (1975–1976). *"Society must be defended": Lectures at the College de France*. Trans. D. Macey. New York: Picador, 2003.

Freud, S. (1900). The Interpretation of dreams (first part). In J. Strachey, ed. and trans., *The standard edition of the complete psychological works of Sigmund Freud, 24 vols*. London: Hogarth Press, 1953–1974. 4.

Freud, S. (1905). Three essays on the theory of sexuality. *Standard ed.*, 7:125–245.

Freud, S. (1910). Leonardo da Vinci and a memory of his childhood. *Standard ed.*, 11:59–137.

Freud, S. (1914). On narcissism. *Standard ed.*, 14:67–104.

Freud, S. (1915). The unconscious. *Standard ed.*, 14:159–204

Freud, S. (1917). Introductory lectures on psycho-analysis (Part III). *Standard ed.*, 16:241–463.

Freud, S. (1920). Beyond the pleasure principle. *Standard ed.*, 18:1–63.

Freud, S. (1921). Group psychology and the analysis of the ego. *Standard ed.*, 18:65–143.

Freud, S. (1923). The ego and the id. *Standard ed.*, 19:1–66.

Freud, S. (1926). Inhibitions, symptoms and anxiety. *Standard ed.*, 20:75–175.

Freud, S. (1933). New introductory lectures on psycho-analysis. *Standard ed.*, 22:1–182.

Gadamer, H.-G. (1973). To what extent does language preform thought? In *Truth and method.* Trans. G. Barden & J. Cumming. London: Sheed and Ward, 1975.

Garcia, T. (2010). *Form and object: A treatise on things.* Trans. M.A. Ohm and J. Cogburn. Edinburgh: Edinburgh University Press, 2014.

Gilbert, P. and Andrews, B. (1998). *Shame: Interpersonal behavior, psychopathology, and culture.* Oxford: Oxford University Press.

Hazard, PA. (1969). Freud's teaching on shame. *Laval théologique et philosophique*, 25(2), 234–67.

Heraclitus of Ephesus (c. 500BCE). *The art and thought of Heraclitus: An edition of the fragments with translation and commentary.* Trans. C.H. Kahn. Cambridge: Cambridge University Press, 1979.

Hilgers, M. (2013). *Scham.* Göttingen: Vandenhoeck & Ruprecht.

Hobbes, T. (1651). *Leviathan.* In the Three-text edition of Thomas Hobbes's political theory: *The elements of law, De cive* and *Leviathan,* D. Baumgold ed. Cambridge: Cambridge University Press, 2017.

Kroonen, G. (2013). *Etymological dictionary of Proto-Germanic.* Leiden: Brill.

Kühn, R., Raub, M. and Titze, M. (1997). *Scham – ein menschliches Gefühl. Kulturelle, psychologische und philosophische Perspektiven.* Opladen: Westdeutscher Verlag.

Lansky, M.R. and Morrison, A.P. (1997). *The widening scope of shame.* Hillsdale, NJ and London: The Analytic Press.

Lewis, H.B. (1971). *Shame and guilt in neurosis.* New York: International Universities Press.

Lewis, M. (1992). *Shame: The exposed self.* New York: The Free Press.

Maibom, H.L. (2010). The descent of shame. *Philosophy and Phenomenological Research,* 80(3), 566–94.

Marx, K. (1857). Introduction. In *Economic manuscripts of 1857–58.* Volume 28 of *Marx/ Engels collected works (MECW).* Trans. E. Wangermann. New York: International Publishers, 1986.

Metcalf, R. (2000). The truth of shame-consciousness in Freud and phenomenology. *Journal of Phenomenological Psychology*, 31(1), 1–18.

Morrison, A. (1989). *Shame: The underside of narcissism.* New York: Routledge.

Morrison, A. (1996). *The culture of shame.* New York: Ballantine.

Nathanson, D. (1987). *The many faces of shame.* New York: Guilford Press.

Nathanson, D. (1992). *Shame and pride.* New York: Norton.

Nussbaum, M. (2004). *Hiding from humanity: Disgust, shame, and the law.* Princeton: Princeton University Press.

Plato (c. 385–370 BCE). *The Symposium.* Trans. M.C. Howatson. Cambridge: Cambridge University Press, 2008.

Pokorny, J. (1959). *Indogermanisches etymologisches Wörterbuch.* Bern: A Francke AG Verlag.

Sadger, I. (1910). Ein Fall von multipler Perversion mit hysterischen Absenzen. *Jahrbuch für psychoanalytische und psychopathologische Forschungen*, 2, 59–133.

Samnotra, M. (2020). *Worldly shame: Ethos in action*. Lanham, MD: Lexington Books.

Sartre, J.-P. (1943). *Being and nothingness*. Trans. H.E. Barnes. New York: Simon & Schuster, 1956.

Scheler, M. (1913). Shame and feelings of modesty. In *Person and self-value*. Trans. M.S. Frings. Dordrecht: Martinus Nijhoff, 1987.

Tangney, J.P. and Dearing, R.L. (2002). *Shame and guilt*. New York: The Guilford Press.

Tangney, J.P. and Fischer, K.W. (1995). *Self-Conscious emotions: The psychology of shame, guilt, embarrassment and pride*. New York: Guilford Press.

Thomason, K. (2018). *Naked: The dark side of shame and moral life*. New York: Oxford University Press.

Vanderheiden, E. and Mayer, C.-H. (2017). Introduction. In *The value of shame: Exploring a health resource in cultural contexts*. Cham, Switzerland: Springer International Publishing.

Werden, R. (2015). *Schamkultur und Schuldkultur: Revision einer Theorie*. Münster: Aschendorff Verlag.

Westerink, H. (2005). *Het schuldgevoel bij Freud: Een duister spoor*. Amsterdam: Uitgeverij Boom.

Wurmser, L. (1981). *The mask of shame*. Baltimore: Johns Hopkins.

Zahavi, D. (2015). *Self and other: Exploring subjectivity, empathy, and shame*. Oxford: Oxford University Press.

Chapter 5

The clinical narrative and bisexuality

The 1914 paper by Burrow has served so well in previous chapters to uncover the concept of primary identification and reconstruct the bisexuality thesis, but Burrow's aim was not only to produce a universal theory of homosexuality via primary identification, i.e. irrespective of biological sex, he also aimed to establish a link between the repression of this universal homosexuality and psychopathology. This second thrust of his paper is less well developed and leaves more questions than answers, but it does introduce the very useful distinction to universal homosexuality of latent and manifest forms of homosexuality. In Burrow's view, the universal homosexuality of primary identification is subject to repression and is most often transformed into unconscious homosexuality. It is this unconscious material of latent homosexuality which he suggests may become pathogenic. By contrast, he is very clear that manifest homosexuality is not pathogenic because "in manifest homosexuality the libido is released, free and untrammeled" (Burrow, 1914, p. 272). The idea of a universal repressed and unconscious homosexuality is fascinating and will serve as the focus for much of this chapter, to some extent in the light of Burrow's brief initial suggestion that this repressed material has pathogenic value. Burrow's argument about pathogenesis itself is the least developed part of his paper, however, and is undermined by his appeal to the essentialist idea of a person being "mentally feminine" or "mentally masculine" (p. 282), exactly the error Freud himself warned against (1905, p. 142). There is limited scope for directly re-evaluating Burrow's ideas about the pathogenesis of unconscious homosexuality, and the concern in this chapter is rather to develop more broadly the idea of a universal unconscious homosexuality, and from that to examine the potential for conflict to arise from this repressed material within the individual, and in the larger social structure.

This chapter therefore ties in with and relies on Freud's foundational ideas about the origins of repression, its symptoms and the potential for reversing or releasing repression through treatment. Freud uses the powerful image of the ego serving three difficult masters: external reality, the id and the superego (1923, p. 56; 1933, p. 77), with the potential for conflict to arise and the genesis of repression. However, to evaluate the question of the clinical situation from the full perspective of bisexuality, my approach here is to explore further dimensions to form a broad

DOI: 10.4324/9781003498919-6

understanding of repression and conflict, namely language, metaphor and narrative. As the title of this chapter indicates, the concern is with the *clinical narrative*. The clinical situation in psychoanalysis especially is an overtly narrative situation. The analysand enters and is engaged in a narration to the psychoanalyst, and while this narrative may appear unstructured and free flowing, it is in fact already tightly written in advance in the metaphors of primal unity. The earliest roots of this personal narrative may appear to lie in the acquisition of human language (as Lacan's famous mirror stage metaphor suggests), but human language is introduced from outside, much like the superego, and it is a secondary form of language that is a later and uneven acquisition on the basis of substitution (metaphor) for the first, primal language of the self. In fact, the id itself has no language, in the sense of a human language like English, nor does the id ever acquire language. My view stands in firm distinction to Lacan's now-clichéd claim that the unconscious is structured by language (1955–1956, p. 119), and the first part of the chapter lays out in detail my perspective of the early linguistic period of the infant and how it is firmly inflected by primal unity to produce a model of language that proceeds (inversely to Lacan's model) from the unconscious to the world. While this may seem paradoxical, it is premised on an understanding of the basic structure of language derived from the model developed by Saussure (1906–1911), which I show proceeds from primal unity. The new linguistic model I put forward is developed not only on the basis of the structure of language but also the important linguistic sub-structures of metaphor and narrative. These are integral to an understanding of language and the speaking subject, particularly from the perspective of a clinical narrative. Human language and its organisational structure, especially the concept of time, more generally belong to the ego and the superego, and only through the ego is human language introduced as a substitute for primal unity.

Human language is a later substitute because there is an earlier primal language and signification at work in the unconscious that develops as a consequence of primal unity. This primal language predates the advent of human language. My view is premised on the understanding that the unconscious is not commensurate with but certainly underpinned by the id. This presents an interesting linguistic situation during the period of primary identification, before the advent of any external language, that can be characterised as a self-language, and the first section of the chapter demonstrates how the self-language of primal unity is implicated in the origin of language, metaphor and narrative.

Building on the model of primal unity and its repression presented in the linguistic model and relying on the foundation already laid in Chapter 4 (pp. 106–26), the focus of the chapter then shifts to the precise nature of repression, and I develop a novel formulation drawing inspiration from a term Freud introduced but never expanded, namely *primal repression*. An extensive discussion of this early stage of repression expands considerably Freud's theory of repression and symptoms and their clinical treatment. The narrative of pre-linguistic origin is as important for any clinical consideration as the unconscious material of repressed homosexuality. After all, the spoken cure is about speaking and being listened to, and without this full narrative aspect, the underlying and important early period of the narrative is doomed to clinical silence.

Narrative and the linguistic subject

This section explores and integrates three central linguistic areas: the structure of language, of metaphor and of narrative. These interrelated linguistic structures are employed in a synthesis with the bisexuality thesis. Before launching into this detailed discussion of language and the human subject, it is important to state that comprehensive knowledge of linguistics is not necessary to follow the argument. Certain concepts from the fields of semiotics and narratology are adopted and adapted, but these are outlined in sufficient detail to formulate the synthesis coherently. The initial purpose is to challenge the orthodox but inadequate conclusions that theorists like Lacan have made about Saussure's linguistics, and I will revise and correct the erroneous deployment of these linguistic aspects to develop a narrative model, which in turn serves as a frame for the remaining sections of this chapter.

The first thing to consider is the observation that there is a distinct pre-linguistic period in the early life of the child, a period without human language that is analogous in important ways to the period before the child is aware of the difference in biological sex. This period is pre-linguistic in the sense that it precedes the advent of human language. My own view is that there is in fact a primal linguistic element present during this time, but it does not have its roots in the human language system or external linguistic environment of the child, nor is it causally linked to or a function of the child's later introduction to human language. This view is novel in itself, but it also inverts Lacan's formula about language and the unconscious and introduces the idea of a *pre-language language* present in the primal unity of the child. For this discussion, the term *human language*, also sometimes called *natural language*, is defined as the linguistic system of English or any other language such as German and French. The earlier pre-language language I will call the infant's *primal language*.

Perhaps one of the most widely recognisable and frequently invoked Lacanian clichés is the claim that *the unconscious is structured like a language*. Relying on the analogy of human language, much of Lacan's subsequent theoretical model of psychopathology and its signification are based on this initial conceptualisation, and so it bears critical examination. This popular and well-known version of the statement is actually an incorrect paraphrase of a far more complex statement from the third seminar (Lacan, 1955–1956). Today, the paraphrase is the form that is encountered most often in both French and English, and generally it is invoked without direct reference to or quotation from the original source text, where, in fact, Lacan does not compare the unconscious to language in a simile (i.e. "like"); he claims instead that human language itself structures the unconscious. His exact phrase in the English translation reads: "The unconscious is fundamentally structured, woven, chained, meshed, by language" (p. 119; the published English version is a close translation of the published French text: "*l'inconscient est dans son fond structuré, tramé, chaîné, tissé de langage*", p. 135). In typical Lacanian style (*il veut le beurre et l'argent du beurre*), he also appears to claim the opposite in a brief and undeveloped comment earlier in the third seminar: "the unconscious is a language" (p. 11, "*l'inconscient, c'est un langage*", p. 20). Nevertheless, the cliché simile prevails and remains the main version in academic and popular circulation, where it has achieved considerable stature; see e.g. Dor's (1985) extensive guide to this statement by Lacan; both Ricoeur's (1965) critique of and Žižek's (2006) praise for Lacan also rely on the incorrect paraphrase; even Lacan adopts the popular cliché in later seminars (e.g. Lacan, 1964). Lacan and others (e.g. Laplanche & Leclaire, 1960) deploy this argument to support his central model of psychopathology in which he uses metaphor and metonymy to construct a crude analogy with Freud's condensation and displacement. While the subsequent broken transmission of the cliché no doubt does a disservice to Lacan, even his actual formulation is problematic. To say that the unconscious is structured (and thus "woven, chained, meshed") *by* language implies that language has the claim of genesis and dominance, at least inasmuch as the unconscious can be said to show structure at all, because of course for Freud the unconscious does not have internal organisation or structure except by virtue of its necessary share in each of the three structural components of the mental apparatus (Freud, 1923). Lacan's cliché relates to his equally hackneyed and highly problematic theory of the mirror stage (1949), which has also gained widespread circulation. More broadly, Lacan's view of the dominance of human language interfaces neatly with and fuels inhospitable critiques by Anglo-American analytic philosophers and materialists, such as Fredric Jameson's (1972) simplistic characterisation of language as a prison.

Lacan's formula of language is deployed to produce an understanding of the unconscious itself, but the problem with Lacan's model of the unconscious commences right from the start because the Lacanian model stands in contrast to Freud's concept of the unconscious in crucial areas. Freud's first topography (1900, especially Chapter 7) builds a spatial model of *unconscious* (*Ucs.*), *preconscious* (*Pcs.*) and *conscious* (*Cs.*) mental states and their interaction. Significantly though, this initial nebulous mental structure is replaced by the fully integrated structural model of the second topography and its three agencies: the id, ego and superego. While Freud retained the concept of unconscious material, the structural model recognises that the unconscious plays a role and exists in all three agencies. Although certainly underpinned by the id, the unconscious is not limited to this one agency. This corresponds to Freud's overall shift in perspective from the exploratory first topography to an integrative understanding of the mental structure in the structural model. Not only the id but also the ego and superego have an important share in the unconscious. For Freud, the organisational agency – in the sense of integration – is the ego, while the id retains the character of disorganisation. The superego plays an organisational role, but this emerges later and in relation to the dynamic between the id and the ego.

Freud's concept of the unconscious, with a special focus on repression and integration, returns to detailed focus later in this chapter. For the moment, it is sufficient to accept that unconscious material is simply material that has never risen to consciousness or (more significantly) has been forced into repression. This presents an interesting situation during the period of primary identification, before the advent of any external language. Obviously, the infant in this early period has no language, in the sense of a human language like English, so Lacan's position would lead to the conclusion that the child therefore has no differentiated mental structure yet, no unconscious and no id or ego. Primal unity and primary identification show entirely the opposite, however. There is an id at the start, and it produces an ego in primary identification before the advent of language. My suggestion is that there is a language at this stage, but it exists before human language: it is a language of primal unity. The babbling or baby talk of the infant is vigorous evidence of a primal language, although the primal language is mostly unconscious and unexpressed. In babbling, the infant is *talking with itself.* Primal language is a highly individual and inward instance of language, and yet it shows itself to contain within it the germ of later human language. I am not suggesting that a particular child spontaneously develops or learns human language, or that a particular human language develops out of something like babbling. This would be absurd. Rather, I am suggesting that the infant's own primal language serves as the origin of language in toto by virtue of providing the basic structure for human language. The conclusion must be that language is structured by the unconscious because this primal linguistic seed produces a foundation and model of language that proceeds in direction *from* the early unconscious to the world. This is the inverse of Lacan's model.

Primal unity and the subsequent primary identification produce a basic structure of language, which characterises all human languages. The structure of the primal language matches precisely the structure of human language defined in Saussure's *signifier-signified* pair. Interestingly, this linguistic pairing also models exactly the emergence of the ego from the id in primary identification. Only later on, when secondary identification commences, is human language introduced to the child (in the form of the mother tongue as first human language) through the process of language acquisition as the child grows, but this human language and its linguistic structure as a system take root on the foundation of the already existing primal language and its signifier-signified system of signification in the unconscious that developed as a consequence of primal unity. Like secondary identification, human language is a subsequent formation; it belongs to the ego and the superego, and only through these two agencies is human language introduced to the unconscious, but here it finds the fertile foundation of the earlier primal language, which it appropriates, builds on and overrides.

Lacan claims to base his argument on Saussure's synchronic linguistics, but in fact the Lacanian formulation is an opportunistic misreading of Saussure and relies heavily on the concepts of metaphor and metonymy, rather than Saussure's core linguistic model of the structure of language. The Introduction (pp. 11–13) has already outlined some aspects of Saussure's epistemology, notably langue and parole. In this chapter though, the relevant concept for describing the nature of the linguistic sign is Saussure's famous signifier-signified pairing (1906–1911, especially Part 1, pp. 65–78). Language is composed of signs, and each sign is made up of two elements: the sound of the word (or its written equivalent) and the mental concept associated with the word. This is straightforward enough. The radical insight that Saussure's work adds to this equation is more difficult to comprehend because it profoundly challenges all commonplace suppositions about language as representation of the world. Saussure's *Course* demonstrates that there is nothing inherent to the bond between the signifier and the signified. Their pairing is arbitrary and entirely conventional. There is no reason the word tree is associated with the concept of a tree (pp. 65–7). Through the historical development of a language in a specific linguistic community, the conventions that join sounds and concepts emerge and become established. The conventions may change over time (hence: historical or diachronic linguistics), but at a given synchronic moment in the use of a language like English, the signifier-signified bond is made so solid and immutable by usage that it seems natural and self-evident. At least part of the challenge in understanding the conventional character of language rests on the fact that human language is acquired incrementally as a child, and so the signifier-signifier bonds – the meanings of words like tree and cat – feel intrinsic and obvious. Entirely the opposite is the case. There is no *positive* and inherent bond between the signifier and the signified. Stated differently, words (signifiers) have no positive link to their referents (signifieds). In principle, the linguistic community could decide to change the convention so that any other word – e.g. cat – becomes the signifier for the signified tree, and if the community uniformly keeps to the new convention then cat will mean tree. The absence of an external, positive referent for the sign causes great consternation, and yet it is fundamental to understanding everything else in the world.

The implications of this linguistic structure are profound for an epistemological understanding of how language works, not as representation but as an interrelated matrix of signs that generate meaning by their relations. The structure itself generates meaning. Three laws about signs (semiotic laws) can thus be derived from the signifier-signified structure defined in the *Course*: words and relations between words are always arbitrary and conventional; words have no positive meaning or content; the meaning of a particular word is determined by the relations of signification between it and other words. Simply put, each word is a conventionalised pairing of a signifier and a signified, and a word has no inherent meaning but derives meaning from its relation to other words. Despite appearances, no word has a positive and essential meaning. All meaning is generated by the conventions. This produces a paradoxical situation because the convention is based on negative relations between words. Think about it like this: each word can only be defined (e.g. in a dictionary) by other words, and yet that word exits by virtue of *not* being any other word. This gives the linguistic sign the character of a negative value. Even if the definition of a word proceeds via a simple physical gesture towards an object while making the sound of the word, this meaning still depends entirely on the system and convention underpinning the word. No other word can be substituted for the indicated word, but only because within the linguistic system that word is the conventionalised word in that instance.

The negative and relational character of language leads the discussion of language to the concept of substitution. Each word stands in a relationship of negative substitution with other words. Technically, substitution within the linguistic system is called *metaphor*. When people hear or use the word metaphor, they generally think in very restricted terms of the literary device of metaphor, which in this narrow sense stands in contrast to *literal* language. This is a very limited understanding though of metaphor. In fact, I am suggesting that the entire structure of language is based on relations of negative substitution, and I call this situation *language as metaphor*. This is reminiscent of Nietzsche's observation:

> We believe that when we speak of trees, colours, snow, and flowers, we have knowledge of the things themselves, and yet we possess only metaphors of things which in no way correspond to the original entities.
>
> (1873, pp. 144–5)

Perhaps the first and most notable such metaphor is the child's name: the child must exchange the fullness of its primal unity for a single proper noun in negative substitution. This is followed by the words for mother and father, and so on, as the linguistic universe of human language is gradually conjured into place for the child. The concept of language as metaphor is discussed below in the specific and unique context of primal language; given the complexity and novelty of my semiotic model of language as metaphor, readers interested in a wider understanding will find it explained in detail elsewhere (Olver, 2021).

Before returning to the primal language situation, however, there is a third aspect of language to consider and adopt, namely narrative. In addition to the grammar of a language, the key integrative aspect of language is narrative, and this occurs at a higher level of organisation than the basic linguistic structure. It may be possible to put forward an argument that narrative can take place outside of language, but for the purposes of this discussion the focus is on the integrative function of *language as narrative*. Freud observes that the ego plays a central organisational role: "The ego is, indeed, the organized portion of the id" (1926, p. 97). He does not say much directly about the introduction of language, but he is clear that the organisation achieved by the ego is tightly related to the introduction of *the concept of time*. As Freud repeatedly observes, the unconscious itself is *timeless* (1915b, p. 187; his view remains unchanged over the entire period of his output, as the incisive editorial footnote details, with significant references: 1915b, fn 1, p. 187). This character of being timeless is a fundamental characteristic of the id:

> There is nothing in the id that corresponds to the idea of time; there is no recognition of the passage of time, and – a thing that is most remarkable and awaits consideration in philosophical thought – no alteration in its mental processes is produced by the passage of time.
>
> (1933, p. 74)

The closest Freud comes to a philosophical consideration is his reference to the Kantian theorem that "space and time are necessary forms of our mental acts" (p. 74, and previously in 1920, p. 56). Lacan's cliché clearly aspires to give a philosophical consideration of this situation, but Lacan simply creates a paradox by negating Freud's principle of the timelessness of the unconscious. Language by its very nature is time, so if (as Lacan avers) language were to structure the unconscious, it would lose its timeless character.

Freud himself does not directly consider the fundamental role of language in the introduction of time, so the following suggestion is mine, but it is obvious that language introduces time, if the syntax (grammar) of language is considered. Language is not only a lexical entity (vocabulary); language is built on the crucial temporal expression of *tenses*. While time as a concept is potentially conceivable outside of language, this conception is only possible a posteriori to language. Human time is inherently a function of human language. Time – or more specifically tense – is therefore also the factor that distinguishes human language from the first primal language. Primal language is a language without tense, positioned in an eternal present. Time commences when the primal unity begins to decay and pass into the substitute of primary identification. Speculatively, this point when time commences is also where consciousness in its specific human character enters the picture. Compared to animal consciousness or life without a distinction between conscious and unconscious, the human inflection of consciousness is the recognition of time, an awareness and mental organisation of past and future in relation to the present. Time is the domain of the ego. The ego is where temporal organisation takes place, via human language, whereas the id always remains out of time and in the eternal present tense of the primal language.

Human time, like human language, follows a simple and irrevocable pattern. The name for this temporal organisation is *narrative*. This happened and then that. In the study of literary narratives, this temporal structure of language is termed *plot*. A plot in a story can be defined briefly as the relationship of incidents and objects (including people) to time. Upon examination, this relationship is entirely predictable as a sequence and is also universal by virtue of its linguistic structure. Beyond the obvious case of literary narratives, however, the same narrative function is observable in the way people organise, understand and represent their lives and the world. It is therefore necessary to analyse the structure of narrative, derived from the linguistic structure itself, and to consider this structure in the form of a universal plot. Such a plot structure is directly analogous to the distinction between langue and parole (Introduction pp. 11–13).

Events (instances) in a narrative do not happen randomly; they are organised in relation to each other in a very specific and invariable structure (system). To understand this universal plot structure, it is useful to start from the model of literary plots. Working from the fabric of language itself, the structuralist Tzvetan Todorov (1971, pp. 108–19) shows that the action in a narrative can be reduced to three basic states: equilibrium-> disequilibrium-> equilibrium regained. A state of initial equilibrium is disturbed, and this initiates the action of the plot; the action of the plot in turn seeks to restore the equilibrium. There are thus three states, entirely relative to each other. Disequilibrium exists only because there is equilibrium, and vice versa. These states derive their meaning in relation to each other. The equilibrium regained is not the same as the initial equilibrium, because the original state has been inexorably transformed by the action that has transpired during the disequilibrium. Crucially, each state can often only be identified retrospectively when it comes to analysing and interpreting the plot. While a particular outcome (instance) is not predetermined, the outcome is always a dialectic struggle between equilibrium and disequilibrium, driven by the desire to restore equilibrium. In a literary narrative, the plot has an ending: the dialectic is suspended, and an outcome is selected (nominated) as permanent. The formula is familiar: *and they all lived happily ever after*, or just: *The End*. It is important to emphasise, however, that the narrative structure says nothing about the *content* of a narrative, only its temporal form. In this way, there is no ideological teleology to the model, in the sense of the end being "happy" or otherwise. The end is simply a relation to the beginning, with the modification between the two points formed by and forming time. In the absence of time there would be no modification, and no narrative. Nothing to tell.

This tripartite model of literary narratives can be extended more broadly to all narrative situations, and indeed it is clear that the entirety of human life becomes structured as a narrative by the inescapable relationship of human lives to time. Furthermore, the narrative situation and its segmentation and analysis clearly come into play in the psychoanalytic model of treatment. The object of psycho-*analysis* is surely to review and understand the narrative, and to determine on the basis of this review how a particular narrative or narrative element has been arrested in a specific state of disequilibrium that is preventing the progress of the narrative as a whole.

Todorov's narrative model makes a very useful distinction between the central plot and embedded plots. In any given narrative there is always a central plot line that follows this dynamic tripartite structure, but a central plot may be augmented by embedded plots (pp. 70–3); these in turn follow the same structure and are also prone to further embedded narratives. The methodology of segmenting and then analysing a narrative flows from this universal structure. Given the significance of narrative to the method of psychoanalytic analysis, this basic narrative structure is a useful model to apply to the broad analysis of human life; in addition, the narrative model is equally applicable in situations that are simple or complex. In a rough extension of this model to explain the concept of repression: the repressed material is moved *out of time* and into the unconscious, but it remains an embedded disequilibrium in the plot that holds back the progress of the rest of the narrative. To the extent that the plot line is able to continue at all in this holding pattern, it will always be under the influence of the repression until the repressed is brought back from the id into the domain of time: which is the ego.

There is one further important link that the narrative structure shows: the tripartite narrative model (equilibrium-> disequilibrium-> equilibrium regained) brings to mind and reflects the triple action of the dialectic (thesis-> antithesis->

synthesis) so that in a fundamental manner the action driving narrative is the action of the dialectic. This is no mere coincidence. Both narrative and the dialectic are human responses to the phenomenon of time. The dialectic is a profoundly human condition reflected in human language as narrative. At the heart of this, the ego is the human narrative function. The birth of the ego is both the genesis of time and narrative itself and also the dialectic. This has significant clinical implications, which are explored in the last section of this chapter. The starting point, however, of human language and the dialectic narrative of time lies in the primal language of the infant.

In my initial proposal, I suggest that the primal unity of being and having the same object contains the germ of a universal linguistic model that flowers into primal language. Primal unity is a primary and foundational sign, unique in all linguistic sign systems because (quite surprisingly) it takes on the character of a positive and non-relational sign. Every other linguistic sign strictly adheres to the three laws of semiotics. The primal self-sign is thus different to all other signs in that it is not a negative substitution. For the primal language, *the signifier is the signified*. The child in primal unity is a primal signifier (itself) of the primal signified (itself). This sign does not – at the start – signify in relation to any other signs. There is definitely a discrete signifier and signified, but they point only to each other in the child's cathexis with itself. This apparent unity will seem contradictory to an external observer who is observing from within the established language system, a system of negative and relative signs. The contradiction is a clue to the situation because in part the primal sign only exists as a primal sign because it occurs still on the outside of human language. There is no discreet linguistic subject or object yet, and this unity cannot be expressed in language proper, which is a relative system, a system of subjects and objects. The self-sign is the pure signification of existing, and signifying such existence only to itself. This is also the definition of primary narcissism and primary identification. Some trace or residue of this pure signification remains in the emerging subject and its desire, even or especially in the repressed part of desire, which is expressed later by the will to signify again in such an impossible positive and non-relational manner.

After the advent of human language, this primal structure persists, but there is a linguistic and mental division into discreet signifiers and signifieds via the substitution (metaphor) of human language for primal language, of which the first substitution is the name of the child. In this way, cathexis is the signifier for the signified of identification. The ego is the signified of the id, and later the ego also becomes the contested signified of the superego as the signifier. As the signifier-signified structure shows, the ego is initially a direct experience as the metaphor of the id in primal language; the ego then seeks human language metaphors (substitutes and equivalents) for the primal cathexis; these metaphors are the sum total of human language, but this is also the language of the superego, leaving the ego poised between the two languages and trying to translate. Human language can be thought of as a reservoir of all the previous primal languages, derived from the amalgamation of a multitude of primal cathexes and still reflecting the primal language pattern of signifier-signified. Keeping in mind that narrative is the organisation brought by the ego via the introduction of time, the ego becomes the central plot, *the master story*; but its story is the combined narrative of the three masters the ego serves. The master story and the masters' story. The ego's organisation is also the will striving to regain some semblance of the original equilibrium of unity, albeit in and via language, the mental apparatus and bisexuality. The libido is not only the search for the (reproductive) object but also the relentless will for unity with the object that is the subject, the original unity. The will in search of its original equilibrium.

On closer examination, the primal sign born in this period of primary unity is not actually positive and non-relational, but it creates this impression under observation (from outside and always subsequent to the advent of human language) because the signifier and the signified are identical and reversible. They have the appearance – or more precisely the *experience* – of a non-relational value. The primal sign also takes on this positive and non-relational appearance by virtue of being the first sign, and in this way comes to function as the model for later signs and for all signification, albeit that later signification becomes channelled via the substitutive negation introduced by human language. In its dualism of having and being the same object, the primal sign serves as the model for language and signification built on the basis of a signifier and a signified. As a model of language, however, the self-sign leaves behind a longing for positive and non-relational signs, but these do not exist later in human language except by the act of nomination, so the primal sign inadvertently also serves as a model for nomination. It may even be suitable to call this primary signification the aim of all subsequent signification. All subsequent signification points back to this initial primal unity, the state in which the signifier and signified were experienced as identical with each other. This is the primal narrative equilibrium against which all subsequent states of disequilibrium are measured, and the equilibrium that the will seeks to restore.

This definition of the primary sign as initial equilibrium coincides with the definition for the self-cathexis of primary narcissism. After the loss of this cathexis and its replacement as primary identification, the surrogate period is an attempt to revert back to that primary equilibrium state, but it is complicated by the cycle of being destroying having. Such a search is also difficult because there is little or no conscious memory, no full knowledge, of what it is exactly that is being sought, since primal unity cannot be consciously known, only experienced as an infant and remembered indistinctly by the sensation of its absence. This memory trace, this unconscious groping backwards, leaves the subject open and vulnerable. In the quest to re-establish primal unity by way of surrogates, the infant can only proceed by trial and error, and this opens the process up to exploitation of memory by the insertion of surrogates from outside. These are mediated objects with vested interests beyond the infant, of which the parents and caregivers are the first instance. These surrogates insert themselves via shame and the concomitant injunctions. Here is the advent of the law, society and the economy, the neat little triumvirate of exploitation that has already been described in detail (Chapter 4, pp. 111–27). This is also the point where shame and rivalry trigger a fundamental initial repression by inhibiting and preventing the complete transformation of primary cathexis into primary identification.

The surrogate signifiers (including human language) are nothing but placeholders: first for the original signifier, but later the surrogates take on the appearance of primacy themselves, as they seek to usurp the dominion of the child. These placeholders become signifiers of loss but bring with them also other significations – starting with language as the most comprehensive social system, and also parental identification, as the self-authorising universal or transcendental signifier. This is how the phallus, for example, could be confused (metonymically) as the transcendental signifier by Lacan. The phallus is nothing but another placeholder for parental identification, which seeks to make the child a suitable surrogate for the parent's own purposes. The privileging of the phallus in (e.g. Lacan's) theory reflects only the phallocentrism of such theory itself. Any other biological marker of sexual difference could be symbolically privileged in the manner of the phallus because the phallus is in effect only the psychological representation of a biological marker of sexual difference. The breast, for example, would have far greater claim to such a master surrogate placeholder role, if only because of the necessary and universal presence of the breast for the child in the chronologically earlier preoedipal period that is undifferentiated by biological sex. The ancient Romans and Greeks understood this, calling the galaxy of stars that dominates the night sky the Milky Way (*Via Lactea, galaxías kýklos*) in recognition of the powerful trope of the breast. The concomitant consequences of a mastocentric (or mammocentric) theory would still be a form of rivalry established on the binary principle of having and not having (or losing) the signifier, but this would be accentuated by the preceding universal experience of plenitude and the stoppage or withdrawal of flows of pleasure in the earliest period of infancy, which the Greek myth of the formation of the Milk Way highlights. From a mastocentric perspective, the penis is a vastly shrunken and poorly functional replica (metaphor) of the breast. In mastocentric nomination, for example, it would be the male child who suffers from envy, the female who fears castration. Indeed, there are ample clinical and cultural indications of male envy for the functional breast, and of the traumatic consequences of cancer-related mastectomy for females, which motivate recognition of the breast as surrogate signifier on a par with the phallus. This comparison invites a revaluation of the repression of the female breast by phallocentric theory, and a subsequent reworking of the theory as *parental* rather than phallo or masto centric. Such revaluation is fully anticipated and facilitated by the bisexuality thesis.

There is a further dimension not directly recognised by Freud, namely the possibility of male anxiety about and envy of the creative power of the female body to bring forth new life. A vague (or perhaps unconscious) awareness of male anxiety underlies Freud's concept of the death drive (1920), which emerges around the same time as the structural model, and there is an obvious and direct parallel between the death drive and the anxiety and envy surrounding castration, but the matter of *gestation and natal envy* is not considered by Freud. The death drive is probably one of the most difficult areas of Freud's theory to interpret without recourse to biographical details: the catastrophic impression made on him by the devastating First Word War and the collapse of Austro-Hungry. Still, male anxiety and envy surrounding the unique female creative power in reproduction would certainly help explain why a destructive drive is present. There are two universal empirical features of life: the reproduction of the species and the end of life. Both produce indisputable and inescapable intersections between human psychological reality and empirical reality. Although death and the creation of life offset each other on balance, the physical experience is unevenly shared between men and women. The diminished male share of the creative process can understandably lead to anxiety and envy, and in turn it is possible that this could be expressed in a countervailing drive to destruction and death. Furthermore, any broader sense of creative or productive ability in human culture is a dim reflection of sexual reproduction, which is the prerogative of the human female body. It is therefore valuable to consider human history in simple material terms as a struggle for control of this reproductive potential. In the struggle, groups of men may appear to fight between themselves for control, but on a more profound level one half of the species is forever pitted against the other. The fundamental power of sexual reproduction vested in the female body and the anxiety and envy this may cause to the male are issues that deserve far greater investigation. Beyond this biological bedrock, the only creative paths to which the human species may aspire are extremely rudimentary and largely limited to the creation of signs, and this is of necessity bound – directly or indirectly; consciously or unconsciously; manifestly or latently – to the conventions of human language.

Secondary or surrogate identification functions on the basis of language as metaphor: finding linguistic equivalents – metaphors – for all the conditions of having and being. Like language itself, the human subject is the residue of its previous signification in the form of identification. In the understanding of language as metaphor, all signs point to each other, but they also point back to the signifier-signified (sign) of primary identification as the model for signification. The primary sign is always receding – in memory and under the assault of new signs that seek to lend the primary sign their shapes and colours. The advent of language plays a special role in this process of substitution. These secondary signs stand on the foundation of the primary sign, the primal unity, but they also obscure it and gradually erase it by forcing it into repression. This is the special form of substitution (metaphor) that Freud finds reflected in symptoms. From that unconscious place where the primal self is banished, the secondary signs draw on the primal libidinal and homosexual energy of the self – it is homosexual because of primary identification, but unconscious because of repression – in order to give life to their own vast and expansive projects of sublimation: to produce servitude, domestication, tameness, captivity. The primary sign lives on in the unconscious, in the shadowy corners of the mind and memory, and from there infuses the surrogates with meaning in a dialectic movement, even as the secondary signs seek both to repress the primary sign and arrest the dialectic in this negation. This is how the substitutes revive the primary sign – while keeping it unconscious through repression – and draw on it for their own purposes. The stasis produced by this mechanism is *nomination*. If narrative is the story of the dialectic, then nomination stands in contrast to the dialectic. Nomination arrests the dialectic by repression.

Primary repression and unconscious homosexuality

Notwithstanding the broader criticism by Foucault of the "repressive hypothesis" (1976), repression in the way Freud conceives it remains one of the most interesting and important dimensions of Freud's metapsychology. Since his repression theory is generally well known, only the main points and references are given here. The theme of repression has also been discussed extensively in previous chapters (pp. 69–73; 110–19) under the matrix of the two developmental mechanisms responsible for repression: shame and rivalry. Much of Freud's metapsychology in the area of repression (1915a) and the unconscious (1915b) was developed in the period of his first topographical model, as already mentioned in the previous section, and is therefore inflected by the systems of that model: *unconscious* (*Ucs.*), *preconscious* (*Pcs.*) and *conscious* (*Cs.*). Freud did not comprehensively revise the theory of repression in the wake of the structural model, and the result is a relatively backward- looking theory when it comes to repression and the unconscious that has to be read in combination and synthesised with the new structural model. The paper on *Inhibitions, symptoms and anxiety* (1926) offers Freud's main subsequent revision of his understanding of repression and the unconscious; Freud's footnote on p. 142 of this text is especially useful for a synthesised overview of his thinking about repression.

Repression is the route by which a symptom is constructed to interrupt a mental process. The original mental process is forced to remain unconscious through repression and is replaced by a substitute, which is the return of the repressed force in the form of a symptom (1917, pp. 280, 294; 1926, p. 95), although it may also return as a dream. Condensation and displacement play a role in how repression works to produce symptoms (1917, pp. 366–7). The original process is an undesirable impulse that can be aroused by external provocation, such as anxiety, or internally, such as via the libido's desire for satisfaction (1926, p. 94). By repression, these original impulses are inhibited and deflected from their aim (p. 142). The repression is effected by means of withdrawing cathexis (presumably leading to an incomplete identification) and also by a counterforce (*die Gegenbesetzung*), which the *Standard edition* translates as an *anti-cathexis*; this force steps in to hold the original force from breaking through into consciousness (1917, p. 360). Perceptive readers will immediately recognise that I am steering towards an explanation of heterosexuality and gender as an anticathexis in the repression of homosexuality.

In the paper on repression (1915a), it is interesting to note that Freud distinguishes between two different kinds of repression: primal repression (*die Urverdrängung*) and repression proper (p. 148), although the distinction is already present much earlier in less precise terminology (1900, pp. 303–4). The exact distinction between the two is not entirely clear and appears to have the element of a chronological nature, implying two stages of repression. Freud's terminology adds to the imprecision with his neologism *die Nachdrängen* for repression proper (*die eigentliche Verdrängung*). The *Standard edition* only expands the confusion with its inadequate translation of *die Nachdrängen* as "after-pressure", although the editor's footnote comment (1915a, fn 2, p. 148) does connect the German neologism to the more obvious form of *die Nachverdrängen* that Freud uses in a later text (1937). The *Revised standard edition* makes no change to the clumsy term *after-pressure*. In German, this term suggests a subsequent repression, confirmed by the semantic sense of the definition Freud offers of the two stages. Primal repression is "a first phase of repression, which consists in the psychical (ideational) representative of the instinct being denied entrance into the conscious". It becomes a fixation that "persists unaltered from then onwards" (1915a, p. 148). Repression proper applies to later derivatives of the material that is primally repressed, and these derivatives then too become repressed, hence their status as subsequent repression. Freud is at pains to stress the dual nature of the force at work in repression proper. Not only is there

> the repulsion which operates from the direction of the conscious upon what is to be repressed; quite as important is the attraction exercised by what was primally repressed upon everything with which it can establish a connection. Probably the trend towards repression would fail in its purpose if these two forces did not cooperate, if there were not something previously repressed ready to receive what is repelled by the conscious.
>
> (p. 148)

This early supposition of a primal repression leads Freud to propose the concept of anticathexis as:

> the permanent expenditure [of energy] of a primal repression ... which also guarantees the permanence of that repression. Anticathexis is the sole mechanism of primal repression; in the case of repression proper ('after-pressure') there is in addition withdrawal of the *Pcs.* cathexis. It is very possible that it is precisely the cathexis which is withdrawn from the idea that is used for anticathexis.
>
> (1915b, p. 181)

In Freud's (1926) subsequent revision of this material, the concept of primal repression retains its central role in relation to later stages of repression, with the admission that "Far too little is known as yet about the background and preliminary stages of repression", and a very cautious suggestion is made that it is "the emergence of the super-ego which provides the line of demarcation between primal repression and after-pressure" (p. 94). This implies that primal repression is a form of early repression linked to the advent of the superego.

This fascinating though ill-defined concept of primal repression holds much promise as a category of repression for the early period of primary identification.

The following discussion adopts the distinction between two types or stages of repression suggested by Freud, but I will call the first stage *primary* repression in deference to the fact that Freud's term (*die Urverdrängung*) with the prefix *ur* implies a general primal state and avoids reference to the word primary, as he uses it in other contexts, such as primary identification (1923, p. 31) and primary narcissism (1914). While primal repression seems to indicate a link to the period of primal unity as discussed in the previous chapter, the phrase *primary repression* is more precise in linking the foundational repression of this kind to the primary identification in the period before the introduction of the superego. The distinction between primal and primary, however, is not essential to my argument; the point now is to turn to and examine the phase of early repression corresponding to the infant's period of primal unity and primary identification. The main characteristics that will be covered in the following discussion are the universality of primary repression, its strength and its dominating influence over later repression, the mental structure and society in general. These aspects will be considered in both the object and subject dimensions of bisexuality.

Starting first by considering the *object dimension*, the discussion is premised on the idea that there is an unconscious component of the overall bisexual object desire that has been forced into repression at an early time in the child's life. Primary repression applies to all sexual impulses to begin with – both reproductive and non-reproductive – through the introduction of shame and rivalry. A portion of the sexual impulse is then partially released from repression by a combination of the withdrawal of injunction over the reproductive component and the biological upwelling of the reproductive impulse, especially at puberty. One feasible conclusion is that most desire is ultimately repressed and unconscious. Most desire has never been released from the early repression, and so it exists in the way a victim of extreme malnourishment does: starved and desperate but too weak to do much to satisfy the hunger. Desire persists in the repressed form but always and only on the condition that it remains below the surface.

Given the premise of a universal bisexuality, however, this general answer does not explain why some people manifest as exclusively heterosexual (or homosexual, for that matter), nor does it explain why manifest heterosexuality dominates. A revised conclusion therefore is that primary repression is applied in particular to the homosexual component of universal bisexuality. While the sexual impulse in each person is fully bisexual in origin and nature, the homosexual object component of the bisexuality of desire is thus kept mostly latent and unconscious by the action of primary repression while the heterosexual – and especially reproductive – object component is released from the repression. More than this, by the action of primary repression splitting the original bisexual desire into its component parts, and the repression of one component (homosexuality), the other component of heterosexuality is actually an anticathexis. This explains the heteronormative bias of society and leaves only the questions of why and how the homosexual component of bisexuality does not break through from the repressed unconscious state into the manifest form in a more generalised or frequent manner. These questions require further exploration of the way in which both the object and subject homosexual component of bisexuality is repressed in the first place and kept unconscious by the restraint of primary repression. Furthermore, even the more recently permitted manifest forms of exclusive object homosexuality and bisexuality are limited and offer a restricted alternative that remains a straitjacket for expressing desire in society, albeit a less severe outcome than the previous outright persecution of homosexuality.

Observation of the social expression of desire shows that there appears to be an *impenetrable barrier* between unconscious and manifest desire. This is attributable to the phenomenon I am calling primary repression. The mechanism of primary repression appears to allow the unconscious repressed impulses of desire to hold sway and operate beneath the surface in impressive ways, and yet in such a manner that these impulses never break through into consciousness. In fact, observation shows the opposite to be the case for the repressed components. The more these are approached (in life, in dreams, in analysis) and the closer they seem to rise to the surface, the more unlikely they are to break through into consciousness. These impulses are so deeply repressed that even when they come towards the surface there seems to be a remaining and final impenetrable barrier to keep them from breaking through. This impervious strength of primary repression relates to its universality and accounts for the numerous areas in individual lives and society more broadly over which primary repression maintains its influence and draws its substantial strength.

For the inhibited desire of primary repression to be homosexual, the impulse being repressed would need to arise early via the route of primary identification. That much is obvious. Primary repression is early in the sequence of repressions, at a time of limited psychological range and experience, by necessity; it is after all the infancy period. This suggests that the repression of this early infantile period is the most severe of all repressions, and for two obvious reasons: the sexual impulse of this period is subject to the extremely powerful shame complex, and this period is defined by the solitary nature of primary identification. This early repression is the counterpart and product of shame, which is so powerful in its inception because it meets so little resistance from the infant, while the solitariness of the process means that there is no ally from outside, only the nascent ego to contend with the repression. This is not to underestimate the strength of primary identification, which claims its own power by virtue of its incumbency and novelty. It is primary also in the sense of being the first in the long line of identifications that is to come. However, the early primary desire predates and therefore can draw no reinforcement from the hormonal and biological storm that is unleashed at puberty. These pubertal forces are most often quickly and fully co-opted by rivalry, which builds on the grand foundation of shame that has already been laid in advance in the earliest of ages. The amalgamation of shame and rivalry produces fixed gender and privileges an exclusive heterosexual orientation. In turn, the subsequent repressions therefore both lend their strength to and draw reinforcement from primary repression, in exactly the dual nature of this early repression Freud recognises. In most cases then, the primary identification fully accedes to the repressive forces and the child emerges with a fixed heterosexual orientation and a fixed construction of gender that is aligned with biological sex. However, there must also be some element at work to account for the manifest form of homosexuality even (or especially) given the historical persecution of homosexuality.

In the face of primary repression, to speculate about the reasons for the appearance of manifest homosexuality, either in isolation as exclusive homosexuality or in the form of adult bisexuality, it is worth considering that in some cases the pubertal force might be harnessed by primary identification, perhaps because primary identification is stronger in some individuals, rather than seized and deployed by secondary identifications as heterosexuality. This would explain the conditions under which manifest homosexuality or bisexuality emerges in some individuals. There is also presumably the potential at some stage of development for an alliance between the child's primary identification and the non-rival bisexual component of the parent(s)/caregiver(s), even if such an alliance is unconscious or imagined. This mechanism would be interesting to understand and is anticipated by the bisexuality thesis. To return to (and rephrase) Freud's call to explain "the exclusive sexual interest felt by men for women" (i.e. heterosexuality), it does seem that the real mystery is why a majority of people accede to primary repression (of whatever form and combination), and then in addition why this repression is able to maintain itself for life with such tenacity. Clearly primary repression is not unassailable, but it is certainly strong enough to withstand challenge.

Even if the impenetrable barrier of primary repression is put aside for a moment, and the focus is given to the potential of a manifest form of homosexuality or bisexuality to break through the repression, although sometimes only later in life, so that homosexuality is now fully on the conscious side, this process is hardly ever simple nor does it necessarily produce a harmonious outcome for the individual or society. To demonstrate the possibility of such a scenario, take the common gay or lesbian *coming out* narrative. This is a potent and often quite early form of breaking through the barrier of primary repression, and for most of the individuals involved, the breakthrough takes place in a fundamental, permanent manner. Even so, in coming out and living as openly gay/lesbian/bisexual it seems there can often be a residue of self-conflict that produces certain typical individual symptoms, such as incomplete self-acceptance, internalised homophobia and an inability to accede fully to same-sex love. These symptoms are only aggravated by societies that are intolerant of and persecute manifest homosexuality. Presumably, this would explain why it was possible in the historical context to force manifest homosexuality back into repression, albeit never fully, by the re-application of the original forces or some other variety of negation. This is the fantasy of curing manifest homosexuality played out by psychoanalysts like Charles Socarides at enormous cost to thousands of their patients, but the reversal of manifest homosexuality is never quite as strong as the original primary repression, and there is always a residue, at least, in the consciousness.

The impenetrable barrier of primary repression is all the more remarkable because of its ability to indulge the homosexual component very close to the surface. Perhaps it is exactly because of the close proximity that the repression barrier is able to withstand the pressure of primary desire. This is the special and specific character of primary repression where the libidinal energy is redirected away from homosexual (self-)objects into a broader more diffuse and unconscious form of homosexual object cathexis that is social; and away from manifest sexual aims into diffuse and unconscious social forms of non-sexual or desexualised behaviour. This is the argument of sublimation that Freud puts forward in *Group psychology* (1921) and then later explains in more detail as desexualised social feelings (1923, pp. 30, 43), to sketch a form of identification called group identification which is able to contain diffuse and latent but also partially manifest homosexuality. Group identification thereby becomes the barrier to greater release of individual manifest homosexuality, or it allows for partial releases that are always temporary and socially condoned or ignored as a pressure-release valve.

Group identification on the basis of a common and shared primary repression produces a generalised unconscious social desire, which by the nature of repression in most human societies is first and foremost unconscious homosexuality. It is not simply that homosexuality produces the possibility of social bonds in parallel to the limited familial bonds of reproductive heterosexual object relations, but rather the repression of homosexuality and its unconscious existence actually make possible the non-reproductive bonds in human society. Thus the repressed and unconscious universal homosexual impulse is the material factor that produces the possibility of a social dimension beyond mere biological kinship. The social aspect of repressed homosexuality was introduced in Chapter 4 (pp. 123–6) in the context of bisexual non-rivalry.

Keeping in mind that the unconscious material of latent homosexuality thus forms the cement of the social structure, the conclusion must be: these unconscious non-reproductive homosexual bonds of non-rivalry are as essential for human survival as sexual reproduction because, by counter-balancing rivalry, the non-reproductive sexual regime produces all social formations greater than the necessarily small units of direct biological kinship. More than this, however, the non-reproductive regime produces not only manifest homosexuality but also relationships of a homosexual kind even between men and women, if the perspective is shifted from the sexual object to the level of subject homosexuality. In a complex interplay of active and passive impulses in men and women, subject bisexuality allows a man to see a woman *as himself*, and not only the means to his reproductive end, and vice versa. If trust and empathy are taken as the social expression of non-rivalry par excellence, it would be interesting to consider the degree to which trust and empathy are a function of homogeneity; this in turn is the ability to recognise sameness in others, which is simply an extension or sharing of primary identification.

Turning now to explore in more detail the *subject dimension* of primary repression, this may play an even more important role by becoming the proximate and perpetual force that maintains the barrier of repression. The terminology confounds the discussion, and I attempt some clarification, although it remains clumsy and unsatisfactory to a significant degree. In fact, the terminological difficulties play a useful defamiliarising role in the discussion to foreground orthodox assumptions about socially constructed gender. *Subject bisexuality* is easily explained as the intricate interplay of the full range of active and passive impulses (sexual and otherwise) in each man or woman, irrespective of biological sex. Since the repression commences at such a young age, I must picture this interplay in a somewhat speculative and idealised manner as a continuum of activity and passivity that is fluid and situational for each person. As terms, activity and passivity can be considered in their widest meaning, and not only in the limited sense of stereotypical social or sexual roles. Following this formula, I use *subject homosexuality* to reflect the component of the active-passive range that is repressed: the bisexual continuum is polarised to become static, and subject homosexuality is then repressed by socially constructed gender. In the social stereotypes, passivity is repressed for men, and activity for women. The original bisexual fluidity is both polarised and reduced to a vastly more limited range of activity or passivity as the social representation of biological sex. *Subject heterosexuality* is left as the unrepressed component of activity or passivity socially affirmed and aligned to biological sex. While this socially constructed alignment is claimed to be congruent with biological sex, it merely expresses arbitrary and still prevalent social stereotypes for men and women, even as the precise content of these stereotypes is gradually adjusted to the prevailing economic and social conditions.

The primary repression mechanism for the original subject bisexuality follows the same logic as for repression of object homosexuality, but here the social construction of gender is the repression of the opposite polarity, and the necessary anticathexis is the stereotypical social sex of a particular man or woman aligned and fixed to their biological sex. The subject component of primary repression is a permanent repression of activity or passivity nominated (perceived and designated) as incongruent with the constructed parameters of gender socially aligned with biological sex. Furthermore, the subject dimension of primary repression is an auxiliary factor that is integral to the formation of the homosexual object anticathexis by reducing the active and passive components of both the object and the subject to the stereotypes of socially constructed gender. Primary repression of subject homosexuality is therefore central to the ego's compromises between primary and secondary identification, which in turn are the foundation of the developing ego. These compromises commence after the awareness of biological sex sets in and are extremely complicated. Any potential disruption by the force of the repressed homosexual component coming to and breaking the surface becomes a significant threat to the stability of the ego itself. Unlike object desire, which is brought to expression in more intermittent and brief private episodes, the subject's socially constructed gender is on display almost constantly in the expression of social sex by virtue of its public nature, and so the ego's stability in this area is always potentially at risk from the superego. The anticathexis of socially constructed gender is merely an armistice or stasis the ego has negotiated in the rivalry of the superego, but the treaty is on public display at any given time.

In the early stage before the superego is fully established, the inhibition by shame plays the direct role of subject homosexuality repression, focused in particular on the child's body. This is to be expected and gives the repression the important physical dimension later found in the social stereotypes. The repression manifests as general obedience to the parents. Later, the role of the superego in homosexual subject repression is more pronounced when the ongoing ego formation is dominated (as it is in most cultures) by the rivalry of the superego. At that later point, the position of the immediate parents is often diminished and the group or social nature of the identification can be fully appreciated as a broad amalgam of this ego anticathexis with its repressed subject homosexuality redirected and diffused into the social sphere to produce: universal gender affirmation, in obvious socially constructed but unobtainable physical and behavioural stereotypes; socially approved deviations that serve to affirm the stereotypes; and also sublimations, like passivity and obedience in men towards such figures as the leader, the hero, the superhero. The homosexual foundation of primary repression goes some way to explaining why a threat by the unconscious homosexual subject material to break through the barrier of repression is experienced so strongly as transgression and anxiety by the unrepressed heterosexual subject component. Any such break, even momentary, is felt as a transgression because it threatens the grip of the superego, which in turn will lead to "moral anxiety" (Freud, 1933, p. 78) and a disruption of the existing mental balance and anticathexis of social sex negotiated by the ego. Here again is seen the abiding power of rivalry, which arises in the Oedipus complex but continues for life in the often figurative and ritualised forms of social competition which serve to maintain and reinforce the anticathexis.

The sheer force of primary repression of subject homosexuality is exemplified by the solidity of social sex constructed supposedly on the basis of and aligned with biological sex. Any dissonance ("gender dysphoria") felt between social sex and biological sex threatens to undo the anticathexis of social sex and release the subject homosexual material under primary repression; the dissonance probably also threatens the object orientation anticathexis. In this situation, primary repression and the social sex anticathexis prove to be so strong that the incongruence manifests in a form of physical *subject homophobia*, which could also be seen as *heterophilia of the subject*. Via the anticathexis, the unconscious homosexual material prompts a corresponding conscious and practical series of endeavours to make physical incursions on the somatic markers of biological sex in order to align the body's outward appearance with the internal unconscious structure of social sex, thereby eliminating the external dissonance and threat to primary repression of subject bisexuality. This is a stark realignment of the physical with psychological reality and shows the disproportional importance the early inhibition of the child's body can assume in the anticathexis. Often, subject homophobia is found in tandem with a parallel object homophobia, which is then implicitly involved in the physical realignment. An alternative form of dissonance (what I would term "gender inadequacy") can also occur, where physical interventions in the body are implemented to heighten the appearance of congruent social sex and similarly reinforce the anticathexis, producing hyper-stereotypes of masculinity and femininity. All these interventions coincide because all social sex is constructed on the basis of psychological stereotypes, and it is difficult to draw any clear distinction or come to any understanding of the stereotypes themselves. I cannot emphasise sufficiently that these constructed psychological realities are circular: self-referential and mutually reinforcing with no empirical basis or reference in empirical reality.

Subject and object heterosexuality clearly demonstrate not only the negative and repelling aspect of repression but also the attracting force of primary repression to enhance later social compliance. Some people are able to make the homosexual content manifest, presumably via the boldness of the ego in standing up to the superego, i.e. by the residual and comparative strength of primary identification in comparison to the secondary identification, which is the superego, although it still does not explain why this would happen in some cases and not others beyond the individual aspect. Perhaps in situations of manifest homosexuality the superego is not so well endowed, due to a less-pronounced development of rivalry in the immediate family context, or perhaps the ego forms a stronger link to the id than the superego is able to form because there was less application of shame in the early repression period. These would all represent individual outcomes, and the underlying system of primary repression only stands out more clearly as a result of the variety of outcomes. In addition to individual variability, there are certainly also cultural and social factors that play a role, reflected in the way the superego is constructed in secondary identification; this is seen in the difference between a society that is more tolerant of sexual diversity and one that rigorously reinforces primary repression and works to maintain this internal repression in a permanent state through external legislation and persecution. These variables reflect once again the dialectic discussed in Chapter 4 (pp. 126–8) and highlight how exclusive heterosexuality and homosexuality and the fixing of gender are forms of a nominated stasis produced when the dialectic is arrested.

In overview, the phenomenon of primary repression can be summarised as the initial repression via shame of primal unity and primary identification that produces the ego. Rivalry and secondary identification, which produce the superego, reinforce primary repression as well as produce subsequent repression. Some factors that are conducive to the development of weaker primary repression and manifest homosexuality include: strong primary identification; weaker initial repression via shame; and weaker subsequent secondary identification via rivalry. The inverse factors would be indicators of more effective primary repression producing a less penetrable unconscious barrier.

In all cases, identification (i.e. the subject) and the object go hand in hand: primary identification has its "natural" object, as does secondary identification. The question for manifest and latent homosexuality is the degree to which the object of the secondary identification is able to link to and align with the primary object. In concrete terms, this reflects if the more complete form of the Oedipus complex is able to connect with the primary identification or if the superego (the parental secondary identification) is so strong it is able to override the primary and thus reinforce the early repression of homosexuality. In light of the bisexuality thesis, there is an additional variable that is initiated by non-rivalry, Freud's "It may also be ..." (1923, p. 33). This all points to a substantial degree of latitude and variability in the outcome of secondary identification and superego formation. Such variability is indexed by the cultural, social and historical tolerance or persecution of manifest homosexuality, and allows for a predictive index as follows: more (or less) tolerant models of secondary identification will admit a more (or less) manifest form of homosexuality; and inversely, more (or less) tolerant models produce less (or more) diffusion of the unconscious homosexuality into group identifications. A similar degree of variability in the social construction of gender can be observed, with greater or lesser emphasis on individual adherence to social sex stereotypes composed around activity and passivity. Invariably, these stereotypes are also directly linked to the social and political activity accorded or denied to women.

Cultural specificity and variability suggest the possibility of a bisexual type of society, with far diminished or even absent primary repression, linking to the idea of a society that is more or less warlike, depending on the degree it tolerates or represses bisexuality (Chapter 4, pp. 125–6). Specific cultural and social dimensions also often obscure the universality of bisexuality and its repression, where repression is clothed in other cultural and social anticathexes such as religions and affiliations of class, nation and race.

At this point though the situation becomes somewhat abstract and theoretical, and it is not easy to pinpoint a precise and material social, economic or even evolutionary causal factor which the phenomenon of primary repression would suggest. To some significant extent, this opaqueness simply highlights again the universality of the incest taboo. In the tradition of the scholarship of Claude Levi-Strauss, there may be something to gain in exploring the ultimate goal served by an incest taboo, and there are two obvious potential candidates: reproduction and rivalry. Either and both would certainly offer a route to a material (social, economic, evolutionary) level of analysis. For example, the social and economic *value* of exogamy could be examined from an evolutionary perspective.

In thinking about primary repression in this material way, however, it is striking that the reproductive regime is itself the force of repression and anticathexis. This is simply the repression through evolution of the non-reproductive regime, where this regime is pressed into unconscious service and dominated by the regime of reproduction. If the species is to survive, reproduction must contend with and find a way to dominate the chronologically earlier non-reproductive regime, which is the realm of primary identification, but the non-reproductive regime is paradoxically necessary, if only for the central role it plays in the genesis of the human psyche. It is also necessarily and chronologically anterior to the reproductive regime by virtue of uniquely human factors like a long period of infancy and childhood dependency, social bonding, economic cooperation and so on. This brings the discussion directly to Darwin's paradox. In its most direct form, the reproductive regime is also an expression of primary identification; this is the involuntary subordination and circularity that Freud is pointing to with the germ-plasm metaphor (1914, p. 78, quoted in the Introduction p. 17). Burrow, in his paper on primary identification, incorporates exactly the same idea but independently of Freud's germ-plasm metaphor: "there is a teleological independence ... between the immediate, individual impulse, and the broader purpose of evolution which the individual impulse subserves" (Burrow, 1914, p. 276, fn 9). In his metaphor, Freud also uses the idea of two purposes to the reproductive act, but there is far more going on from the perspective of the individual than even Freud recognises (or acknowledges). The reproductive regime in an individual seeks to reproduce not only the species but also the specific specimen of the species that is the biological parent, who seeks to recreate itself in an act of reproductive primary identification that is only confirmed by subsequent secondary parental identifications. This brings the discussion back to the problem of circularity (Chapter 4, p. 109) and, while I optimistically suggested this is solved by non-rivalry and primary identification, all that remains is to behold the utter ubiquity of narcissism in the human species bequeathed by evolution.

The clinical narrative

The initial proposition of a clinical narrative is based on the idea that the ego is a narrative function, which means the ego is both integrative and linear, linking to the idea in Chapter 4 of a dialectic bisexual subject. There I suggested the goal is to keep the dialectic open. Keeping this in mind, the discussion of primary repression shows that the dialectic is halted by the repression of homosexuality. The broad goal then of any clinical intervention is to release the primary repression and restore the dialectic motion.

Before proceeding with a discussion about the clinical value of this dialectic narrative view, however, I must state briefly some comments about my overall scepticism on the matter of clinical treatment. The premise of clinical intervention is that there is a preceding pathology. However, psychology and psychiatry in general and psychoanalysis in particular show the inverse to be the case: the clinical intervention is the pathology it produces. The obvious example is homosexuality and the institutional development of categories, e.g. in the APA's *Diagnostic and statistical manual of mental disorders* (DSM), to determine and distinguish in a binary and exclusive manner the supposedly diseased form of sexuality from a healthy form. At minimum, such severe and systemic assaults on individual human rights and welfare must throw all the diagnostic and classificatory nominations of psychopathology into question. Quite simply, if the DSM was wrong about something as simple and self-evident as homosexuality, how can a diagnostic approach ever be accepted as the authority on any other "mental disorder"? I can only conclude that the act of pathologising specific conditions and behaviour is a special and central type of prohibition, in the long catalogue of secular prohibitions that produces the modern superego, and a type moreover that is heavily inflected with a fundamental and extreme conflict of interests. The psychiatrist-doctor defines the subject as diseased and in the same act of diagnosis also appoints himself (or herself, though more often than not the doctor is still a male) as the authority who will bring the cure to the patient, and naturally at a monetary price. The individual doctor in turn relies for his authority on an entire self-ordained institution that has previously codified these pathologies in a crudely standardised and *depersonalised* matrix. Both the handbook and the institution are regarded as immutable in their authority and yet they are themselves forever in flux as they respond to the other social and economic manifestations of the id, ego and superego.

No doubt, most clinicians approach their work with the best of intentions, yet their inherent conflict of interest as agents of an institutionalised psychopathology does not seem to be a concern voiced very often, and they appear largely unperturbed that their clinical role in a secularised arrangement blending pastoral care with social control simply replaces the earlier religious priesthood. Even progressive and enlightened members of the clinical profession seem able to live comfortably with this conflict of interest, and daily ignore their role as agents of the superego. This struck me forcibly during a recent seminar I attended of progressive-minded analysts, where one speaker was advancing a programme to divest the psychoanalytic profession of prejudice against transgender patients. Her formulations and the way she was using the term *prejudice* struck me as precisely a placeholder (unconscious?) for the way the term *pathology* had previously been the predominant focus of the psychoanalytic discourse after Freud. Her appeal for colleagues to expel prejudice from the profession reminded me starkly of the discussions around removing homosexuality from the DSM. This apparent shift in the discourse (from pathology to prejudice) is interesting, but what was more striking to me is that pathology and prejudice are structurally the same thing in the end; the concept of pathology and its enabling clinical discourse are simply the entrenchment and enforcement of one particular set of prevailing prejudices at a given moment in the clinical profession. Even the counter-movements of depathologisation, such as the efforts to remove homosexuality from the DSM in the 1970s and the debate around gender dysphoria today, fall into this structural category and demonstrate the fundamentally mutable and socially determined nature of pathology and prejudice. During the seminar, I was also struck by how neither the presenter nor the audience seemed to realise that while they were vocally rejecting "prejudice" (or, in effect, one particular prejudice), they still wished to retain the overall concept and category of psychopathology, which of course they must because their profession (and income) depends on there being a pathology to fix.

Such qualms of mine aside, I must concede that a phenomenon of primary and subsequent repression exists, and it does produce harmful effects – for individuals and for society. For the sake of the full exploration of this topic, it is necessary to explore repression not only in its causes and development but also in the potential for its cure. My supposition and the underlying focus of the remainder of this discussion is that a release from repression will support the chief goal of individual and social emancipation. The following is a generalised and condensed summation that does not consider pathology in discreet diagnostic categories but rather regards primary repression as a general origin of conflict and in that way a problem for treatment.

Freud's theory of repression (outlined above) goes hand in hand with the observation of symptoms. For Freud, the origin of symptoms lies in repression. While the symptom is evidence of the problem, the goal is not to treat the symptom but to find a way of releasing the repression that is generating the symptom.

> What we make use of must no doubt be the replacing of what is unconscious by what is conscious, the translation of what is unconscious into what is conscious. Yes, that is it. By carrying what is unconscious on into what is conscious, we lift the repressions, we remove the preconditions for the formation of symptoms, we transform the pathogenic conflict into a normal one for which it must be possible somehow to find a solution.
>
> (1917, p. 435)

The therapeutic task consists, therefore, in freeing the libido from its present repressive attachments. Treatment involves a two-step process: "First, the search for the repression and then the removal of the resistance which maintains the repression" (pp. 436–7; a detailed overview of the five kinds of resistance is given in 1926, p. 160). For the treatment of repression, the problem is that repression removes the repressed material from the domain of the ego so that "the repressed is now, as it were, an outlaw; it is excluded from the great organization of the ego and is subject only to the laws which govern the realm of the unconscious" (1926, p. 153). In brief, these laws of the unconscious are: exemption from mutual contradiction; mobility of cathexes; timelessness; and replacement of empirical reality by psychological reality (1915b, p. 187). This essentially means the repressed content has escaped from the narrative that the ego is weaving. The narrative is left stuck in a loop of plot repetition. The repression is outside of time in the unconscious, and the treatment goal is to bring the repressed content back into the ego's domain of time so that the narrative can resume.

The solution lies in focusing on the resistance (anticathexis) that sets up the repression, which is still located in the domain of the ego's narrative. This anticathexis is the expenditure of energy to keep the libido under repression and ward off its assaults (1917, p. 454). Anticathexis produces an attachment to the symptoms, which is how the anticathexis can be discovered in the first place, tracing its existence back from the symptoms. For Freud, therefore, treatment entails working with the ego as a collaborator in the task of "freeing the libido from its present attachments, which are withdrawn from the ego, and in making it once more serviceable to the ego" (p. 454). This collaboration combines "the patient's desire for recovery" with the support provided by the analyst. Freud goes on to characterise the collaborative approach by his now well-established concept of *transference*:

> The decisive part of the work is achieved by creating in the patient's relation to the doctor—in the 'transference'—new editions of the old conflicts; in these the

patient would like to behave in the same way as he did in the past, while we, by summoning up every available mental force [in the patient], compel him to come to a fresh decision. Thus the transference becomes the battlefield on which all the mutually struggling forces should meet one another.

(p. 454)

Freud's early focus on supporting the ego in treatment is only reconfirmed by his later comments (1926, p. 154) and the elaboration of the structural model. Here the complicated position of the ego is given more precision by describing the ego as a *frontier creature* (*das Grenzwesen*); in this precarious existence the ego stands on the frontier of various provinces, and here it must serve the three tyrannical masters: the external world, the libido of the id and the severity of the superego (1923, p. 56; 1933, p. 77). Freud here directly links the role of the ego and the role of the analyst. In effect, the role of the ego is to mediate between the three forces and to organise the individual's narrative; the resulting narrative is therefore composed of integrating these three elements, the demands of the world, the id and the superego. Freud offers a concise overview of the clinical situation: "Psycho-analysis is an instrument to enable the ego to achieve a progressive conquest of the id" (1923, p. 56), and this is further summarised succinctly in Lecture 31:

the therapeutic efforts of psychoanalysis have … [the] intention to strengthen the ego, to make it more independent of the super-ego, to widen its field of perception and enlarge its organization, so that it can appropriate fresh portions of the id.

(1933, p. 80)

This lecture ends with the famous statement: "Where id was, there ego shall be", using the metaphor of the Dutch impoldering and draining of the Zuider Zee.

In my own understanding of treatment, more can be said about narrative and organisation. Clearly, there needs to be some kind of synthesis (or organisation, as Freud calls it) between the various agencies and forces at play in the mental terrain. The ego is the organisational and synthesising role; it is the central narrative agency. When the ego is ascendant, the narrative is characterised by fluidity, balance, efficiency, durability, resilience and similar effects. The ego is able to manage the dialectic interplay of equilibrium and disequilibrium. An imbalance between the forces is invariably produced by the domination of one of the other mental agencies or by the neglect of reality. If the superego dominates the narrative, the result is an excess of self-hate; if the id dominates there is an excess of self-love; if external reality dominates or is ignored, there is also a deleterious outcome. The ego strives for a balance between the demands of the two agencies and the demands of external reality. An ideal narrative balance could be called *ego dominance* by mastery of the mental apparatus, and the ego achieves this in relation to the id and the superego via identification. Attainment of a balance is anticipated by the bisexuality of the subject and the object. Such a balance is the ongoing synthesis of the dialectic in the form of transformation to produce a satisfactory identification, whereas the stasis of repression does not achieve balance; it pauses the narrative in imbalance and prevents synthesis.

Echoing this structure, it is therefore possible to identify and characterise three main approaches to clinical intervention, based on the structural areas the clinical focus bolsters. Treatment can be supportive of the ego, in line with Freud's conception, but in principle the clinical thrust could just as easily be focused on bolstering the disorder of the id or reinforcing the prohibitions and later repressions put in place by the superego. In principle, too, each approach would deliver results. Since the ego is serving three masters – and in particular the id and superego – there is thus always the potential for conflict to arise, and if this conflict is seen as the source of repression and its symptoms in individuals (and in society, for that matter), any reduction in conflict would reduce the symptoms. Each of the three potential clinical routes to bolstering the mental apparatus would potentially reduce conflict by promoting one of the three agencies over the others. Conflict is thus reduced by one of the three component forces of the mental structure gaining the upper hand over the others. Of course, the clinician can also use combinations of the three, and also adopt approaches that broaden the three main routes via their opposites, e.g. undermining the ego to support the superego.

Naturally this is a very coarse characterisation, but it does serve as a way of understanding the clinical approach of somebody like Charles Socarides and even explains how it is possible to "cure" something like homosexuality. A clinician enlisting and enhancing the force of the patient's superego over the libido can no doubt strengthen a repression so that it is more easily and durably maintained; presumably this *hyper-repression* could be done so effectively in the clinical situation that the symptoms themselves are significantly reduced or even converted into other manifestations, such as the famous gain from illness. This admittedly simplified view of the clinical situation offers a microcosm of the macro social interventions and interpellations that take place all the time focused on the mental agencies of the individual, such as the *in loco parentis* education system of schools with the harsh superego emphasis on uniformity and rules; or commercial advertising that appeals to the unrestrained and unrealistic lusts of the id, or the insecurities of the ego or to the vanity of the superego.

To further illustrate this overview of treatment styles, it is possible to characterise the approach of Lacan as reinforcing the superego, while the route of the *schizoanalysis* of Deleuze and Guattari supports the disorder of the id. For example, it is striking how Lacan's work is so firmly entrenched in the language of psychopathology and diagnostic classification. Furthermore, his system of diagnosis is derived entirely from the child's negotiation of the simple Oedipus complex. Not only does Lacan's approach validate the simple form of the Oedipus complex to the exclusion of homosexuality, but it also assumes and promotes a crude and harsh alignment of biological sex with socially constructed gender; any variance from either validated construct (heterosexuality, gender) is directly implicated in Lacan's diagnosis as pathological, recalling Brunswick's vulgarised formula (discussed in Chapter 1, pp. 31–3). In their turn, Deleuze and Guattari are positioned in an Oedipal struggle with Lacan, whose concepts and idioms they take over and use uncritically but in a project of asserting an anti-Oedipal and anti-Lacanian analysis. *Anti-Oedipus* (1972) is steeped in Lacanian thought but is also strikingly oppositional to Lacan, reinforcing the counter-positionality implicit in this project. Lacan in turn was also opportunistic in his so-called return to Freud. Neither Lacan nor Deleuze and Guattari's theories have any allegiance to Freud's epistemology, demonstrated by their vast proliferations of new terminology. These armies of new metaphors seem designed largely to obscure the wholesale borrowing from Freud.

Of greater concern though is that both approaches (Lacanian psychopathology and Deleuze and Guattari's schizoanalysis) are quick to embrace violence, which is an ostentatious tool equally of the superego and the id. That the violence is nominally symbolic makes no difference to its purpose. Lacan does not hesitate to deploy the disciplinary superego violence of diagnosis and cure, while Deleuze and Guattari repeatedly invoke an amorphous force of wild destruction driven by the id that is (deliberately?) reminiscent of the Reign of Terror in the French Revolution: "Destroy, destroy. The task of schizoanalysis goes by way of destruction" (1972, p. 311). Like all rebellious zeal, the practical value of such bloodletting is limited to its menace as a means of forcing the renegotiation of contractual terms with the brutal diagnostic superego. The incumbent power of deploying diagnosis, meanwhile, serves only to reinforce the authority of the physician. Once violence and destruction are (re)admitted by either party to the clinical exchange, however, it effectively terminates further negotiations and treaties, and it is hardly possible to view such performances as clinical treatment in the sense of anything healthy.

These two approaches seem locked in each other's embrace, and to the exclusion of Freud's radical ideas. No doubt, Lacanian psychopathology and Deleuze and Guattari's schizoanalysis are both responding to the circularity implicit in the Oedipus model – the regressive chicken-and-egg problem of which comes first, the father/parent or the child (as discussed already in Chapter 4, p. 109). Each approach seeks to arrest the circularity by and for the purposes of clinical intervention, and each has its favoured area of intervention within their appropriated form of Freud's structural model, but both approaches rely on a deployment of violence that is fundamentally incompatible with Freud's incremental dialecticism of the ego based on reason. While reason often seems out of favour in contemporary discourse, I still see the appeal and value of an approach that assumes reason can prevail over violence, or at least produce a better outcome.

The clinical approaches of Freud, Lacan and Deleuze and Guattari illustrate three different clinical styles, but the approaches to treatment by all psychoanalytic schools and also the many schools of general psychology and psychiatry will fall broadly into one (or perhaps more) of these three general areas. The clinical intervention always boils down to bolstering a structural area of the psyche. Even in a simplified overview, this is quite a striking observation. My sympathy lies with Freud's approach and his focus on the ego, but very little of the clinical practice carried on in the name of Freud and psychoanalysis has been loyal to his radical vision of bolstering the ego. There would also be some benefit in an informed approach that is at least aware of and able to recognise the three broad styles of treatment. A clinical approach that focuses on supporting the ego is by definition an integrated approach because it is the ego that has to integrate and manage the demands of the two other agencies and of reality. An analysis that is cogently established in and striving for this form of ego-led integration will only help to reinforce clinical intervention.

Returning then to the initial proposition of a clinical narrative with an integrative function, the following comments explore the possibility and value of a clinical method using a narrative approach that is focused on supporting the ego. I should make clear that the focus of my interest is treating the primary repression. While integrative, this approach also requires the auxiliary elements of interpretation and understanding in order to integrate the components of the structure, be it by the ego or with the aid of the analyst. Interpretation implies a degree of metaphorical translation between the various speakers and languages involved, linked also to the premise that symptoms are metaphors, which is an obvious extension of the initial idea of clinical narrative. Taking these techniques of interpretation, translation and integration together, the proposed clinical approach can loosely be called hermeneutic. Much of this is already present in Freud's understanding of treatment, and in psychoanalytic clinical practice today, but there are some key points to emphasise. It is also important to underscore from the start that case studies are not the aim or focus of a narrative hermeneutic approach. As paradoxical as this may seem, case studies and clinical vignettes are mere instances and have little substitutive or comparative value in a narrative system. More than any epistemological claims, the high professional regard for case studies today reflects the clinician's need to make sense of and master individual cases for himself/herself via retelling and repetition. Small professional support groups of colleagues would be a better forum for such working through. Although there is value in case notes as a private tool for segmenting and analysing a particular narrative instance, these details have little to offer as theory. At best, the published case study is mere gossip, and it seems inappropriate to recount these vignettes outside of the analytical relationship, even though the case is anonymised. Whatever salacious details they reveal, many case studies display only the need of the clinician to assert authority and overcome insecurity.

In the hermeneutic approach, exploring symptoms from a narrative perspective means learning to understand how these symptoms point to integral but as yet unintegrated elements of a narrative. In even simple cases, there may be a large degree of re-assembly necessary to produce the linear narrative underlying the narrative elements that have been repressed and found expression instead as symptoms. This is a long and time-consuming process of reconstruction, and will be a chronic form of analysis, although there is also the possibility of an intense application in acute ways to treat specific traumatic episodes, especially if they are recent. Like any narrative analysis, the hermeneutic approach relies on segmenting the text and identifying patterns. The symptoms are obvious segments, and their patterning is recognised by their frequency and repetition, which Freud characterises as the compulsion to repeat (1926, pp. 153–4).

The next step or goal in the clinical intervention is a process where the analysand and the analyst accept these reconstructed past narratives as accurate in their reconstruction and as events that are *past but not past*. The repression is located in the chronological past of the ego's time, but it is held in the eternal present of the unconscious, where the narrative is never over and prevents integration. Developing the skills for segmentation and interpretation can be hard at the start, but in principle the narrative function is present in each person, and the analyst simply has to offer the terminology and methods for developing these hermeneutic skills. Once the therapeutic narrative has been reconstructed from the various elements, this shared text can lead to the next stage of the process, which is releasing the present and future narrative from the tyranny of past narratives. Of course the past, and especially those aspects of the past reflected in the symptoms, will remain part of the narrative for the present and into the future, but once these repressions have been undone and their symptom-producing elements integrated or reintegrated (as the case may be), they lose their ability to dominate and freeze the narrative. As embedded plots in the main narrative, they are restored to equilibrium, and they are no longer a chronic or acute disequilibrium in the main plot. This is to characterise repression as an embedded plot stuck in disequilibrium and able to exert a constraining force on the central narrative.

An obvious focus of the hermeneutic approach to treatment is to identify and acknowledge the underlying causes of symptoms. Clearly this is a more difficult level of interpretation, but it lies at the heart of Freud's ambition to move towards a causal treatment (1917, p. 436). Invariably, symptoms are the consequence of repression. In turn, repression as the underlying cause of symptoms is a position occupied by the ego somewhere between cathexis and identification. Repression can be defined as an incomplete identification that has been stabilised by an anticathexis – a counter-investment of attachment by the ego – and maintained in the unconscious, from where the symptom arises. Previous cathexes and identifications may be harmful or problematic for a number of reasons, but these are all reducible to their ability to provoke anxiety. The challenge at this point is not only to release the repression by undoing the anticathexis but to do so without unsettling the existing mental structure, which would trigger further anxiety. This is akin to fixing a car's engine while it is still running; because the engine can never cease turning over, the clinical situation aims to create a safe workspace for the ego where the movement can be slowed and managed for the purpose of the hermeneutic process. This is where the analyst's support for the ego comes fully to the fore, so that the ego is buttressed in the process of discovering and releasing the anticathexis and reclaiming the energy previously dedicated to maintaining the repression.

In essence, what happens in this task of integration is that *the identification is completed*: where previously the identification had retained an element of unreleased libidinal cathexis to the original object upon which the identification was constructed by the ego, thereby requiring the anticathexis, now the original cathexis and the anticathexis are released and the lost or prohibited object becomes integrated fully as a component of the ego. Through this completed transformation into identification, the id (for loss) or the superego (for injunction) can come to accept the ego as a suitable compromise replacement for the original object, which is the definition of identification and the prerequisite foundation of stability for the entire structural model created in the process. In primary repression, there is a struggle by both the id and the superego to assert mastery. The id seeks the original self-object, the superego seeks its elimination. The ego's anticathexis is an incomplete substitution to meet the incompatible demands of id and superego.

The unreleased object and the concomitant inability to complete the identification is the underlying problem to which the symptoms only point. Remember that the object itself is already lost or prohibited, and so the reluctance to accept the ego's substitution for the object may come from either side, from the id or the superego. The ego is also required to find a compromise that meets the demands of reality. It cannot simply submit to the demands of any one of the three masters, and hence allow that one to dominate. Such complete submission or obedience, while necessary to some significant degree in the early childhood years of complete dependence, would lead to serious complications in adulthood so that the ego is weakened to the point of dysfunction. As the ego grows stronger, through the active physical assertion of autonomy; by appropriating fresh portions of the id; and by engaging with the demands of reality independently of parental mediation, the ego is able to establish itself more confidently. The ego does this in relation to the id and the superego through the process of identification. By contrast, the partial or intermediary compromise of the anticathexis is a holding pattern that isolates the partially unreleased object – still as a kind of identification but incomplete and repressed in the unconscious from where it is able to produce anxiety and symptoms. The ego is weakened by the constant necessity to maintain the unconscious repression and by the anxiety and symptoms, but it is not defeated. With the necessary clinical support, the ego can renew the battle to complete the identification, release the energy charge reserved for the repression and assert its role in stronger and more efficient ways.

The analyst stands as an ally, and helps to create a field of non-rivalry, a zone where the ego can begin to recognise and resolve the incomplete identification. Bisexuality of the subject and the object have profound implications not only for the content of the narrative but also for the transference itself, which must be fully bisexual for it to be effective in reaching and releasing primary repression. For ego dominance, a full embrace of bisexuality is necessary in the style of analysis and the focus area (the ego). It is the bisexual channel of the transference that determines the clinical style and outcome. If the transference channel itself retains elements of repression and incomplete identification, then this will severely hamper the clinical outcome.

In this idea of the clinical narrative, there is a strong case for understanding symptoms as metaphors for the underlying components of the narrative that are caught in repression. These metaphors require interpretation and translation, so that they can be understood and resolved. Freud himself describes psychoanalytic treatment as a form of translation (1917, pp. 435–7), from the medium of symptoms into the medium of language. In primary repression, the primal language has not been fully understood and translated, and this is the part of the narrative that is caught in primary repression. The struggle to translate the primal language into language proper and to understand the primal narrative reflects the main challenge of intelligibility between these two linguistic systems. It must also be conceded that some individual conditions will be beyond the intervention of the clinical narrative, as Freud himself says: "Our therapy works by transforming what is unconscious into what is conscious, and it works only in so far as it is in a position to effect that transformation" (p. 280). "Where no repressions (or analogous psychical processes) can be undone, our therapy has nothing to expect" (p. 435). To this must be added the problem of external oppression – dominance by an external reality; this is a problem of scale that the individual ego and clinical intervention are less equipped to resolve, but individual emancipation still holds out hope for broader change.

Emancipation

This chapter concludes with some final thoughts on the treatment of primary repression going back to the language and narrative of primal unity. In his writings on clinical method, Freud often talks about treatment in the evocative metaphor of a conflict and a war, like "the Battle of the Huns in Kaulbach's painting" (1923, p. 39), and it would not be a stretch of these images to characterise both the repression and the clinical situation as a war within, an internal struggle between the provinces and identifications of the mental structure.

Conflict and pathology are linked on two levels in this struggle. On one level, conflict between the agencies is the genesis of repression. Certain conflicts overwhelm the ego's ability to integrate or find a workable compromise, and the result is repression of the conflict in the unconscious and symptom formation. On a second level, the clinical treatment itself is a form of conflict: the original repressed conflict is resolved by reviving it and battling it out anew but on a battlefield of the ego's choosing and a context where the ego is now adult and equipped with better resources and a new ally in the person of the analyst.

In exploring this struggle in light of the reconstructed bisexuality thesis, I am most interested in how primary repression can be addressed by analysis. Clearly, primary repression is the result of an early and defining germinal conflict, and it plays a central role in subsequent conflicts and repressions. It also seems probable that many if not all subsequent repressions and symptoms can be traced back to primary repression as the generative and reinforcing configuration, so the clinical possibility of directly engaging with and releasing primary repression is of great interest also from a holistic perspective. Not only does the resolution (even if only partial) of this primary conflict hold the promise of a significant total boost to the standing of the ego, but the resolution of primary repression will also offer the potential to prevent, short-circuit and help to resolve subsequent conflicts and repressions. This assumes, as Freud suggests, a combination of attraction and causation between primary repression and subsequent repressions, but even if such a direct linkage is not the case, a strengthened ego unchained from the need to maintain the primary repression will be in a far better position overall to navigate the conflicts it must face throughout life.

To gauge the treatment of primary repression, it is necessary to remember that this early repression is the consequence of inhibition (via shame) and prohibition (via rivalry) of the primal unity of self. The general symptoms of this repression will always reflect the genesis in shame and rivalry. To the extent that the symptoms of primary repression can be told apart from the symptoms of later repressions, these include: an inhibited and weakened ego and its narrative function, and consequently, the ego will show deep reliance on external structure and organisation; a general social desexualisation and sublimation of the libido, paired with strong valorisation of reproductive sexual activities and conformity with social gender stereotypes; in primary repression, the libido has been damned and channelled into heterosexuality and social sex; any non-reproductive aims and objects may therefore also become symptomatic of primary repression. These aims and objects come to resemble the traditional pathological and diagnostic symptoms as the primary repression becomes stronger, to the point that the symptoms are increasingly disruptive, overtly violent and destructive in nature.

In light of the bisexuality thesis, primary repression is intimately involved in producing the static forms of socially constructed categories of gender and sexual orientation as anticathexis. While primary repression is a repression of subject and object bisexuality, this gives the repression a general unconscious homosexual character precisely because it is the component of subject and object homosexuality that is repressed and kept from integration. Heterosexuality and gender function as the anticathexis in maintaining primary repression. The very act of fixing people in roles of socially constructed gender and sexual orientation is not only the anticathexis of primary repression but also the underlying impetus and reinforcement of a range of individual and group conflicts and symptoms. The repression of universal bisexuality/homosexuality is therefore productive of internal conflicts and broader social friction.

This preliminary overview of some symptoms of primary repression suggests the direction for clinical intervention. The resolution of this repression will entail making conscious and integrating or reintegrating the unconscious homosexual component from primary repression. This will entail returning to the earliest foundation of conflict in shame and rivalry. The process will vary in detail for each individual, but there will be an underlying and general reinforcement of the ego because it is the ego that suffers most from the consequences of primary repression. In exchange, there will need to be a radical devaluation of the superego demands and its channels to the id. The ego is reinforced by completing and transforming id and superego cathexes into ego identifications, thereby restoring the linear and temporal narrative organisation of the ego. In practical terms, the clinical situation will entail individual liberation from primary repression by full bisexual liberation. Ego dominance in combination with a far diminished superego is the foundation and prerequisite for full bisexual liberation. For transference to work, the analyst's own unrepressed and integrated bisexuality is a prerequisite.

I am suggesting nothing less than my hope for a clinical mode and method of individual liberation. Such emancipation will be the immediate manifestation of freeing up energy by releasing primary repression and lifting the anticathexis of heterosexuality and social sex. Furthermore, the gain to the ego will enable it to manage subsequent repressions and conflicts better. There will be a net benefit to the organisational capacity of the ego and its ability to integrate the demands of the id, the superego and reality. In place of primary repression, it is possible to imagine a primary liberation. If this is extrapolated over the wider population, there is an enormous potential capacity unleashed for synergy, cooperation and the resolution of conflict in a broader social project of emancipation brought about through multitudes of individual emancipations from primary repression. The multiplier effect is potentially limitless: an army of unshackled and emancipated egos building an allied narrative of conscious association within the full range of bisexual potentiality where the libido is released, free and untrammelled.

Individual emancipation holds out the promise of overall greater emancipation through multitudes of individual emancipations. Where previously post-Freudian psychoanalysis was "an institution of bourgeois society charged with controlling the libido" (Hocquenghem, 1972, p. 77), psychoanalysis can now potentially play a role in liberating the libido and society from primary repression by embracing Freud's radical bisexuality thesis.

Reference list

Please note: References follow the system of historical layering, with a distinction between source texts and access texts. If the source date is different to the access date, page references are always for the access text, but the reference year is that of the source text. For more in this regard, please see the comment on historical layering in the Introduction, p. 5.

Burrow, T. (1914). The genesis and meaning of "homosexuality" and its relation to the problem of introverted mental states. First presented on 5 May at the fourth annual meeting of the American Psychoanalytic Association. Published in 1917 in *The Psychoanalytic Review*, 4(3), 272–84.

Deleuze, G. and Guattari, F. (1972). *Capitalisme et schizophrénie: L'anti-Œdipe*. Paris: Éditions de Minuit. Trans. by R. Hurley, M. Seem and H. Lane as *Anti-Oedipus: Capitalism and schizophrenia*. Minneapolis: University of Minnesota Press, 1983.

Dor, J. (1985). *Introduction à la lecture de Lacan, I: L'Inconscient structuré comme un langage*. Paris: Denoël. Trans. by Susan Fairfield as *Introduction to the reading of Lacan: The unconscious structured like a language*. New York: Other Press, 1998.

Foucault, M. (1976). *Histoire de la sexualité: La volonté de savoir*. Paris: Éditions Gallimard. Trans. by R. Hurley as *The history of sexuality. Volume 1: An introduction*. New York: Pantheon Books, 1978.

Freud, S. (1900). The interpretation of dreams (second part). In J. Strachey, ed. and trans., *The standard edition of the complete psychological works of Sigmund Freud, 24 vols*. London: Hogarth Press, 1953–1974. 5.

Freud, S. (1905). Three essays on the theory of sexuality. *Standard ed.*, 7:125–245.

Freud, S. (1914). On narcissism. *Standard ed.*, 14:67–104.

Freud, S. (1915a). Repression. *Standard ed.*, 14:141–58.

Freud, S. (1915b). The unconscious. *Standard ed.*, 14:159–204.

Freud, S. (1917). Introductory lectures on psycho-analysis (Part III). *Standard ed.*, 16:241–463.

Freud, S. (1920). Beyond the pleasure principle. *Standard ed.*, 18:1–63.

Freud, S. (1921). Group psychology and the analysis of the ego. *Standard ed.*, 18:65–143.

Freud, S. (1923). The ego and the id. *Standard ed.*, 19:1–66.

Freud, S. (1926). Inhibitions, symptoms and anxiety. *Standard ed.*, 20:75–175.

Freud, S. (1933). New introductory lectures on psycho-analysis. *Standard ed.*, 22:1–182.

Freud, S. (1937). Analysis terminable and interminable. *Standard ed.*, 23:209–53.

Hocquenghem, G. (1972). *Le desir homosexuel*. Paris: Editions Universitaires. Trans. by D. Dangoor as *Homosexual desire*. Durham: Duke University Press, 1993.

Jameson, F. (1972). *The prison-house of language: A critical account of structuralism and Russian formalism*. Princeton University Press.

Lacan, J. (1949). The mirror stage as formative of the *I* function as revealed in psychoanalytic experience. A paper delivered on 17 July in Zurich at the Sixteenth International Congress of Psychoanalysis. In *Ecrits* (Complete edition in English). Trans. B. Fink. New York: W.W. Norton and Company, 2006.

Lacan, J. (1955–1956). *Le Séminaire, Livre III – Les Psychoses*. Paris: Éditions du Seuil, 1981. Trans. by R. Grigg as *The seminar of Jacques Lacan: Book III: The psychoses 1955–1956*. New York: Norton, 1993.

Lacan, J. (1964). *Le Seminaire, Livre XI – Les quartre concepts fondamentaux de la psychanalyse*. Paris: Éditions du Seuil, 1973.

Laplanche, J. and Leclaire, S. (1960). *L'inconscient, une étude psychanalytique* (colloque de Bonneval, automne 1960), originally published in H. Ey, *L'Inconscient, 6e Colloque de Bonneval, 1960*. Paris: Desclée de Brouwer, 1966. Also in J. Laplanche. *Problématiques IV. L'inconscient et le ça*. Paris: PUF, 1981, pp. 261–321. Trans. by P. Coleman as *The unconscious: A psychoanalytic study*. *Yale French Studies*, (48), 118–75.

Nietzsche, F. (1873). Über Wahrheit und Lüge im aussermoralischen Sinne, unpublished in Nietzsche's lifetime; published in *Sämtliche Werke Kritische Studienausgabe Band 1: Die Geburt der Tragödie, Unzeitgemäße Betrachtungen I–IV, Nachgelassene Schriften 1870–1873*. Berlin: Walter de Gruyter & Co., 1967–77. Trans. by R. Speirs as "On truth and lying in a non-moral sense". In *The birth of tragedy and other writings*. Cambridge: Cambridge University Press, 1999.

Olver, T. (2021). Language as metaphor. *Spline*, *2*, 3–26.

Ricoeur, P. (1965). *De l'interprétation: Essai sur Sigmund Freud*. Paris, Éditions du Seuil. Trans. by D. Savage as *Freud and philosophy: An essay on interpretation*. New Haven: Yale University Press, 1970.

Saussure, F. de. (i.1906–1911). Lectures delivered at the University of Geneva and published from auditors' notes by Charles Bally and Albert Sechehaye under the title *Cours de linguistique générale*. Paris: Payot, 1916. Trans. by W. Baskin as *Course in general linguistics*. New York: The Philosophical Society, 1959. Subsequently edited by Perry Meisel and Haun Saussy. New York: Columbia University Press, 2011; references are to this edition.

Todorov, T. (1971). *Poétique de la prose*. Paris: Éditions du Seuil. Trans. by R. Howard as *The poetics of prose*. Ithaca: Cornell University Press, 1977.

Žižek, S. (2006). *How to read Lacan*. London: Granta Books.

Conclusion

The bisexuality of indiscriminate sex

Reconstructing Freud's bisexuality thesis shows Freud's work to contain at least two viable theories of universal bisexuality. The first theory I have called the rivalry thesis; it is found in the bisexual continuum of the full form of the Oedipus complex. The second theory is the now reconstructed thesis that bisexuality is the defining component of an early self-identification in the infant, which predates the advent of human language and the Oedipus complex. Primary identification then enters the primary repression of sexuality established by shame and rivalry, where it later becomes caught up in the rivalry of the Oedipus complex. The degree to which primary repression is released during the Oedipus complex and transformed into secondary identifications with parents and society determines the manifest form of subject and object bisexuality in an individual, but an important share of primary bisexuality is not released and remains in repression where it is held by the anticathexis of heterosexuality and socially constructed gender. Universal primary bisexuality is the bedrock for later socially determined and qualified forms of sexuality, not only by the release of manifest components of sexuality but also through the ongoing powerful influence effected by repressed components of bisexuality in the unconscious.

Everything returns to the Oedipus complex. In summary, the reconstructed bisexuality thesis is very similar to the complete form of the Oedipus complex as Freud describes it in *The ego and the id*: there is a four-way cathexis and identification with both biological sexes as subject and object. The bisexual object character is a primary homosexuality that must contend with the secondary demand of reproductive biology, with the additional proviso and paradox of a demand for the repression and sublimation of homosexuality into social identifications. The bisexual subject is best understood in the neutral terms of active and passive, rather than male and female. This opens the way for a proper analysis free of social constructions of gender, which must be the goal: freedom from a pre-defined and fixed psychological tether to biological sex. The crucial element of difference between the two theses is rivalry, which is only present in the Oedipus complex. Later rivalry within the self in the form of conflict between the agencies of the mental apparatus merely reflects an internalisation of the initial rivalry introduced by the superego of the parents. This is rivalry with others.

DOI: 10.4324/9781003498919-7

The crucial factor of rivalry in the Oedipus complex is mediated by a universal incest taboo. Without the incest taboo, there is no universal mechanism for this rivalry. The function and material basis of the incest taboo is difficult to fathom. The obvious value of an incest taboo is the introduction and expansion it brings of the scale of social group formations beyond the reproductive biological family. An incest taboo facilitates and regulates kinship and exogamy, which are both key aspects of larger social formations. It is remarkable, however, that the incest taboo is a relatively recent development in human history. In the historical record, there is evidence in many different cultures of the absence of a universal incest taboo until fairly recently, such as the consanguine marriage practices of ruling dynasties in ancient Egypt or more recent empires. From an evolutionary perspective, the cognitively complicated and higher conceptual order incest taboo is unlikely to have played a decisive role in evolution until fairly recently. The incest taboo certainly requires the presence of human language, which is also a late-stage element of evolution, and also tightly linked to the expansion it brings of social groups. This affirms the relatively recent pedigree of the incest taboo and its importance for exogamy. Primary identification by contrast is a far earlier feature of individual development (ontogenesis) and presumably also of the evolution of the species (phylogenesis) for the central role it plays in the genesis of the human psyche.

If the evolutionary horizon of rivalry is pushed back and considered as a far more generalised rivalry in natural and sexual selection (i.e. not limited to an incest taboo), then the evolutionary role and benefit of such rivalry for selection can conceivably also become counterproductive, especially as populations grow larger, and such rivalry may eventually undermine the survival of the species. This is pronounced in environments where human survival is made more difficult by exogenous factors like harsh climates, extreme seasonal variations, irregular food sources or reaching the limits of migratory expansion; the counter-productivity of rivalry therefore translates into the necessity for cooperative strategies (as an index of bisexuality) to overcome these environmental factors. In these circumstances, survival is threatened by rivalry and enhanced by cooperation. Presumably there is a goldilocks zone somewhere between the two extremes, and it is in this zone of balance that universal bisexuality has co-evolved with rivalry to ensure both cooperation and competition. The necessity for balance only becomes more pronounced as human populations grow in size and density, adding new pressure to survival of the species. Presumably, cooperation not only facilitates the population growth; it is also a prerequisite for survival and is thus a selected factor.

Here again is the circularity of human reproduction. The incest taboo is a step that produces sharp growth in the size of human populations via exogamy, but it also reinforces rivalry, and this translates into an increase in conflict generally, potentially even a predisposition to conflict. It may also be that the opposite is the case: perhaps rivalry is a relatively recent social development that is not an advantage for human survival in the long run. The incest taboo may introduce an element of rivalry that was not present before in the eons of human evolution. In all these scenarios, the absence of rivalry in the reconstructed bisexuality thesis is a critical consideration. Purely from the perspective of the theory itself, a valuable impetus and key advantage of the bisexuality thesis is that it eliminates the generally assumed dominance and exclusivity of the reproductive regime and restores a balanced theoretical consideration of both regimes.

This returns the discussion to the original paradox of evolution and the freedom-evolution problem. Freedom in its simplest form is freedom from need. However, the need to reproduce in the sense of a libidinal drive can probably never be satisfied or deactivated. Satisfaction is an inbuilt impossibility by the very nature of evolution and survival of the species. The conclusion must be that freedom is always proscribed by evolution, as long as bisexuality is repressed and exclusive heterosexuality and homosexuality are the limiting terms defining the investigation. However, once the universal and indiscriminate sex of bisexuality is acknowledged, it is clear that there is no conflict between evolution and freedom. On the contrary, it is the work of emancipation to ensure that the instrumentalised forms of rivalry introduced in recent human history are not allowed to persist in inhibiting the natural bisexuality of the species.

... ...
... ...

Index

For Product Safety Concerns and Information please contact our EU
representative GPSR@taylorandfrancis.com
Taylor & Francis Verlag GmbH, Kaufingerstraße 24, 80331 München, Germany

www.ingramcontent.com/pod-product-compliance
Lightning Source LLC
Chambersburg PA
CBHW070340270326
41926CB00017B/3925